Wrestling with Faith

Printed in the United States of America

by THE ROHR JEWISH LEARNING INSTITUTE
822 Eastern Parkway, Brooklyn, NY 11213

Cover Art: *Jacob Wrestles with Esau's Angel,* Yoram Raanan, 2014.

(888) YOUR-JLI/718-221-6900
WWW.MYJLI.COM

Wrestling with Faith

STUDENT TEXTBOOK

PILLARS OF JEWISH LITERACY

KEVIN BERMEISTER
Sydney, Australia

PABLO AND SARA BRIMAN
Mexico City, Mexico

ZALMAN AND MIMI FELLIG
Miami Beach, FL

YOSEF GOROWITZ
Redondo Beach, CA

DR. VERA KOCH GROSZMANN
S. Paulo, Brazil

HERSCHEL LAZAROFF
Monsey, NY

JENNY LJUNGBERG
New York, NY

DAVID MAGERMAN
Gladwyne, PA

DR. MICHAEL MALING
Deerfield, IL

YITZCHAK MIRILASHVILI
Herzliya, Israel

BEN NASH
New Jersey

YAIR SHAMIR
Savyon, Israel

LARRY SIFEN
Virginia Beach, VA

PRINCIPAL BENEFACTOR

GEORGE ROHR
New York, NY

ADVISORY BOARD OF GOVERNORS

YAAKOV AND KAREN COHEN
Potomac, MD

YITZCHOK AND JULIE GNIWISCH
Montreal, QC

BARBARA HINES
Aspen, CO

DANIEL B. MARKSON
S. Antonio, TX

DANIEL AND ROSIE MATTIO
Seattle, WA

DAVID MINTZ
Tenafly, NJ

DR. STEPHEN F. SERBIN
Columbia, SC

LEONARD A. WIEN, JR.
Miami Beach, FL

PARTNERING FOUNDATIONS

WILLIAM DAVIDSON FOUNDATION

MEROMIM FOUNDATION

KOHELET FOUNDATION

CRAIN-MALING FOUNDATION

WORLD ZIONIST ORGANIZATION

AVI CHAI FOUNDATION

OLAMI—WOLFSON FOUNDATION

RUDERMAN FAMILY FOUNDATION

ESTATE OF ELLIOT JAMES BELKIN

KOSINS FAMILY FOUNDATION

SPONSORS

MARK AND REBECCA BOLINSKY
Long Beach, NY

DANIEL AND ETA COTLAR
Houston, TX

GORDON DIAMOND
Vancouver, BC

AMIR AND DAFNA ELYASHAR
Ramat Aviv, Israel

SHMUEL AND SHARONE GOODMAN
Chicago, IL

ELLEN MARKS
S. Diego, CA

FRANK (A"H) AND FRUMETH POLASKY
Saginaw, MI

MOSHE AND YAFFA POPACK
Fisher Island, FL

HERCHEL AND JULIE PORTMAN
Denver, CO

DR. ZE'EV RAV-NOY
Los Angeles, CA

CLIVE AND ZOE ROCK
Irvine, CA

ZVI RYZMAN
Los Angeles, CA

ALAN ZEKELMAN
Bloomfield Hills, MI

MYRNA ZISMAN
Cedarhurst, NY

THE ROHR JEWISH LEARNING INSTITUTE

gratefully acknowledges
the pioneering and ongoing support of

George and Pamela Rohr

Since its inception,
the Rohr JLI has been
a beneficiary of the vision, generosity,
care, and concern
of the Rohr family.

In the merit of
the tens of thousands of hours of Torah study
by JLI students worldwide,
may they be blessed with health,
Yiddishe nachas *from all their loved ones,*
and extraordinary success
in all their endeavors.

Dedicated by

Joe and Shira Lipsey

in honor of their children
Joseph and Louise

JLI is indebted and deeply grateful
for their partnership in bringing Torah study
to all corners of the world.
In the merit of the Torah study by thousands of students worldwide, may they be blessed with good health, happiness, *nachat* from Joseph and Louise, and success in all their endeavors.

Endorsements

Wrestling with Faith brings to the forefront some of the central questions of our times, as faith and science seem to clash now more than ever. How do we reconcile the Torah with modern scientific findings? How do we find a place for a personal relationship with G-d in modern times? How can we reconcile the teachings of the Torah with the social and moral struggles of today, including gay rights and the rights of all peoples and faiths? We humans are creatures in search for meaning, and our lives are defined by this quest. *Wrestling with Faith,* as the name suggests, examines the core issues that may threaten the Jewish faith head-on, offering a path anchored on the constructive engagement between science and religion. I can see no better way to move forward than to propose a complementary approach to our many ways of knowing.

MARCELO GLEISER, PHD
Director, Institute for Cross-Disciplinary Engagement
Appleton Professor of Natural Philosophy
Professor of Physics and Astronomy, Dartmouth College

The Rohr Institute is to be commended for tackling the challenges to faith that trouble many Jews. The goal of the course is not only to engage these challenges intellectually, but to sensitize people to the interplay between mind and heart—to lift emotional obstacles that stand in the way of commitment and make a life built around G-d and Jewish tradition inspiring and meaningful.

DAVID SHATZ, PHD
Ronald P. Stanton University Professor of Philosophy, Ethics, and Religious Thought
Yeshiva University

Can God and science coexist? We live in an era where being secular appears synonymous with being a "modernist and thinking" person. According to this view, rejecting religion is a virtue because science and religion are incompatible, and we live in a scientifically based age of enlightenment.

In my humble opinion, both science and religion attempt to understand the Truth from two different perspectives. In fact, science ends where religion begins. Thus, science and religion are complementary, not adversaries.

Complex issues of faith and contemporary society are addressed in *Wrestling with Faith* in a comprehensive and extensive matter. It should make for a thought-provoking series of lectures.

MICHAEL SZYCHER, PHD
CEO and President, CardioTech International, Ltd.
Author and lecturer

The new course offering, *Wrestling with Faith,* continues JLI's provocative series of courses that refuse to shy away from controversy. Instead, it promises to take on the most challenging issues facing both faithful Jews and those who may have decided that Judaism provides no guidance in a world of changing values.

Some contend that there is an unbridgeable divide between reason and faith. Superficial thinkers, whether believers or atheists, confidently reject one side of what they take to be a binary. This course will demonstrate that reason and faith are not mutually exclusive, but are mutually supportive. Judaism not only tolerates critical thinking and reasoned debate, but demands that we approach our religion with an inquiring mind, not a slavish one. Modernity, reason, and science are not the enemies of Judaism, but neither is every new idea or innovation necessarily good simply because it is novel.

Modern life poses many painful dilemmas that challenge traditional values. Fortunately, courses like this one offered by JLI reveal to learners that the resources that Judaism provides for navigating today's treacherous waters are not antiquated or irrelevant, but timely and enduring.

JAN FELDMAN, PHD
Professor of Political Science
University of Vermont

The greatest biblical figures and founding leaders of the Jewish people have not shied away from the most fundamental perplexing questions at the core of belief in G-d, as beneficent, omniscient, omnipotent, and all-encompassing. The challenge of theodicy, along with reconciliation of articles of Jewish faith with day-to-day experience, and so much more are woven through Talmudic discourse and beyond and are highlighted by Maimonides in the *Guide for the Perplexed*. In fact, permission to question is nearly a unique feature of Jewish theology, coupled with the realization that the tools and concepts to address these and many more apparent dilemmas are themselves divine gifts.

Looking through the curriculum of topics in the Rohr Institute's adult education course, entitled *Wrestling with Faith,* reveals the course to be a high-level continuation of this tradition. While we may not be at the spiritual and intellectual levels of our forefathers and sages of the past, nevertheless, for our own sake and especially for the sake of future generations we dare not withdraw from continuing in this tradition, always from a basis of humility in our limited capacity to ultimately resolve challenges to what are ultimately principles of faith. The connection to our Jewish heritage is strengthened by the kind of in-depth discussions under the guidance of the superb teachers who will participate in this course.

More than ever, scientific breakthroughs, societal interconnection, and democratization of knowledge render this kind of in-depth discussion course more important than ever. Therefore, I am happy to lend my endorsement, and I look forward to receiving outcomes of the discussions and teachings that will emerge.

KARL SKORECKI, M.D.
Director, Molecular Medicine Laboratory
Professor of Medicine, Israel Institute of Technology

At a time when science and technology dominate the mechanics and framing of our modern lives, it is more important than ever to ask the bigger questions of life's purpose and values. This course enables the seeker to embrace the achievements of modern science while seeking the higher gifts of wisdom, meaning, and a personal relationship with G-d.

JENNIFER WISEMAN, PHD
Senior Astrophysicist, NASA Goddard Space Flight Center
Director, Dialogue on Science, Ethics, and Religion
American Association for the Advancement of Science

Endorsements, continued

Being occupied with minutiae of life, the fundamental questions dealt with in *Wrestling with Faith* are often postponed until later in life. But one can always pause and pose intriguing queries that will surely lead to unanticipated, deep insights accumulated over millennia.

If God wants something from us, that means that we are not insignificant. Contrary to Rousseau, who stated that "Man is born free, and he is everywhere in chains," we are all free-willed individuals who can have a profound influence on the world around us. And, indeed, as many will testify, science and religion are not mutually exclusive.

Make a difference, take the course on *Wrestling with Faith*—whether you have retired or are expecting to do so only decades from now—to discover God, the world, and (yes!) oneself.

ISAAC ELISHAKOFF, PHD

Distinguished Research Professor, Department of Ocean and Mechanical Engineering, Florida Atlantic University

JLI courses are life-changing. This new course, *Wrestling with Faith,* will help us work though the most important and challenging issues in our life. In today's world, where science seems to explain almost everything, humans seem—well—unimportant. This course will bring alive the depth of Judaism and really show you how significant we are as partners with G-d in achieving the divine purpose.

DANIEL FRIEDMANN, MS, P. ENG.

Chairman, Carbon Engineering,
Former CEO, MacDonald, Dettwiler and Associates
Best-selling author of three books on Torah and science, including *The Genesis One Code*

Contents

Lesson 1

FIRST IMPRESSIONS

REDEFINING G-D

Jaffa seashore. Yaacov Ben-Dov, gelatin silver print, c. 1920.

As we mature, our understanding of nuanced topics matures too. For many of us, however, our conception of G-d has not evolved much beyond what it was when we were in Hebrew school. If we want to have a relationship with G-d, we need to know: Who is He really? Who is He ***not****? And how is He relevant to our lives?*

Exercise 1

What are some issues that commonly challenge a person's faith in God and/or their desire to have a relationship with Him?

a.	
b.	
c.	

QUESTION FOR DISCUSSION

How important is God to Judaism?

TEXT 1

SEFER HACHINUCH, MITZVAH 25

מִצְוַת הָאֱמוּנָה בִּמְצִיאוּת הַשֵּׁם: לְהַאֲמִין שֶׁיֵּשׁ לָעוֹלָם אֱלוֹ-הַּ אֶחָד . . .

שׁוֹרֶשׁ מִצְוָה זוֹ אֵין צָרִיךְ בֵּאוּר. יָדוּעַ הַדָּבָר וְנִגְלֶה לַכֹּל כִּי הָאֱמוּנָה הַזוֹ יְסוֹד הַדָּת, וַאֲשֶׁר לֹא יַאֲמִין בָּזֶה, כּוֹפֵר בָּעִיקָר וְאֵין לוֹ חֵלֶק וּזְכוּת עִם יִשְׂרָאֵל.

וְעִנְיָן הָאֱמוּנָה הוּא שֶׁיִּקְבַּע בְּנַפְשׁוֹ שֶׁהָאֱמֶת כֵּן וְשֶׁאִי אֶפְשָׁר חִילוּף זֶה בְּשׁוּם פָּנִים. וְאִם נִשְׁאָל עָלָיו, יָשִׁיב לְכָל שׁוֹאֵל שֶׁזֶה יַאֲמִין לִבּוֹ, וְלֹא יוֹדֶה בְּחִילוּף זֶה אֲפִילוּ יֹאמְרוּ לְהָרְגוֹ.

The mitzvah to believe in God consists of the obligation to believe that the world has one God. . . .

The origins of this mitzvah are obvious. All know that this belief is the foundation of Judaism, and that one who rejects it is in denial of the most fundamental principle and has no share in and merit with Israel.

This mitzvah requires us to affix in our soul the truth [of God's existence] and the impossibility of any other option. If asked about our belief, we will affirm to any inquirer that [the belief in one God] is our heart's conviction. We will never submit to a contrary belief, even at the cost of our lives.

ספר החינוך

פה ברין

SEFER HACHINUCH

A work on the biblical commandments. Four aspects of every mitzvah are discussed in this work: the definition of the mitzvah; ethical lessons that can be deduced from the mitzvah; basic laws pertaining to the observance of the mitzvah; and who is obligated to perform the mitzvah, and when. The work was composed in the 13th century by an anonymous author who refers to himself as "the Levite of Barcelona." It has been widely thought that this referred to Rabbi Aharon Halevi of Barcelona (Re'ah); however, this view has been contested.

Exercise 2

Which adjectives or qualities describe God?

Which adjectives or qualities do not describe God?

GOD IS	GOD IS NOT

TEXT 2a

MAIMONIDES, *MISHNEH TORAH*, LAWS OF THE FOUNDATIONS OF THE TORAH 1:1–8

יְסוֹד הַיְסוֹדוֹת וְעַמּוּד הַחָכְמוֹת לֵידַע שֶׁיֵּשׁ שָׁם מָצוּי רִאשׁוֹן, וְהוּא מַמְצִיא כָּל נִמְצָא, וְכָל הַנִּמְצָאִים מִשָּׁמַיִם וָאָרֶץ וּמַה שֶּׁבֵּינֵיהֶם לֹא נִמְצְאוּ אֶלָּא מֵאֲמִתַּת הִמָּצְאוֹ.

וְאִם יַעֲלֶה עַל הַדַּעַת שֶׁהוּא אֵינוֹ מָצוּי, אֵין דָּבָר אַחֵר יָכוֹל לְהִמָּצְאוֹת.

וְאִם יַעֲלֶה עַל הַדַּעַת שֶׁאֵין כָּל הַנִּמְצָאִים מִלְּבַדּוֹ מְצוּיִּים, הוּא לְבַדּוֹ יִהְיֶה מָצוּי וְלֹא יִבָּטֵל הוּא לְבִטּוּלָם. שֶׁכָּל הַנִּמְצָאִים צְרִיכִין לוֹ וְהוּא בָּרוּךְ הוּא אֵינוֹ צָרִיךְ לָהֶם וְלֹא לְאֶחָד מֵהֶם. לְפִיכָךְ אֵין אֲמִתָּתוֹ כַּאֲמִתַּת אֶחָד מֵהֶם.

הוּא שֶׁהַנָּבִיא אוֹמֵר, "וַה' אֱלֹקִים אֱמֶת" (יִרְמְיָהוּ י, י): הוּא לְבַדּוֹ הָאֱמֶת וְאֵין לְאַחֵר אֱמֶת כַּאֲמִתָּתוֹ. וְהוּא שֶׁהַתּוֹרָה אוֹמֶרֶת, "אֵין עוֹד מִלְּבַדּוֹ" (דְּבָרִים ד, לה), כְּלוֹמַר, אֵין שׁוּם מָצוּי אֱמֶת מִלְּבַדּוֹ כְּמוֹתוֹ.

הַמָּצוּי הַזֶּה הוּא אֱלֹקֵי הָעוֹלָם אֲדוֹן כָּל הָאָרֶץ . . .

וִידִיעַת דָּבָר זֶה מִצְוַת עֲשֵׂה, שֶׁנֶּאֱמַר, "אָנֹכִי ה' אֱלֹקֶיךָ" (שְׁמוֹת כ, ב). וְכָל הַמַּעֲלֶה עַל דַּעְתּוֹ שֶׁיֵּשׁ שָׁם אֱלוֹ-הַּ אַחֵר חוּץ מִזֶּה, עָבַר בְּלֹא תַעֲשֶׂה, שֶׁנֶּאֱמַר, "לֹא יִהְיֶה לְךָ אֱלֹהִים אֲחֵרִים עַל פָּנָי" (שָׁם, ג), וְכָפַר בָּעִיקָּר, שֶׁזֶּהוּ הָעִיקָּר הַגָּדוֹל שֶׁהַכֹּל תָּלוּי בּוֹ.

אֱלוֹ-הַּ זֶה אֶחָד הוּא, וְאֵינוֹ שְׁנַיִם וְלֹא יָתֵר עַל שְׁנַיִם, אֶלָּא אֶחָד שֶׁאֵין כְּיִחוּדוֹ אֶחָד מִן הָאֲחָדִים הַנִּמְצָאִים בָּעוֹלָם. לֹא אֶחָד כְּמִין שֶׁהוּא כּוֹלֵל אֲחָדִים הַרְבֵּה, וְלֹא אֶחָד כְּגוּף שֶׁהוּא נֶחְלָק לְמַחְלָקוֹת וְלִקְצָווֹת, אֶלָּא יִחוּד שֶׁאֵין יִחוּד אַחֵר כְּמוֹתוֹ בָּעוֹלָם . . . וִידִיעַת דָּבָר זֶה מִצְוַת עֲשֵׂה, שֶׁנֶּאֱמַר, "ה' אֱלֹקֵינוּ ה' אֶחָד" (דְּבָרִים ו, ד).

הֲרֵי מְפוֹרָשׁ בַּתּוֹרָה וּבִנְבִיאִים שֶׁאֵין הַקָּדוֹשׁ בָּרוּךְ הוּא גּוּף וּגְוִיָּה, שֶׁנֶּאֱמַר, "כִּי ה' אֱלֹקֵיכֶם הוּא אֱלֹקִים, בַּשָּׁמַיִם מִמַּעַל וְעַל הָאָרֶץ מִתָּחַת" (יְהוֹשֻׁעַ ב, יא), וְהַגּוּף לֹא יִהְיֶה בִּשְׁנֵי מְקוֹמוֹת. וְנֶאֱמַר, "כִּי לֹא רְאִיתֶם כָּל תְּמוּנָה" (דְּבָרִים ד, טו). וְנֶאֱמַר, "וְאֶל מִי תְדַמְּיוּנִי וְאֶשְׁוֶה" (יְשַׁעְיָהוּ מ, כה). וְאִילּוּ הָיָה גּוּף, הָיָה דּוֹמֶה לִשְׁאָר גּוּפִים.

The foundation of all foundations and the pillar of all wisdom is to know that there is a primary being Who

RABBI MOSHE BEN MAIMON (MAIMONIDES, RAMBAM) 1135–1204

Halachist, philosopher, author, and physician. Maimonides was born in Córdoba, Spain. After the conquest of Córdoba by the Almohads, he fled Spain and eventually settled in Cairo, Egypt. There, he became the leader of the Jewish community and served as court physician to the vizier of Egypt. He is most noted for authoring the *Mishneh Torah*, an encyclopedic arrangement of Jewish law, and for his philosophical work, *Guide for the Perplexed*. His rulings on Jewish law are integral to the formation of halachic consensus.

brings all things into being. All that exists in the heavens, the earth, and what is between them came into existence only from the truth of His being.

In theory, if He does not exist, no other thing could possibly exist.

In theory, if all things aside from Him would not exist, He would continue to exist; He would not cease to exist because all else ceases to exist. For all things need Him, but He does not need any of them. His truth, therefore, does not resemble the truth of any other being.

This is implied by the prophet's statement, "God, the Lord, is true" (JEREMIAH 10:10): He alone is true and no other entity compares to His truth. This is the meaning of the Torah's statement, "There is none besides Him" (DEUTERONOMY 4:35): outside of Him, there is no comparable true existence.

This being is the God of the world, the master of the entire earth. . . .

Knowing all this is a mitzvah, as it says, "I am the Lord your God" (EXODUS 20:2). It is forbidden to presume that there is another god besides this being, as it says, "You shall have no other gods before Me" (IBID., 20:3).

[Moreover, belief in another god] is a denial of a fundamental principle of the Jewish faith—[for belief in One God] is the great principle upon which all [of Judaism] rests.

This God is one; not two or more, but one. His unity surpasses any unity present in the things of the world. His unity is not like that of a [single] species that comprises many members, nor like a [single] body that contains various parts and dimensions. There exists in this world no unity similar to God's unity. . . . Knowing all this is a mitzvah, as it says, "[Hear, O Israel,] the Lord is our God, the Lord is One" (DEUTERONOMY 6:4).

It is explicitly stated in the Torah and [the works of] the prophets that God is not a body or physical form. It says, "For your God is the Lord in the heavens above and the earth below" (JOSHUA 2:11); and a body cannot [simultaneously] exist in two places. It is also stated, "For you did not see any image [on the day that God spoke to you at Horeb from the midst of the fire]" (DEUTERONOMY 4:15). Further it is said, "To whom will you compare Me? Who is My equal?" (ISAIAH 40:25). Were He a body, however, He would be comparable to other bodies.

TEXT 2b

MAIMONIDES, IBID., 1:11

וְכֵיוָן שֶׁנִּתְבָּרֵר שֶׁאֵינוֹ גוּף וּגְוִיָּה, יִתְבָּרֵר שֶׁלֹּא יֶאֱרַע לוֹ אֶחָד מִמְּאוֹרְעוֹת הַגּוּפוֹת. לֹא חִיבּוּר וְלֹא פֵּירוּד, לֹא מָקוֹם וְלֹא מִדָּה, לֹא עֲלִיָּה וְלֹא יְרִידָה, וְלֹא יָמִין וְלֹא שְׂמֹאל, וְלֹא פָּנִים וְלֹא אָחוֹר, וְלֹא יְשִׁיבָה וְלֹא עֲמִידָה. וְאֵינוֹ מָצוּי בִּזְמַן עַד שֶׁיִּהְיֶה לוֹ רֵאשִׁית וְאַחֲרִית וּמִנְיַן שָׁנִים. וְאֵינוֹ מִשְׁתַּנֶּה, שֶׁאֵין לוֹ דָּבָר שֶׁיִּגְרוֹם לוֹ שִׁינּוּי. וְאֵין לוֹ לֹא מָוֶת, וְלֹא חַיִּים כְּחַיֵּי הַגּוּף הַחַי, וְלֹא סִכְלוּת, וְלֹא חָכְמָה כְּחָכְמַת הָאִישׁ הֶחָכָם, לֹא שֵׁינָה וְלֹא הֲקִיצָה, וְלֹא כַּעַס וְלֹא שְׂחוֹק, וְלֹא שִׂמְחָה וְלֹא עַצְבוּת, וְלֹא שְׁתִיקָה וְלֹא דִּבּוּר כְּדִבּוּר בְּנֵי אָדָם.

Because it has been established that He does not have a body or corporeal form, it is clear that He is not subject to any properties or incidents that characterize the physical: neither integration nor disintegration, space nor measure, ascent nor descent, right nor left, front nor back, standing nor sitting. He is not subject to time, so He does not have a beginning, end, or an age. He does not change, for there is nothing that can cause Him to change. Death, life (in the context of physical life), foolishness, wisdom (in terms of human wisdom), sleep, waking, anger, laughter, joy, sadness, silence, and speech (in the human understanding of speech) are not applicable to Him.

Exercise 3

According to Maimonides, which adjectives or qualities describe God, and which adjectives or qualities do not describe God?

GOD IS	GOD IS NOT

Figure 1.1

Divine Parameters

WE BELIEVE THAT . . .

a. there is an underlying fundamental reality.

b. everything that exists is a product of this fundamental reality.

THIS FUNDAMENTAL REALITY . . .

c. is **essential**.

d. is **unchanging**.

e. is **one**.

f. is **bodiless** and **formless**.

TEXT 3

RABBI YEDAYAH HAPENINI, *BECHINOT OLAM* (VILNA, 1879), PP. 70–71

תַּכְלִית מַה שֶּׁנֵּדַע בְּךָ,
שֶׁלֹּא נְדָעֲךָ.

וְאוּלָם נֵדַע הֱיוֹתְךָ נִמְצָא,
זֶה חֶלְקֵנוּ מִכָּל עֲמַל הַהִשְׂתַּכְּלוּת וִיגִיעַת הַהַשְׁקָפָה.

לְבַד בְּהַשָּׂגַת קְצַת שׁוֹלְלִיּוֹת,
יִלְבַּשׁ צְדָקָה מְבַקֵּר בְּהֵיכָלֶךָ.

וּבַהֲבָנַת הַהַרְחָקוֹת,
יִקְרַב אִישׁ לְהִשְׁתַּחֲוֹת לְךָ.

The ultimate knowledge of You
is [the knowledge] that we cannot know You.

Our philosophic exertion and inquiry
is only to know that You exist.

Only the comprehension, though negligible, of what You are not
drapes with righteousness the seeker in Your sanctuary.

By appreciating distance,
a person can approach and bow to You.

אגרת
שמים לרום
בחינות עולם
פה קק לובלין
שער

RABBI YEDAYAH BEN AVRAHAM HAPENINI
C. 1270–C. 1340

Poet, physician, philosopher. Rabbi Yedayah ben Avraham HaPenini was born in Béziers. Among his numerous writings is an ethical work, *Bechinat Olam*, and a philosophical commentary on various *Midrashim*. During the controversy surrounding the study of philosophy, he wrote *Igeret Hitnatselut* ("Apologetic Letter"), addressed to Rabbi Shlomo ben Aderet, in defense of philosophical study, entreating him to withdraw his ban against such study.

TEXT 4

DEUTERONOMY 6:4

שְׁמַע יִשְׂרָאֵל: ה' אֱלֹקֵינוּ, ה' אֶחָד.

Hear O Israel, the Lord is our God, the Lord is One!

TEXT 5

"WHEN AMERICANS SAY THEY BELIEVE IN GOD, WHAT DO THEY MEAN?," PEW RESEARCH CENTER, APRIL 25, 2018

Previous Pew Research Center studies have shown that the share of Americans who believe in God with absolute certainty has declined in recent years, while the share saying they have doubts about God's existence—or that they do not believe in God at all—has grown.

These trends raise a series of questions: When respondents say they don't believe in God, what are they rejecting? Are they rejecting belief in any higher power or spiritual force in the universe? Or are they rejecting only a traditional Christian idea of God—perhaps recalling images of a bearded man in the sky? Conversely, when respondents say they do believe in God, what do they believe in—God as described in the Bible, or some other spiritual force or supreme being?

A new Pew Research Center survey of more than 4,700 U.S. adults finds that one-third of Americans say they do *not* believe in the God of the Bible, but that they do believe there is some other higher power or spiritual force in the universe. A slim majority of Americans (56%) say they believe in God "as described in the Bible." And one-in-ten do not believe in any higher power or spiritual force.

In the U.S., belief in a deity is common even among the religiously unaffiliated—a group composed of those who identify themselves, religiously, as atheist, agnostic or "nothing in particular," and sometimes referred to, collectively, as religious "nones." Indeed, nearly three-quarters of religious "nones" (72%) believe in a higher power of some kind, even if not in God as described in the Bible.

TEXT 6a

MARCUS DU SAUTOY, PHD, *THE GREAT UNKNOWN: SEVEN JOURNEYS TO THE FRONTIERS OF SCIENCE* (NEW YORK, N.Y.: VIKING, 2016), PP. 416–417

What happens if I try to be creative with some of our unknowable questions? What if, for example, I were to define God as the solution to the question "Why something rather than nothing?" This concept is meant to be nothing more than the solution to that question. It doesn't have any other properties. Even if we gain more knowledge about the answer to the question, it will just mean that we know more about this particular God. . . .

The trouble with most religions is that the God that is served has so many properties that have nothing to do with the definition. It's as if we are working backwards, focusing on the strange properties conjured up over the generations without really understanding the original definition. We come across this bastardized picture early on as kids, and then when we ask the question "Why something rather than nothing?" it doesn't really work as a solution. But we've been shown the wrong thing.

Being an atheist means, for me, that I reject the classical solutions that religion seems to offer for these unknowns. But maybe I shouldn't throw everything out. There are things that will always remain unknown, so perhaps God does exist. . . .

MARCUS PETER FRANCIS DU SAUTOY, PHD
1965–

British scientist and mathematician. Du Sautoy is a highly awarded professor of mathematics.In 2008, he succeeded Richard Dawkins as chair of the Simonyi Professorship for the Public Understanding of Science at the University of Oxford (U.K.). He has written numerous articles and books on mathematics, including the best seller, *The Music of the Primes*.

I wonder, though, whether, as I come to the end of my exploration, I have changed my mind about declaring myself an atheist. With my definition of a God as that which we cannot know, to declare myself an atheist would mean that I believe there is nothing we cannot know. I don't believe that anymore. In some sense I think I have proved that this God does exist. The challenge now is to explore what quality this God has.

Le Penseur (The Thinker) (detail), Auguste Rodin, bronze sculpture, 1880. (National Gallery of Art, Washington, D.C.)

TEXT 6b

MARCUS DU SAUTOY, PHD, IBID.

The trouble with this definition of God is that it doesn't really get you much further. . . . Defining something as the solution to "Why something rather than nothing?" doesn't give rise to anything new. You need to make up properties for this thing that don't follow from its definition. As Karen Armstrong put it, this high God is too high. . . .

I reject the existence of a supernatural intelligence that intervenes in the evolution of the universe and in our lives. This is a rejection of the God that people assign strange properties to—such as compassion, wisdom, love—that make no sense when it comes to the idea that I am exploring.

TEXT 7

MIDRASH, *BEREISHIT RABAH* 42:8

"וַיַּגֵּד לְאַבְרָם הָעִבְרִי" (בְּרֵאשִׁית יד, יג) . . .
רַבִּי יְהוּדָה אוֹמֵר: כָּל הָעוֹלָם כּוּלּוֹ מֵעֵבֶר אֶחָד וְהוּא מֵעֵבֶר אֶחָד.

"[A fugitive] reported to Abraham the Hebrew [that Lot had been taken captive]" (GENESIS 14:13). . . .

Rabbi Yehudah said: [Abraham is called "the Hebrew"] because the entire world was on one side, and he was on the other side.

BEREISHIT RABAH

An early rabbinic commentary on the Book of Genesis. This Midrash bears the name of Rabbi Oshiya Rabah (Rabbi Oshiya "the Great"), whose teaching opens this work. This Midrash provides textual exegeses and stories, expounds upon the biblical narrative, and develops and illustrates moral principles. Produced by the sages of the Talmud in the Land of Israel, its use of Aramaic closely resembles that of the Jerusalem Talmud. It was first printed in Constantinople in 1512 together with four other Midrashic works on the other four books of the Pentateuch.

Abraham Contemplates the Stars, Ephraim Moses Lilien, illustration from F. Rahlwes (ed.), *Die Bücher Der Bibel (The Books of the Bible)* (Braunschweig, Germany: Georg Westerman Publ., 1908).

TEXT 8a

PSALMS 113:3–6

> מִמִּזְרַח שֶׁמֶשׁ עַד מְבוֹאוֹ; מְהֻלָּל שֵׁם ה׳.
> רָם עַל כָּל גּוֹיִם ה׳; עַל הַשָּׁמַיִם כְּבוֹדוֹ.
> מִי כַּה׳ אֱלֹקֵינוּ; הַמַּגְבִּיהִי לָשָׁבֶת.
> הַמַּשְׁפִּילִי לִרְאוֹת; בַּשָּׁמַיִם וּבָאָרֶץ.

From where the sun rises to where it sets, God's name is praised.

God is exalted above all the nations; His glory is upon the heavens.

Who is like our God, Who is seated on high,

Who lowers Himself to look on the heavens and the earth?

Genesis (detail), Shalom Moskovits, gouache on paper, 1958.

TEXT 8b

THE REBBE, RABBI MENACHEM MENDEL SCHNEERSON, *SEFER HAMAAMARIM MELUKAT* 1:53

דְהִנֵּה, "רָם עַל כָּל גּוֹיִם ה', עַל הַשָּׁמַיִם כְּבוֹדוֹ". שֶׁהֵן אוֹמְרִים שֶׁהוּא רָם וְנִשָּׂא, וְעַל כֵּן רַק "עַל הַשָּׁמַיִם כְּבוֹדוֹ", אֲבָל עַל הַנִּבְרָאִים הַתַּחְתּוֹנִים וְהַשְּׁפֵלִים הֲרֵי זֶה הַשְׁפָּלָה לְגַבֵּי' לְהַשְׁגִּיחַ עֲלֵיהֶם, וְעָזַב ה' אֶת הָאָרֶץ בִּידֵי הַכּוֹכָבִים וּמַעַרְכוֹת הַשָּׁמַיִם...

אֲבָל בֶּאֱמֶת אֵינוֹ כֵּן, דְּ"הַמַּגְבִּיהִי לָשָׁבֶת, הַמַּשְׁפִּילִי לִרְאוֹת בַּשָּׁמַיִם וּבָאָרֶץ". דִּלְהִיוֹתוֹ מַגְבִּיהִי לָשָׁבֶת, בִּבְחִינַת הַבְדָּלָה, עַל כֵּן הוּא מַשְׁפִּילִי בַּשָּׁמַיִם וָאָרֶץ בְּשָׁוֶה.

“God is exalted above all the nations; His glory is upon the heavens.” The nations claim that because God is exalted and lofty, His glory is *only* “upon the heavens.” It would be degrading for Him to oversee the affairs of the lowliest of creations. He therefore left the world to be administered by the various forces of nature [that He created]. . . .

In truth, however, God “is seated on high,” and “lowers Himself to look upon the heavens and the earth.” God sits on high, beyond all. He therefore lowers Himself equally to [look upon] heaven and on earth.

RABBI MENACHEM MENDEL SCHNEERSON 1902–1994

The towering Jewish leader of the 20th century, known as “the Lubavitcher Rebbe,” or simply as “the Rebbe.” Born in southern Ukraine, the Rebbe escaped Nazi-occupied Europe, arriving in the U.S. in June 1941. The Rebbe inspired and guided the revival of traditional Judaism after the European devastation, impacting virtually every Jewish community the world over. The Rebbe often emphasized that the performance of just one additional good deed could usher in the era of Mashiach. The Rebbe’s scholarly talks and writings have been printed in more than 200 volumes.

TEXT 9

JERUSALEM TALMUD, BERACHOT 9:1

בָּשָׂר וָדָם יֵשׁ לוֹ פַּטְרוֹן. אִם בָּאתָ לוֹ עֵת צָרָה אֵינוֹ נִכְנַס אֶצְלוֹ פִּתְאוֹם, אֶלָּא בָּא וְעוֹמֵד לוֹ עַל פִּתְחוֹ שֶׁל פַּטְרוֹנוֹ, וְקוֹרֵא לְעַבְדּוֹ אוֹ לְבֶן בֵּיתוֹ. וְהוּא אוֹמֵר, "אִישׁ פְּלוֹנִי עוֹמֵד עַל פֶּתַח חֲצֵירָךְ", שֶׁמָּא מַכְנִיסוֹ וְשֶׁמָּא מַנִּיחוֹ.

אֲבָל הַקָּדוֹשׁ בָּרוּךְ הוּא אֵינוֹ כֵּן. אִם בָּא עַל אָדָם צָרָה לֹא יִצְוַוח לֹא לְמִיכָאֵל וְלֹא לְגַבְרִיאֵל, אֶלָּא לִי יִצְוַוח וַאֲנִי עוֹנֶה לוֹ מִיַּד. הָדָא הוּא דִכְתִיב, "כֹּל אֲשֶׁר יִקְרָא בְּשֵׁם יְהוָה יִמָּלֵט" (יוֹאֵל ג, ה).

If someone finds himself in distress, even if he has an influential patron, he does not abruptly approach the patron to request assistance. Rather, he stands at the door of the patron's courtyard and asks of the patron's servant or household member [to announce him]. The servant or household member says, "So-and-so is at the door of the courtyard [and seeks to be admitted.]" Permission to enter may or may not be granted.

God's way, however, is different. Therefore, when misfortune befalls a person, one should not seek the intercession of the angels Michael or Gabriel. "Call out to Me," God says, "and I shall immediately respond." Thus the prophet says, "Whosoever shall call on the name of God will be saved" (JOEL 3:5).

JERUSALEM TALMUD

A commentary to the Mishnah, compiled during the fourth and fifth centuries. The Jerusalem Talmud predates its Babylonian counterpart by 100 years and is written in both Hebrew and Aramaic. While the Babylonian Talmud is the most authoritative source for Jewish law, the Jerusalem Talmud remains an invaluable source for the spiritual, intellectual, ethical, historical, and legal traditions of Judaism.

QUESTIONS FOR DISCUSSION

1 Does our newfound understanding of God resolve any of the issues people have with God? If yes, which ones?

2 Does our newfound understanding create any new issues with God or exacerbate any of the ones we've already discussed?

Hear O Israel, Isac Friedlander, etching, c. 1944.

KEY POINTS

1 Belief in God is fundamental to Judaism. We are obliged to believe that there is a primary being and that everything that exists is a product of this being. This primary being is essential, unchanging, bodiless and formless, and one. As this description suggests, what we don't know about God far exceeds that which we do know about Him.

2 Many who profess not to believe in God reject not God, but a package of secondary beliefs. They do, in fact, accept the aforementioned notion of a unified underlying reality that is beyond human understanding. In effect, they believe in God, but by a different name.

3 Some secondary beliefs that people find unpalatable are a product of an immature or uninformed conception of God. Other secondary beliefs are correct—though non-essential to God's definition—and will be explored in this course.

4 The concept of a primary being that is the cause for all subsequent existence is not difficult to embrace. Many believe, however, that this God is too great and transcendent to be relevant to finite beings.

5 The belief in God's oneness, introduced to the world by our forefather Abraham, means that God is the one and only power. No other entity, physical or spiritual, exerts any control. Thus, this being—Who is beyond definition or understanding—is intimately involved with every aspect of Creation.

6 To accept God is to embrace and be in tune with the underlying reality of all of existence; to reject God is to live oblivious to the ultimate reality.

Additional Readings

MEET YOUR CREATOR

BY RABBI ARYEH KAPLAN

> *And the L-rd spoke to Moses, saying,*
> *"Speak to all the congregation of the children of Israel and say to them, 'You must be holy, for I the L-rd your G-d, am holy.'" (Leviticus 19:1-2)*

To understand this quotation from the Torah, we must focus on the word "holy." Precisely what does it mean? And furthermore, what does the Torah intend when it describes G-d as "holy"?

Ordinarily, when we think of something holy, we think of something that is dedicated to G-d. Thus, we would consider a holy person to be one who dedicates his life to serving G-d. Similarly, we call a Torah scroll holy, since its use is dedicated to the worship of G-d. However, if to be holy is to be dedicated to G-d, then describing G-d Himself as holy would seem to be meaningless, a senseless redundancy.

Delving deeper into the semantics of the word "holy" reveals another meaning. "Holy" actually means separated from earthly, worldly things. Thus, a holy person is not only dedicated to G-d, he also relinquishes all worldly things. A holy vessel is not simply used in a worship service; it is never used for any mundane purpose at all.

This, then, is what the Torah means when it describes G-d as holy. He is completely separated from all earthly things, from the physical and material world. His nature is beyond all human comprehension. Even the highest angels cannot fully understand G-d's true nature. Only G-d Himself can truly know Himself.

Maimonides describes this in his *Canon of the Laws of the Foundations of Faith:*

> *Even the very highest spiritual beings cannot understand the true nature of their Creator. . . . Although their knowledge of G-d far transcends that of any mortal man—that of any creature bound to the physical world—still, there is no being, other than G-d Himself, who can understand the nature of G-d. (Ch. I, Par. 8)*

Such an analysis may indeed seem discouraging. Since by definition no one can ever hope to understand fully what G-d is, many people give up trying to understand Him at all. Yet, this attitude is not merely negative, it is in fact very wrong. Although we can never comprehend G-d's true essence, there are many things about Him that we do know.

What is G-d? To Whom do we address our prayers? Whom do we serve? These are questions about which we can learn a great deal.

Our first concept of G-d is that He is the Creator of the universe. "In the beginning G-d created the heaven and the earth" (Genesis 1:1). What does it mean to be the Creator of the universe? And what is this universe that G-d created?

The earth is a ball suspended in space. Its diameter is about 8,000 miles. If a man were to take a trip around the world, he would travel about 24,000 miles. Imagine trying to walk from New York to Chicago. Even after such a long walk, one would have travelled across a very small portion of the earth—about 1/60 of the distance around the globe.

Compared to man, the earth is very big. Yet, vast though the earth may seem to us, it is a mere speck in the greater vastness of space. Ninety million miles

RABBI ARYEH KAPLAN, 1934–1983

American rabbi, author, and physicist. Rabbi Kaplan authored more than 50 volumes on Torah, Talmud, Jewish mysticism, and philosophy, many of which have become modern-day classics. He is best known for his popular translation and elucidation of the Bible, *The Living Torah*; and his translation of the Ladino biblical commentary, *Me'am Lo'ez*.

from the earth is the sun, a fiery ball of gas, 866,000 miles in diameter, and over a hundred times larger than the earth. Even the sun is a mere speck in the great expanse of space. There are billions and billions of suns, for every star in the sky is actually a sun, thousands of times bigger than the earth, yet so far away that it appears to be a mere point of light.

These figures baffle the mind—we simply cannot grasp the concept of millions of miles. An imaginary model will help us to comprehend it. Picture a huge giant, suspended in outer space. Between his fingers he holds a little ball—one inch in diameter—about as big as a ping-pong ball. That is the earth. On its surface are cities and people, but they could only be seen with a microscope.

About three feet from this little ball is another, the size of a pea. That would be the moon. The sun, on the other hand, would be nowhere in sight. It would be placed about a quarter of a mile away—a glowing ball, nine feet in diameter, about the size of a small car.

Nine planets, the solar system, rotate around the sun. The furthest planet, Pluto, would be about 13 miles away. Even a giant holding the earth between his fingers would have a long walk if he wished to visit all the planets in the solar system.

But what if the giant wanted to visit the nearest fixed star, Alpha Centauri—how far would he need to travel? Even a giant could never make the trip on his own. Even he would be forced to take a rocket ship, for in this model, with the earth scaled to a one-inch ball, the nearest fixed star would still be 40,000 miles away! And many stars would be farther still, millions of miles away, even on such a reduced scale.

Comparing the earth to a ping-pong ball may help us conceive of the solar system, but beyond that, the model fails us. The distances still boggle the imagination, so a new measure is required. The one most scientists use in discussing interstellar space is the speed of light.

Light travels 186,000 miles per second—over 600 million miles per hour—a hundred thousand times faster than the fastest rocket. Light travels around the earth in 1/7 of a second, from the earth to the moon in 1½ seconds, and from the earth to the sun in about eight minutes. Yet it would take light, even at this speed, over four years to reach the nearest fixed star. And to reach many of the stars we see in the sky, light would have to travel for many hundreds of years.

Each one of these distant stars is like the sun, thousands and even millions of times bigger than the earth. The stars cluster together in galaxies. In our galaxy alone, astronomers count over one hundred billion stars, each one thousands of times larger than our planet, many with solar systems of their own. Can we imagine the size of a single galaxy? It would take light, travelling at over 600 million miles per hour, over one hundred thousand years to cross our galaxy alone.

Yet this enormous galaxy, with its billions of stars, is but a speck in the universe. Modern telescopes can photograph hundreds of billions of galaxies, each one containing hundreds of billions of stars. Can the human mind begin to comprehend the size of even the visible universe?

Still, our universe is finite. Scientists proved that many years ago. Finite though it may be, the universe is so immense that it staggers the human imagination. Our planet, our solar system, even our galaxy, are like minute bits of dust in the vast expanse of the universe.

Where, then, did this vast universe come from? How did this tremendous amount of matter and energy come into being? There can be only one answer: It was created by G-d. Stars, planets, galaxies, billions and billions of them all—all were created by G-d! What great power G-d must have!

One might think that creating such a huge universe was a lot of work for G-d, even that it tired Him out. Nothing could be further from the truth. The Midrash tells us that G-d created the universe with the Hebrew letter *heh*. That is, G-d created the universe with as little effort as it takes to pronounce the sound "huh." G-d's power is infinite, so that for Him any finite task, no matter how enormous, is nothing.

Many people have asked, if G-d is so great, and if the entire universe is His domain, how can He pay any attention to the tiny speck of cosmic dust that is our planet earth. How can He give any consideration to the prayers, or to the actions, of any single individual?

Such questions underestimate G-d, for just as He has infinite power, He also has infinite wisdom.

Imagine: infinite wisdom, infinite intelligence, infinite mentality.

An ordinary human being has limited mental capacities. He can usually concentrate on only one thing at a time. Even then, his concentration may often waver and drift. Gifted individuals can occasionally concentrate on two or three problems at a time, but again, their concentration drifts from one thing to another; it is not absolute.

Suppose that the mentality of this entire planet were gathered, and the intelligence of all five billion people on earth were placed into a single mind. Presumably, such a mind would be able to concentrate on five billion things at once. Nevertheless, it would still be a finite intellect. But the intellect of G-d is infinite. G-d can concentrate His attention infinitely. He can focus simultaneously on every single atom in the universe. He is aware of each electron and each proton in all of creation, with less mental effort than a man uses to scan the newspaper.

An infinitely powerful G-d Who watches our every move, 24 hours a day—the implications are frightening. At every moment, G-d knows our every thought, for He sees not with light and eyes, as men do. Rather, He has an awareness of everything in the universe—an awareness that is much more than seeing—an awareness that only the Creator can have. It is a terrifying thought, but it is true.

When we first consider G-d's greatness, we are filled with tremendous awe. But if a person were to think awhile, to realize just how great G-d really is, and if he would truly grasp how He watches us every second of the day, that person would become a saint. He would have no alternative. After all, how could a person do wrong if he realized that the Creator of the entire universe is watching him constantly and is interested in everything he does?

So it is indeed possible to know something about G-d. We know that He has infinite power and that He created the universe without effort. We know that He has infinite mentality, that He is interested in us, that He listens to our prayers, and that He loves His creatures. And we understand that there is only one G-d, for there can be only one Infinite Being.

We know that G-d has no body, no shape, and no form. Our very concepts of space and time become meaningless when we try to apply them to G-d's being. But G-d is not an abstract concept. He is very real, as real as we are. In fact, He is more real than we are, for our very concept of reality was created by G-d.

This, then, is the G-d to whom we all pray. When we pray, we are talking to G-d. We speak to the Being Whose power brought the entire universe into existence. We utter this thought in our morning prayers when we say, "Blessed is He who spoke and the universe came into being."

There is a story about the great Chassidic rabbi, Reb Zusia of Anipoli. He would always be the first to arrive in the synagogue each morning. One day, Reb Zusia was late. His students waited and waited. Finally, just before noon, he arrived, a look of awe and wonder on his face. The prayers began. Somehow they seemed more meaningful, more fervent than usual.

After the service, the students asked the rabbi where he had been. "We were so worried," they said.

Reb Zusia replied, "I will tell you. As you all know, every morning when we first awake we say the prayer, 'I give thanks before You, O Living and Eternal King, Who has returned my soul to consciousness in mercy. Great is Your trust.'

"This morning I began the prayer, 'I give thanks before You.' The thought struck me, what am I, and what is 'You'? Who am I to speak to G-d? How can I address the Creator of the universe?

"I began again. 'I give thanks before You'—I, an infinitesimal speck of creation, before You, the Author of all creation. I couldn't continue. It took me hours to gather courage to finish the prayer. That is why I was late."

Reb Zusia was overwhelmed by the implications of the brief and simple *Modeh Ani* prayer. Yet every time we say a prayer, we are speaking to G-d Himself. We are standing before the Master of all creation, before the One Who created the earth, the sun, the stars, the entire universe.

In preparing to pray, we focus our minds on G-d's wonders, until we begin to realize to Whom we are praying. And like the Psalmist we exclaim,

> *O L-rd, our G-d, how mighty is Your Name in all the earth. . .*
> *When I look at Your heavens, the work of Your fingers;*
> *The moon and the stars that You have established.*
> *(Psalms 8:2–4)*

Through this awareness, we may fasten our gaze on G-d Himself, and with true feeling praise the Master of the universe:

> *I will give thanks to the L-rd with my whole heart;*
> *I will tell of Your wonderful deeds. . .*
> *I will sing praise to Your name, O Most High.*
> *(Psalms 9:2–3)*

Excerpt from Aryeh Kaplan, *Encounters* (Brooklyn, N.Y.: Moznaim Publishing Co., 1990).
Reprinted with permission of the publisher

ABRAHAM: THE RENOVATOR

BY RABBI ADIN EVEN-ISRAEL STEINSALTZ

Abraham[1] is the hero of an epos that is peculiar to Israel and stands out with a greatness of its own in the history of mankind.

The Bible story tells us a great deal about the man and his ideas, the way he lived, his friends and enemies, his family, and so on. Having been told so much, the question may well be asked: What, after all, did he do? What makes him a central figure in the memory of the race? Key figures in history are not ordinary persons, and we usually attach some descriptive epithet to a great name: a noble conqueror, an artistic genius, an intrepid explorer, the founder of an empire, and so on. How can we define the greatness of Abraham?

The most accepted answer to this question—throughout the generations—has been the view that Abraham was the innovator of monotheism: that he gave us the faith in one God. He is alleged to have been the first to conceive and develop the idea, and thereby to have founded the Jewish people and all the monotheistic religions and, consequently, much of the philosophy and modes of thought that lie at the source of our civilization.

Nevertheless, despite the vivid legend of the story of the young Abraham smashing the idols, this view of the father of the nation is not accepted by serious scientific scholars. A rereading of the Bible text is enough to show that there is no mention of Abraham's role as a great prophet bringing to the world the belief in a single God. Many wonderful things are related about the man, and his stature holds up to any critical scrutiny. His deeds and character are in fact recollected with love and reverence in many tales, with descriptions of his faith and devotion, his wanderings, his courage, his hospitality, and even his weaknesses. But the fact that he was the originator of monotheism is not mentioned.

In point of fact, a closer reexamination of the Genesis story and of the many exegeses leads to a different view of the man and sheds light on many other developments in religious history. To begin with, according to the Bible itself, the belief in one God is not

RABBI ADIN EVEN-ISRAEL STEINSALTZ, 1937–

Talmudist, author, and philosopher. Rabbi Even-Israel Steinsaltz is considered one of the foremost Jewish thinkers of the 20th century. Praised by *Time* magazine as a "once-in-a-millennium scholar," he has been awarded the Israel Prize for his contributions to Jewish study. He lives in Jerusalem and is the founder of the Israel Institute for Talmudic Publications, a society dedicated to the translation and elucidation of the Talmud.

anything new, nor is it the peak of some evolutionary development. Monotheism is not a higher stage of some process of growth following on a lower stage of polytheism. Monotheism is itself primary and basic; it has been the dominant mode of worship from as far back as human memory goes. All the other modes of religious faith came after it, and not before. For this truth, the scriptural text itself, though it does not say so in precisely this fashion, is the chief evidence. And like Maimonides and other Jewish sages, modern scholarship, especially in the field of anthropology, tends to question whether polytheism, even in its primitive forms such as fetishism or voodoo, is not a degeneration of primary monotheistic cults.

In other words, even the most primitive of peoples evince a faith in a higher power. It may be stretching the point to call this monotheism in the modern sense of the term, because the primitive mentality cannot make abstractions to the same degree. Nevertheless, a basic belief in one supreme basic power that makes everything happen in the universe is common to all—even to the Bushmen of Africa or the inhabitants of the Tierra del Fuego in South America, peoples thoroughly isolated from other cultural influences. Their fundamental belief is not in many gods or even in various forces of nature that have to be propitiated; it is a belief in or worship of one power, one essence or thing that takes on the dimensions of the utmost grandeur their psyche can conceive. This fundamental stance of the human before the holy, which is just within and yet beyond conception, is not necessarily a matter of man's relation to any specific force of nature, or to a person or awesome image, or even to gods and demons. It is the primary sensation of "little me," which is the true feeling of every human being when facing the mystery and the vastness of life in the world.

This is the genesis point in the soul. From it two different courses may be taken. One may hold fast to this primal unity against the impact of the inexplicable and bear up to all that such a position implies. This course would lead to a faith in a single God. The alternative development would be from the unity to the multiplicity. In other words, from simple monotheism—the direct faith in something not specific or clearly oriented (which is perhaps like the faith of a child)—to a complex faith, derived from the endeavor to isolate certain things and subjects. At first, there is the concept of the whole, because man cannot yet define any specific force or thing. Afterward, the whole begins to be analyzed, broken down into parts and categories: fire, water, air, earth, sun, and the like. Feelings of fear, gratitude, and shame lead to rites of worship of that eminent force of nature which seems to be most endowed with a life and consciousness of its own. In turn, it itself becomes a complex and variegated system of forces, each with a character of its own and ultimately with a representative god of its own.

After further development and degeneration, the stage is reached of the image or figure. The graven image is not the father of the god but its offspring. At first, the image is the symbol of the divine's power; but, after a certain decline of the power of faith, men no longer present themselves before the primal force or the symbol but relate to the physical image, the statue. Then follows the worship of these statues and pictures and of whatever else is given to visual perception, touch, caress.

Idolatry of this sort is, therefore, not the first or the most primitive stage of religion. It is a later development in a certain direction. It is a transition from the primal belief in an unknown God to a worship of tangible and comprehensible gods. The great amalgam of the infinite is very difficult to negotiate with. It is much easier to relate to some specific force or image and to propitiate "him" with offerings and to expect certain responses in the way of rewards and punishments.

Polytheism is thus a complicated and sophisticated system of worship springing from the need to establish a "rational" and direct contact with the divine. Instead of trying to communicate with a basic supreme essence, polytheism believes in the possibility of usefulness of intermediaries, such as specific gods or a set of semi-divine forces.

Even the Hindu Scriptures (like those of most other "polytheistic" religions) recognize the existence of a supreme formless divine, the Atman, who cannot be reached by man except through the functional gods—which increase in number the nearer they get to the popular mind. And, of course, this is the perspective of the Bible itself. The first man is seen as a whole, the archetype of a direct relation with a single hidden God. The following generations "began to call on the name of God" and thus, according to a certain exegesis, indicated that men were beginning to attach significance to other forces—of nature, symbols, and images, whether genuine or false. A system of well-defined forces that provide a reasonable explanation for things is the product of an advanced culture, with a philosophy, science, astronomy, and so on.

This intellectual world of polytheistic religion—with all its sophistication and corruption—was the world in which the patriarch Abraham lived. He did not emerge from a pastoral world of wandering shepherds, uncouth and unlearned. He came from great cities, centers of culture and hubs of commerce. In these cities, there were banks and letters of credit, as in our own day, even if documents were written on bricks of clay. A world of elaborate civilization, already ancient and worldly-wise in its own way: Ur of the Chaldees, Babylon, Egypt. . . . It was a polytheistic, idolatrous urbanity, the height of an ancient culture, representing the most advanced ideas and the most refined concepts in science, art, and philosophy.

And in this world, the "modern" world of the ancient past, Abraham found himself believing in a single God. It was not a new discovery on his part; on the contrary, it was a reaffirmation of a very old truth, one that had almost been forgotten and was probably considered by his contemporaries as barbaric and primitive. Abraham was thus not an innovator but an ultraconservative, like someone belonging to a cult of ancient origin. On the other hand, Abraham did represent something very new: he was a prophet in that he called for a renewal of faith, a return (almost a repentance) to the divine Oneness. He tried to restore the faith of a distant past; but his contemporaries probably saw him as a crude and rather old-fashioned preacher.

One of the proofs offered by the Bible itself is the meeting with Melchizedek, King of Salem (Jerusalem), priest of the supreme God. This passage implies that Abraham has companions in faith, that his religion is not his own private invention. These companions were to be found scattered in isolated spots throughout the world, such as this small city on the way from one great center of culture on the Euphrates to another on the Nile. What is more, all along the journey, Abraham called on the name of God; he built altars and sanctuaries and taught people the nature of the divine unity. What he did amounted to a cultural revolution in his time: he tried to revive what was considered an archaic remnant of a primitive religion, and to make it into a new system of faith.

Hence, Abraham was not really an innovator or someone proclaiming an entirely new concept of religious belief. He was simply the first person in a long time to relate seriously to an old religious outlook which was primary and genuine. He was a great man in his own terms—a leader of a tribe, a successful man of the world, a conqueror in battle, a fulfilled man in private life, and a thinker who was not subdued by adverse public opinion. In other words, he was a great leader who fulfilled the same function as in later generations would be attributed to a messiah—the restoration of the ancient system of right relations between man and the divine.

Abraham endeavored to release the precious truth from the hands of a small body of the faithful and to build a new sort of vessel to preserve it and to live it—a tribe, a community and family structure that would become a special nation. And this national unit would be able to renew the old faith in one God and keep it alive by grouping together and living according to its spirit.

For this purpose, Abraham wandered the face of the earth, gathering to him all those people who still believed and trying to awaken others to believe in the divine unity. He called on the name of God and preached to all to come to God. In short, Abraham was actually the first prophet to emerge from the ancient faith who taught it as something vital and true, as something to live by.

Excerpt from Adin Even-Israel Steinsaltz, *Biblical Images: Men and Women of the Book* (Jerusalem: Koren Publishers, 1984).

Endnotes

[1] Genesis 12:1–22:19.

INDIVIDUALITY IN UNIVERSALITY

BY RABBI J. IMMANUEL SCHOCHET

It may appear paradoxical, but the emphasis on the universal, on the ultimate oneness of all, also emphasizes the particular. For everything created by G-d, thus everything that is part of the universal, is created for a distinct purpose, with a distinct task in relation to the whole. "All that the Holy One, blessed be He, created in His world, He created solely for His glory."[1] Every particular, therefore, is indispensable.

The toenails, no less than the heart and the brain, have their individual purpose: each one necessary to, and complementing, the other for the complete and perfect functioning of the body. Affectations of the toes become affectations of the brain, and vice versa. The ill-health or pain of the one affect the well-being and functioning of the other.

To be sure, we do make quite clear distinctions between them. We speak of vital and non-vital, higher and lower, more and less important organs and limbs. We set up qualitative as well as quantitative scales of levels and values. Nonetheless, they are all intertwined, interdependent, interacting, with every particular adding its own contribution for which it was created. This contribution is its very function. To achieve it is to contribute to the well-being, the *yichud*, of the whole. To neglect it leads to *perud*, a division and defect in the whole.

In this context, too, it was said that everyone should always regard the whole world as half meritorious and half guilty. When committing a single sin, therefore, woe to him for turning the scale of guilt against himself and against the whole world. Thus it is said, "One sinner destroys much good" (Ecclesiastes 9:18), that is, on account of the sin of that individual he and the whole world lose much good. On the other hand, if he performs one *mitzvah*, happy is he for turning the scale of merit in his favour and in favour of the whole world, thus bringing salvation and deliverance to them, as it is said, "The righteous man is the foundation of the world" (Proverbs 10:25).[2]

The significance of individuality is poignantly expressed in the words of R. Zusya of Annapol, when he said of his day of judgment that he did not fear the Heavenly Judge's question as to why he had not attained the levels of the patriarchs, the prophets or even his masters; after all, who was he to compare to them? He did fear though, he said, the question of "Zusya, why were you not Zusya?"[3]

Excerpt from J. Immanuel Schochet, *The Mystical Tradition: Insights into the Nature of the Mystical Tradition in Judaism* (*The Mystical Dimension*, Vol. 1) (Brooklyn, N.Y.: Kehot Publication Society, 1990).

RABBI JACOB IMMANUEL SCHOCHET, PHD, 1935–2013

Torah scholar and philosopher. Rabbi Schochet was born in Switzerland. Rabbi Schochet was a renowned authority on kabbalah and Jewish law and authored more than 30 books on Jewish philosophy and mysticism. He also served as professor of philosophy at Humber College in Toronto, Canada. Rabbi Schochet was a member of the executive committee of the Rabbinical Alliance of America and of the Central Committee of Chabad-Lubavitch Rabbis, and served as the halachic guide for the Rohr Jewish Learning Institute.

Endnotes

1 *Avot* 6:11.

2 *Kidushin* 40b; Rambam, *Hilchot Teshuvah* 3:4. Note, though, that this weighing of sin against virtues is not a simple mathematical calculation. There are a number of qualitative computations that come into play, and these are an exclusively Divine prerogative; see *Hilchot Teshuvah* 3:2; *Kad Hakemach, s.v.* Rosh Hashanah-I.

3 This does not contradict the principle that everyone must strive to have his deeds achieve the level of the deeds of the patriarchs (*Eliyahu Rabba*, ch. 25); for just as the patriarchs did their best to live up to their obligations and potential, so can and must every individual.

Lesson

2

MEETING HIS NEEDS

WHAT G-D THINKS OF YOU

Morning Prayer on Subway, Lori Grinker, gelatin silver print, 1984. (The Jewish Museum, New York)

G-d's requests of humankind seem incredibly demanding. Why would a supposedly loving G-d complicate our lives with intrusive instructions? Moreover, can either you or your actions matter to an infinite G-d? This lesson explores the purpose of the universe to discover why G-d needs you and your mitzvot.

PSALMS 8:4–5

> כִּי אֶרְאֶה שָׁמֶיךָ מַעֲשֵׂה אֶצְבְּעֹתֶיךָ, יָרֵחַ וְכוֹכָבִים אֲשֶׁר כּוֹנָנְתָּה.
> מָה אֱנוֹשׁ כִּי תִזְכְּרֶנּוּ? וּבֶן אָדָם כִּי תִפְקְדֶנּוּ?

When I observe Your heavens, the work of Your fingers, and the moon and stars that You set in place, [I wonder:]

What is man that You should be mindful of him? What is a human that You should recall him?

The Creation, James Jacques Joseph Tissot, gouache on board, c. 1896–1902. (The Jewish Museum, New York)

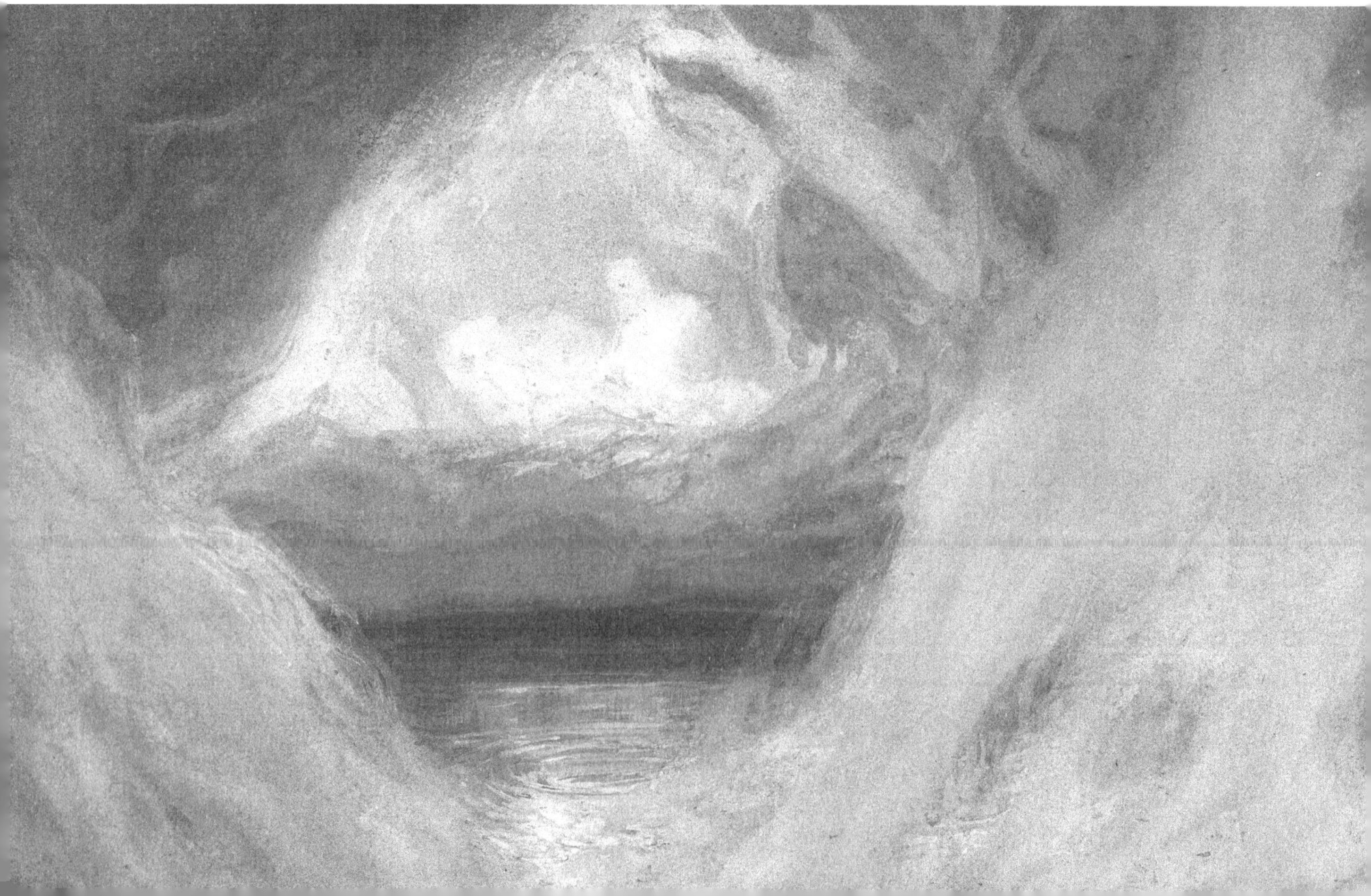

TEXT 2

JOB 35:6–8

אִם חָטָאתָ, מַה תִּפְעָל בּוֹ?
וְרַבּוּ פְשָׁעֶיךָ, מַה תַּעֲשֶׂה לּוֹ?
אִם צָדַקְתָּ, מַה תִּתֶּן לוֹ?
אוֹ מַה מִיָּדְךָ יִקָּח?
לְאִישׁ כָּמוֹךָ רִשְׁעֶךָ, וּלְבֶן אָדָם צִדְקָתֶךָ.

If you sin, how do you affect Him?

If your transgressions are many, what do you do to Him?

If you are righteous, what do you give to Him?

What does He take from your hand?

Your wickedness [only affects] a human like yourself, and your righteousness [only affects] people.

TEXT 3

SIFREI, VEZOT HABERACHAH 2

כְּשֶׁנִּגְלָה הַמָּקוֹם לִיתֵּן תּוֹרָה לְיִשְׂרָאֵל, לֹא עַל יִשְׂרָאֵל בִּלְבַד הוּא נִגְלָה, אֶלָּא עַל כָּל הָאוּמוֹת.

בִּתְחִילָּה הָלַךְ אֵצֶל בְּנֵי עֵשָׂו, וְאָמַר לָהֶם, "מְקַבְּלִים אַתֶּם אֶת הַתּוֹרָה?" אָמְרוּ לוֹ, "מַה כָּתוּב בָּהּ?" אָמַר לָהֶם, "לֹא תִרְצָח" (שְׁמוֹת כ, יג).

אָמְרוּ, "רִבּוֹנוֹ שֶׁל עוֹלָם! כָּל עַצְמוֹ שֶׁל אוֹתוֹ אֲבִיהֶם רוֹצֵחַ הוּא, שֶׁנֶּאֱמַר, 'וְהַיָּדַיִם יְדֵי עֵשָׂו' (בְּרֵאשִׁית כז, כב), וְעַל כָּךְ הִבְטִיחוֹ אָבִיו, שֶׁנֶּאֱמַר, 'וְעַל חַרְבְּךָ תִחְיֶה' (בְּרֵאשִׁית כז, מ)".

הָלַךְ לוֹ אֵצֶל בְּנֵי עַמּוֹן וּמוֹאָב, וְאָמַר לָהֶם, "מְקַבְּלִים אַתֶּם אֶת הַתּוֹרָה?" אָמְרוּ לוֹ, "מַה כָּתוּב בּוֹ?" אָמַר לָהֶם "לֹא תִנְאָף" (שְׁמוֹת כ, יג). אָמְרוּ לְפָנָיו, "רִבּוֹנוֹ שֶׁל עוֹלָם! עַצְמָהּ שֶׁל עֶרְוָה לָהֶם הִיא, שֶׁנֶּאֱמַר, 'וַתַּהֲרֶיןָ שְׁתֵּי בְנוֹת לוֹט מֵאֲבִיהֶן' (בְּרֵאשִׁית יט, לו)".

הָלַךְ וּמָצָא בְּנֵי יִשְׁמָעֵאל. אָמַר לָהֶם, "מְקַבְּלִים אַתֶּם אֶת הַתּוֹרָה?" אָמְרוּ לוֹ, "מַה כָּתוּב בָּהּ?" אָמַר לָהֶם, "לֹא תִגְנוֹב" (שְׁמוֹת כ, יג). אָמְרוּ לְפָנָיו, "רִבּוֹנוֹ שֶׁל עוֹלָם! כָּל עַצְמוֹ שֶׁל אֲבִיהֶם לִסְטִים הָיָה, שֶׁנֶּאֱמַר, 'וְהוּא יִהְיֶה פֶּרֶא אָדָם' (בְּרֵאשִׁית טז, יב).

וְכֵן לְכָל אוּמָּה וְאוּמָּה שָׁאַל לָהֶם אִם מְקַבְּלִים אֶת הַתּוֹרָה.

Before God revealed Himself to the Jews and gave them the Torah, He revealed Himself [and offered the Torah] to all the other nations.

First He approached the children of Esau and offered them the Torah. "What is written in it?" they asked. God responded, "Do not murder" (EXODUS 20:13).

"Master of the World!" they retorted. "Our father Esau was a murderer, as it is stated, 'the hands are the hands

SIFREI

An early rabbinic Midrash on the biblical books of Numbers and Deuteronomy. *Sifrei* focuses mostly on matters of law, as opposed to narratives and moral principles. According to Maimonides, this halachic Midrash was authored by Rav, a 3rd-century Babylonian Talmudic sage.

of Esau' (GENESIS 27:22). In fact, his father Isaac assured him, 'You will live by your sword' (IBID., 27:40)."

Next, God approached the children of Ammon and Moab and offered them the Torah. "What is written in it?" they asked. God responded, "Do not commit adultery" (EXODUS 20:13).

"Master of the World!" they retorted. "Our very existence is due to an illicit relationship, as it is stated, 'The two daughters of Lot became pregnant from their father' (GENESIS 19:36) [and they gave birth to Ammon and Moab]."

God continued and encountered the children of Ishmael and offered them the Torah. "What is written in it?" they asked. God responded, "Do not steal" (EXODUS 20:13).

"Master of the World!" they retorted. "Our father Ishmael was a bandit, as it is stated, 'He will be a wild man, [he will fight everyone and everyone will fight him]' (GENESIS 16:12)."

In a similar fashion, God approached every nation and offered the Torah [and every nation found reason to refuse it].

QUESTION FOR DISCUSSION

What would motivate you to take on a demanding and inconvenient responsibility or task?

Depiction of Moses bringing the tablets down from Mt. Sinai. From the *Braginsky Leipnik Haggadah*, copied and decorated by Joseph ben David of Leipnik, Altona, Hamburg, 1739. (The Braginsky Collection)

Figure 2.1

Forms of Motivation

	SAMPLE TASK	MOTIVATION
Extrinsic reward	Employment	Paycheck
Extrinsic negative consequence	Employment	Fear of poverty, homelessness, etc.
Intrinsic reward and consequence	Brushing and flossing teeth	Healthy teeth and pleasant breath vs. decaying teeth and gingivitis
Relationship	Taking care of a parent, spouse, or child	Love
Importance of the task	Volunteer work/ communal activism	Making a meaningful difference

TEXT 4

MAIMONIDES, COMMENTARY ON THE MISHNAH,
INTRODUCTION TO *PEREK CHELEK*

הַיְסוֹד הָאֲחַד עָשָׂר:
כִּי הוּא, הַשֵּׁם יִתְבָּרֵךְ, נוֹתֵן שָׂכָר לְמִי שֶׁעוֹשֶׂה מִצְוֹת הַתּוֹרָה, וְיַעֲנִישׁ לְמִי שֶׁעוֹבֵר עַל אַזְהָרוֹתֶיהָ.
וְכִי הַשָּׂכָר הַגָּדוֹל הָעוֹלָם הַבָּא, וְהָעוֹנֶשׁ הֶחָזָק הַכָּרֵת.

The eleventh principle:

God, blessed be He, rewards those who observe the commandments of the Torah and punishes those who transgress its prohibitions.

The greatest reward is [to experience the pleasures of] the World to Come; the greatest punishment is to be cut off [from the World to Come].

RABBI MOSHE BEN MAIMON (MAIMONIDES, RAMBAM) 1135–1204

Halachist, philosopher, author, and physician. Maimonides was born in Córdoba, Spain. After the conquest of Córdoba by the Almohads, he fled Spain and eventually settled in Cairo, Egypt. There, he became the leader of the Jewish community and served as court physician to the vizier of Egypt. He is most noted for authoring the *Mishneh Torah*, an encyclopedic arrangement of Jewish law, and for his philosophical work, *Guide for the Perplexed*. His rulings on Jewish law are integral to the formation of halachic consensus.

Figure 2.2

Mitzvah Motivation I

Extrinsic reward	Earthly and Heavenly reward
Extrinsic negative consequence	Earthly and Heavenly punishment

QUESTION FOR DISCUSSION

In your estimation, is the prospect of reward and punishment a sufficient and satisfactory motivation to follow God's instructions? Why or why not?

TEXT 5a

MAIMONIDES, *GUIDE FOR THE PERPLEXED* 3:31

שֶׁכָּל מִצְוָה מֵאֵלּוּ הַתַּרְיַ"ג מִצְוֹת, הִיא, אִם לִנְתִינַת דַעַת אֲמִתִּי, אוֹ לְהָסִיר
דַעַת רָע, אוֹ לִנְתִינַת סֵדֶר יָשָׁר, אוֹ לְהָסִיר עָוֶל, אוֹ לְהִתְלַמֵּד בְּמִדּוֹת
טוֹבוֹת, אוֹ לְהַזְהִיר מִמִּדּוֹת רָעוֹת.

Each of the six hundred and thirteen commandments either conveys an admirable idea or rejects a repugnant idea; either is a principle of justice or wards off an injustice; either endows a noble character trait or cautions against a negative trait.

TEXT 5b

NACHMANIDES, DEUTERONOMY 22:6

"לֹא נִתְּנוּ הַמִּצְוֹת אֶלָּא לְצָרֵף בָּהֶם אֶת הַבְּרִיּוֹת" (בְּרֵאשִׁית רַבָּה מד, א):. . . שֶׁאֵין הַתּוֹעֶלֶת בְּמִצְוֹת לְהַקָּדוֹשׁ בָּרוּךְ הוּא בְּעַצְמוֹ יִתְעַלֶּה, אֲבָל הַתּוֹעֶלֶת בְּאָדָם עַצְמוֹ לִמְנוֹעַ מִמֶּנּוּ נֶזֶק, אוֹ אֱמוּנָה רָעָה, אוֹ מִדָּה מְגוּנָּה, אוֹ לִזְכּוֹר הַנִּסִּים וְנִפְלָאוֹת הַבּוֹרֵא יִתְבָּרֵךְ, וְלָדַעַת אֶת הַשֵּׁם.

וְזֶהוּ "לְצָרֵף בָּהֶם", שֶׁיִּהְיוּ כְּכֶסֶף צָרוּף, כִּי הַצּוֹרֵף הַכֶּסֶף אֵין מַעֲשֵׂהוּ בְּלֹא טַעַם, אֲבָל לְהוֹצִיא מִמֶּנּוּ כָּל סִיג, וְכֵן הַמִּצְוֹת לְהוֹצִיא מִלִּבֵּנוּ כָּל אֱמוּנָה רָעָה, וּלְהוֹדִיעֵנוּ הָאֱמֶת, וּלְזוֹכְרוֹ תָּמִיד.

"The *mitzvot* were given solely to refine human beings" (MIDRASH, *BEREISHIT RABAH* 44:1). . . . The *mitzvot* are not intended to benefit God. Their purpose is to benefit humankind—to keep us from harm, shield us from negative beliefs and base character traits, remind us of the miracles and wonders of the Creator, and to help us know God.

The Midrash says that *mitzvot* "refine" human beings, similar to the process of refining silver. Just as silver is refined to remove all impurities, so, too, *mitzvot* cleanse our hearts of improper beliefs, make us cognizant of the truth, and help us be constantly aware of God.

RABBI MOSHE BEN NACHMAN (NACHMANIDES, RAMBAN) 1194–1270

Scholar, philosopher, author, and physician. Nachmanides was born in Spain and served as leader of Iberian Jewry. In 1263, he was summoned by King James of Aragon to a public disputation with Pablo Cristiani, a Jewish apostate. Though Nachmanides was the clear victor of the debate, he had to flee Spain because of the resulting persecution. He moved to Israel and helped reestablish communal life in Jerusalem. He authored a classic commentary on the Pentateuch and a commentary on the Talmud.

TEXT 6

ROBERT A. EMMONS, PHD, *THANKS!: HOW PRACTICING GRATITUDE CAN MAKE YOU HAPPIER* (NEW YORK: HOUGHTON MIFFLIN, 2008), PP. 205–206

An ingenious series of experiments conducted a number of years ago showed that when people mimicked the facial expressions associated with happiness, they felt happier—even when they did not know they were moving the "happy muscles" in their face. Researchers have found that smiling itself produces feelings of happiness. How were they kept in the dark? Simple. They were asked to hold a pencil with their teeth. Doing so tends to activate the muscle we use when we smile (the zygomatic major). This muscle lifts the corner of the mouth obliquely upwards and laterally, and produces a characteristic smiling expression. Try it now. You will smile. Now, take that pencil and hold it in your lips, pointing it straight out. A different set of muscles are now activated, those that are involved in frowning (these are the ones targeted by Botox treatments). Why this clever ruse? You can't tell subjects in the study that they are supposed to be feeling happy, because that would have unintended consequences on the behavioral rating of interest.

It turned out that the people with the pencil in their teeth, who were, unbeknownst to them, activating their zygomatic muscles, rated cartoons funnier than those

ROBERT EMMONS, PHD
1958–

Professor of psychology. Emmons teaches at the University of California, Davis, and is a leading scientific expert on the psychology of gratitude. Emmons is the founding editor in chief of *The Journal of Positive Psychology* and the author of multiple volumes on the subject of gratitude, including *Thanks! How Practicing Gratitude Can Make You Happier*.

who held the pencils with their lips. It appears that going through the motions can trigger the emotions. Technically stated, involuntary facial movements provide sufficient peripheral information to drive emotional experience.

QUESTION FOR DISCUSSION

How does keeping kosher foster character development?

Matzo Meal, Audrey Flack, oil on canvas, 1962. (The Jewish Museum, New York)

Figure 2.3

Mitzvah Motivation II

Extrinsic reward	Earthly and Heavenly reward
Extrinsic negative consequence	Earthly and Heavenly punishment
Intrinsic reward and consequence	Character development

QUESTION FOR DISCUSSION

In your estimation, is the prospect of character development a sufficient and satisfactory motivation to follow God's instructions? Why or why not?

TEXT 7

PSALMS 42:2–3

כְּאַיָּל תַּעֲרֹג עַל אֲפִיקֵי מָיִם, כֵּן נַפְשִׁי תַעֲרֹג אֵלֶיךָ אֱלֹקִים.
צָמְאָה נַפְשִׁי לֵאלֹקִים לְאֵ-ל חָי. מָתַי אָבוֹא וְאֵרָאֶה פְּנֵי אֱלֹקִים?

As the deer longs for streams of water, so I long for You, O God.

I thirst for God, the living God. When will I come and appear in God's presence?

TEXT 8

NICK SCHWARTZ, "13-YEAR-OLD WITH INOPERABLE BRAIN TUMOR TO CADDIE AT MASTERS PAR-3 CONTEST," *USA TODAY*, APRIL 8, 2015

13-year-old golfer Ethan Couch wished in the hospital two years ago to go to the Masters. After his parents noticed that Couch was suffering from strange symptoms, tests revealed that he had tectal glioma, and there was a benign but inoperable tumor in his brain.

On Wednesday, Couch's wish will come true. Kevin Streelman, whose daughter spent time in intensive care after being born, decided that he wanted to make a difference in a child's life and give them a trip to Augusta National. After contacting the Make-A-Wish Foundation, Streelman was put in touch with Couch, who will serve as his caddie at the Masters Par-3 contest.

Via ESPN:

Streelman [introduced himself to Ethan and] explained that, as a Masters competitor, he was allowed to choose his caddie for Wednesday's event. He was choosing Ethan.

The boy fell silent. His parents, each listening over speaker phone, began crying. When Ethan finally spoke, his voice was shaking.

"I just wanted to go to the Masters," he'd later say. "I didn't expect this."

TEXT 9

RABBI YOSEF YITSCHAK SCHNEERSOHN, CITED IN *HAYOM YOM*, 8 CHESHVAN

מִצְוָה לָשׁוֹן צַוְותָא וְחִבּוּר. וְהָעוֹשֶׂה מִצְוָה מִתְחַבֵּר עִם הָעַצְמוּת בָּרוּךְ הוּא, שֶׁהוּא הַמְצַוֶּה אֶת הַצִּיוּוּי הַהוּא.

וְזֶהוּ "שְׂכַר מִצְוָה מִצְוָה" (אָבוֹת ד, ב), דְזֶה מַה שֶּׁנִּתְחַבֵּר עִם עַצְמוּת אוֹר אֵין סוֹף מְצַוֶּה הַצִּיוּוּי, זֶהוּ שְׂכָרוֹ.

The word *mitzvah* is related to the [Aramaic] word *tsaveta*, which means *connection*. One who performs a mitzvah connects with God, the issuer of the commandment.

This is the meaning of [the Mishnaic phrase,] "The reward of a mitzvah is the mitzvah" (ETHICS OF THE FATHERS 2:4): the reward of the mitzvah is the connection (mitzvah, *tsaveta*) it generates with God Who issued the commandment.

RABBI YOSEF YITSCHAK SCHNEERSOHN (RAYATS, FRIERDIKER REBBE, PREVIOUS REBBE) 1880–1950

Chasidic rebbe, prolific writer, and Jewish activist. Rabbi Yosef Yitschak, the sixth leader of the Chabad movement, actively promoted Jewish religious practice in Soviet Russia and was arrested for these activities. After his release from prison and exile, he settled in Warsaw, Poland, from where he fled Nazi occupation, and arrived in New York in 1940. Settling in Brooklyn, Rabbi Schneersohn worked to revitalize American Jewish life. His son-in-law, Rabbi Menachem Mendel Schneerson, succeeded him as the leader of the Chabad movement.

TEXT 10

RABBI MOSHE ALSHICH, *ROMEMOT KEL*, PSALMS 119:4

לָמָּה הִרְבָּה יִתְבָּרֵךְ לָנוּ תַּרְיַ"ג מִצְוֹת? הֲלֹא בִּהְיוֹת טוֹב לַבְּרִיּוֹת עִם הֶעֱדֵר עַוְלָה הָיָה דַי . . . וְהוּא מַאֲמָר ר' חֲנַנְיָה בֶּן עֲקַשְׁיָא, "רָצָה הַקָּדוֹשׁ בָּרוּךְ הוּא לְזַכּוֹת אֶת יִשְׂרָאֵל, לְפִיכָךְ הִרְבָּה לָהֶם תּוֹרָה וּמִצְוֹת" (מַכּוֹת כג, ב). שֶׁהוּא, כִּי הוּקְשָׁה לוֹ כִּי אַחַר שֶׁהָעוֹשֶׂה מִצְוָה אַחַת וְנִשְׁמַר מֵעָוֹן מְטִיבִין לוֹ וְנוֹחֵל אֶת הָאָרֶץ כוּ', אִם כֵּן לָמָּה הִרְבָּה לָנוּ הוּא יִתְבָּרֵךְ תּוֹרָה וּמִצְוֹת? לָזֶה אָמַר, דַּע כִּי הַטַּעַם הוּא כִּי "רָצָה הַקָּדוֹשׁ בָּרוּךְ הוּא לְזַכּוֹת אֶת יִשְׂרָאֵל, לְפִיכָךְ הִרְבָּה לָהֶם תּוֹרָה וּמִצְוֹת", שֶׁהוּא לְהַרְבּוֹת זְכוּתָם בִּשְׁמוֹר מִצְווֹת הַרְבֵּה. וְגַם, שֶׁלְּרִבּוּיָם לֹא יִבָּצֵר מֵהִזְדַּמֵּן מִצְוָה תָּמִיד, מַה שֶּׁאֵין כֵּן אִם הָיוּ מוּעָטוֹת.

The Talmud teaches (KIDUSHIN 39B) that one who does a single mitzvah and refrains from sin merits the World to Come. If so, why did God give us 613 *mitzvot*? Would it not have been sufficient for Him to admonish us against injustice? . . .

Thus, Rabbi Chananiah ben Akashya taught: "God wished to make Israel meritorious. He therefore gave them an abundance of Torah and *mitzvot*" (TALMUD, MAKOT 23B). God gave us the Torah and *mitzvot* in abundant measure to increase our merit.

Also, the abundance of commandments guarantees that we will always have the opportunity to fulfill a mitzvah. This would not have been so if we had few *mitzvot*.

RABBI MOSHE ALSHICH
1508–1593

Biblical exegete. Rabbi Alshich was born in Turkey and moved to Safed, Israel, where he became a student of Rabbi Yosef Caro, the preeminent codifier of Jewish law. Alshich's biblical, homiletical, and ethical teachings remain popular to this day, most notably, *Torat Moshe*, a commentary on the Torah. His students included Rabbi Chaim Vital and Rabbi Yom Tov Tsahalon. He is buried in Safed.

Figure 2.4

New Mitzvah Perspective

BEFORE	AFTER
Mitzvah = command	Mitzvah = connection
I have to do a mitzvah.	I get to do a mitzvah.
I need to do a mitzvah so that God will love me.	God loves me, so He gave me a mitzvah.

Figure 2.5

Mitzvah Motivation III

Extrinsic reward	Earthly and Heavenly reward
Extrinsic negative consequence	Earthly and Heavenly punishment
Intrinsic reward and consequence	Character development
Relationship	Connection with God

QUESTION FOR DISCUSSION

In your estimation, is the prospect of connection with God a sufficient and satisfactory motivation to follow God's instructions? Why or why not?

TEXT 11

RABBI SHNE'UR ZALMAN OF LIADI, *TANYA*, CH. 37

כִּי בַּעֲשִׂיָּתָהּ מַמְשִׁיךְ הָאָדָם גִלּוּי אוֹר אֵין סוֹף בָּרוּךְ הוּא מִלְמַעְלָה לְמַטָּה לְהִתְלַבֵּשׁ בְּגַשְׁמִיּוּת עוֹלָם הַזֶּה . . .

מִשּׁוּם כִּי זֶה כָּל הָאָדָם וְתַכְלִית בְּרִיאָתוֹ וּבְרִיאַת הָעוֹלָמוֹת עֶלְיוֹנִים וְתַחְתּוֹנִים, לִהְיוֹת לוֹ יִתְבָּרֵךְ דִּירָה בַּתַּחְתּוֹנִים דַּוְקָא, לְאִתְהַפְּכָא חֲשׁוֹכָא לִנְהוֹרָא, וְיִמָּלֵא כְּבוֹד ה' אֶת כָּל הָאָרֶץ הַגַּשְׁמִית דַּיְקָא.

When we perform a mitzvah, we infuse this physical world with the infinite light of the Divine. . . .

This is our entire purpose and the reason we were created—to transform the darkness of this lowly world into light, that God's glory should fill the entire physical world.

RABBI SHNE'UR ZALMAN OF LIADI (ALTER REBBE) 1745–1812

Chasidic rebbe, halachic authority, and founder of the Chabad movement. The Alter Rebbe was born in Liozna, Belarus, and was among the principal students of the Magid of Mezeritch. His numerous works include the *Tanya*, an early classic containing the fundamentals of Chabad Chasidism, and *Shulchan Aruch HaRav*, an expanded and reworked code of Jewish law.

Figure 2.6

Mitzvah Motivation IV

Extrinsic reward	Earthly and Heavenly reward
Extrinsic negative consequence	Earthly and Heavenly punishment
Intrinsic reward and consequence	Character development
Relationship	Connection with God
Importance of the task	Partnering with God; actualizing God's vision for Creation

QUESTION FOR DISCUSSION

In your estimation, is the prospect of partnering with God and actualizing God's vision for Creation a sufficient and satisfactory motivation to follow God's instructions? Why or why not?

A girls' "*kheyder*" (traditional school) in Biala Bilits, Poland. Publ. 1926 in *Forverts/The Forward*. (Photo Credit: Alter Kacyzne) (YIVO Institute for Jewish Research, New York)

Reflection

Is there a mitzvah you would like to adopt but find too difficult? If yes, what piece of advice can you glean from this lesson to help you overcome this obstacle?

1 There are many who take no issue with God per se, but resent His *mitzvot* (instructions), viewing them as burdensome. Fueling this resentment is the belief that our actions cannot possibly matter to God. Resentment fades away when one understands what we accomplish by doing *mitzvot*.

2 Every mitzvah fosters spiritual growth and character development. We might not perceive the intrinsic benefits of each mitzvah, yet we trust that each mitzvah contributes to a more meaningful life.

3 Inasmuch as we are finite and God is infinite, there is no logical way for us to connect with Him. God, however, desires a relationship with us and therefore gave us multiple avenues of connection: the *mitzvot*. Every time we do a mitzvah, we connect with the One Who gave the mitzvah.

4 Each mitzvah we perform reveals God's unity in another element of His Creation, thereby bringing Creation one step closer to fulfilling its destiny. The awareness that God Himself needs us to perfect the world for Him is the ultimate mitzvah motivation.

5 It is illogical to have an "all-or-nothing" perspective with regard to mitzvah observance. Every time we do a mitzvah, regardless of how frequently we do it, we refine our character, connect to God, and make the world a holier place.

Additional Readings

TYING SHOELACES AND OTHER DETAILS

BY SUSAN A. HANDELMAN

"R. Leib, son of Sarah, the hidden *tzaddik* who wandered over the earth, following the course of rivers, in order to redeem souls of the living and the dead said this: 'I did not go to the Maggid in order to hear Torah from him, but to see how he unlaces his felt shoes and laces them up . . . again.'" So goes a well-known Chassidic story somewhat quaint and strange to our ears. What, one wonders, could one great *tzaddik* learn from the way another tied his shoes—and why concentrate on such trivia to begin with?

In fact, the modern Jew tends to ask the same question about much of the body of Jewish Law passed down to us in the *Shulchan Arukh* and various codes—that is, about halakhahh in general. Or perhaps we better say halakhah in its "specifics"; what can one possibly learn from it, and why concentrate on such trivia anyway? That mass of irritatingly minute prescriptions, which cover the pages of the *Shulchan Arukh*, is one of the greatest stumbling blocks for the modern Jew in search of her-or himself. Its laws appear impossible, extreme. Here are directives about matters such as which shoe to put on first, when to wash your hands, when and when not to touch your spouse, how to sleep, eat, drink—even evacuate. Let alone the intricate directives concerning proper observance of the holidays, prayer, litigation, and so forth.

Nonetheless, says the Talmud: "Since the Temple was destroyed, G-d has no place left except the four cubits of halakhah." What kind of G-d, one wonders, cares about my shoelaces? No one will argue about the need to strengthen Jewish "identity," "culture," "values"—but that we need to strengthen ourselves in abiding by Jewish law, in all its sticky specifics, is another matter. What does it matter whether you drive to *shul* as long as you get there, or which shoe you put on first, and so forth. Justice, morality, being a good person, supporting Israel—these are the components of Judaism. *Shabbat, kashrut,* perhaps even *mikveh* make for a nice "lifestyle"; but let's not go too far; let's not be irrational, fanatic; and above all, let's not call it "law."

Halakhah Unites Spiritual and Mundane

In fact, the popular term, "lifestyle," if we stretch it a bit, might serve as a roughly accurate translation of the Hebrew word halakhah, which comes from the root *halakh,* meaning "to walk." The word does not specifically denote "law" (Hebrew *din* or *mishpat*), but "path," the "way to walk," the way to pattern one's life.

But there is more. Style is not always synonymous with substance. There is a profound insight in the popular cliché, "lifestyle"; we desperately search for lifestyle because we lack life-substance. Style can become a substitute for content. And so we try to pick and choose, amalgamate and discard, imitate and absorb bits and pieces of other people's lives, cultures, religions, philosophies, politics, struggling to sew some patchwork of ideas together to clothe our nakedness. Like the era which gave rise to Christianity, ours is one of great religious syncretism.

But halakhah is more than style. Although it contains its own inner mechanism for dealing with the effects of temporal, cultural, and geographical change, the essence of halakhah does not change. Precisely because the essence of halakhah is the unity of the concrete actions it prescribes, with the "theoretical or conceptual" basis of the Torah, halakhah is that which

SUSAN A. HANDELMAN, PHD

Dr. Handelman is a Chicago native and professor of English at Bar Ilan University. She is the author of *Fragments of Redemption, Slayers of Moses,* and *Make Yourself a Teacher.*

unites the most "spiritual" aspects of Judaism with the most physical, mundane details of life. Halakhah is that unique religious expression which—leaping over the boundaries of other non-Jewish concepts of "spirituality"—somehow is able to connect G-d to . . . how you tie your shoelaces. Being good, ethical, spiritual, Zionist etc., is, Halakhah insists, somehow bound up with the way you eat, dress, cook, sleep, keep the *Shabbat*, and so on. Why?

Because in essence, the Torah teaches that nothing, literally nothing, is trivial for the Jew; that there is utterly no aspect of one's life which is unimportant; no action, word, thought, to which you can afford to be insensitive. There is no aspect or moment of life which the Jew does not seek to elevate and sanctify and penetrate with Jewishness. That is why in Judaism, soul and body, idea and action, the most metaphysical and the most mundane realms are not separate. And Halakhah is this very unity of style and substance, soul and body, spirit and letter, daily life and the Divine. We have a G-d who "*mishes* in."

Halakhah Should Not Be Modernized

Precisely in the detail does one find the whole, or to use more philosophical terminology, only though the particular does one reach the universal; concentrate and abstract cannot be separated. Precisely in the seeming small details, in the minutiae, in the concrete *halakhot* is the Torah expressed.

This concept is actually very contemporary. Twentieth-century science teaches us the same lesson. The secret of nature, the ultimate strength and power of the universe lies not somewhere in the vast cosmic expanse, but within the infinitely small world of the atom. The biggest explosive force comes from a highly controlled reaction using the most minute nuclear components.

Those familiar with kabbalah will recognize that the term *tzimtzum*, meaning "contraction, condensation" is central to Jewish mystical thought. The idea is that G-d, so to speak, contracted Himself to make space for the universe, and that He condensed His thought and will through immeasurable contractions into the physical letters and words of the Torah.

Halakhah, for the mystic, is this greatly condensed wisdom of G-d, inseparable from the most abstract metaphysical speculation. And that explains why the very compiler and editor of the *Shulchan* Arukh was none other than the great mystic and kabbalist of the Safed circle, R. Yoseph Caro.

And R. Caro was not alone—our greatest speculative mystics were also our greatest Halakhists. This combination of law and mysticism is unique to Judaism. The most spiritually sensitive of our tradition were also the most attentive to the minutiae of halakhah, for halakhah is the body, the very concrete expression of the soul of Torah. Those who reached the highest levels sought not to abolish, alter, or "modernize" halakhah, but to reinforce it.

We Must Seek Meaning in Halakhah

Can halakhah be attractive today? Yes, because halakhah is the very concrete expression, the very ground and bedrock of Jewish "identity," "culture," "values," and all the other abstract words which don't exist in the Bible, because the word "Torah," meaning "teaching, instruction," includes and indissolubly binds together "religion," "ethics," "politics" with one another and with the way one ties one's shoes. One can't separate them; separate halakhah from the Torah, Jewish action from Jewish thought, and you separate the Jew from Judaism.

To be sure, some *halakhot* are not congruent with some contemporary styles of thought and behavior. That, however, is not a necessary reason for immediately doing away with them, and for rationalizing a Judaism which we adhere to only when it is comfortable for us to observe. And should not we, of all people, be most skeptical of the styles and conceptual fads of modern culture—did we not suffer most in the last century from the hands of those who were most culturally and technologically advanced? Did not "liberal humanism" fail us miserably and does it not appear as if it is beginning to fail us again? Instead of casting away halakhah, let us search for its deeper meaning, its intricate and indissoluble connection to those aspects of Judaism unquestioningly meaningful to us and the world.

But let us search with Jewish eyes. The Torah deals not only with the beautiful and rational elements of ourselves, ignoring the rest, but also (and perhaps more importantly) with what is not beautiful and not rational, and what is spiritually intractable—with our physical behavior in the world of our everyday life, down to the last detail. For if one doesn't pay careful attention to those aspects of human behavior which are non-rational, they can easily become wildly, destructively irrational—rather than guides which can lead us above and beyond the limits of reason.

Even one who is concerned with beauty, proportion, and aesthetics will tell us that details are important. The artist, above all, knows that one incorrect line, awkward angle, off color, can destroy the painting; the poet agonizes over the exact word. Jewish beauty, however, is not ultimately embodied in plaster and paint and poetry, but in deeds, physical actions—the most minute, the most mundane—over which the Jew agonizes and meditates as deeply as does the artist over her or his composition. Meditation over the proper way to tie one's shoes merges into meditation on the secrets of creation, the *Shulchan Arukh* into the kabbalah. In going to the *tzaddik* to learn how he ties his shoes, you learn all. For a Jew's life—way of "walking"—the specifics of halakhah constitute the essence of his or her art and the ultimate masterwork.

Excerpt from Baila Olidort (ed.), *Feeding Among the Lilies: The Wellsprings Reader* (Brooklyn, N.Y.: Wellsprings Journal, 1999).

MITZVOT: THEIR SPIRITUAL ROLE AND FUNCTION

BY RABBI FAITEL LEVIN

It is now time to devote a chapter to bringing the central role and spiritual function of physical mitzvot into sharper relief. We first step back to look at the views of previous thought systems.

Mitzvot in Classic Jewish Writings

Various classic scholars have provided insight into the question of the role of physical mitzvot within Judaism. Maimonides[1] understands mitzvot as a type of springboard designed to aid the masses to overcome their carnality, to free their minds from their bodies towards true spiritual endeavor. That is, the true arena for religious endeavor is indeed the mind. According to Maimonides, man's highest goal in life is metaphysical speculation. G-d is Supreme Logic and in the human, too, logic reigns supreme. Thus, religious experience, or communication between man and G-d, is achieved specifically by way of a rational interchange: man's mind contemplates Divine ideas. It is only as a type of necessary evil, as it were, to provide a cure to help get the body out of the way, that mitzvot enter the picture.

Sefer HaChinuch, a classic medieval compilation, generally offers some philosophical insight into the six hundred and thirteen mitzvot collated in the work. Generally, it might be said that *Chinuch* regards mitzvot as performing a pedagogic, conditioning role.[2] Man's heart is influenced by his actions. Accordingly, each mitzvah aims to have a particular positive effect on the person performing it, refining him, elevating

RABBI FAITEL LEVIN

Chasidic scholar, halachist, and author. Born in England, Rabbi Levin is the author of *Halacha, Medical Science and Technology: Perspectives on Contemporary Halacha Issues* and *Heaven on Earth: Reflections on the Theology of Rabbi Menachem M. Schneerson, the Lubavitcher Rebbe*; and is the founding editor of *The Australian Journal of Torah Thought.* He is currently the rabbi of the Brighton Hebrew Congregation in Melbourne, Australia, and a most sought-after lecturer on halachic issues.

him. In this system then, too, mitzvot are not the primary arena for religious endeavor, not man's ultimate mode for relating to G-d; rather, a vehicle by which to enhance man's true religious standing.

Chasidic literature, too, stresses the value inherent in refining man through the performance of mitzvot (as discussed in chapter ten). It has been in fact erroneously portrayed as anti-legal, as a system that somewhat disregards the externalities of Judaism, in search of the core.

In fact, there is much in Chasidic theology, however, that serves to establish a most significant religious role for mitzvot (subsequently receiving particular emphasis and focus in the Dirah Betachtonim system). Indeed, a very basic argument from general Chasidic literature aims to emphasize the importance of the strict adherence to the minutiae of physical mitzvot.

The Physical Is No Further from G-d

Let us return once again to the very start, to the prevalent notion that meditation rather than physical mitzvot—activities of the mind rather than of the hand, the abstract rather than the concrete, the transcendent rather than the real—are closer to G-d. Upon analysis, apart from all we have said till this point, this attitude is based in part on an erroneous extrapolation from what is common in the human world.

A freshman, for example, would attempt to display nothing but his highest intellectual acumen when speaking to a world authority on his subject. An ordinary person would attempt to display nothing but his best behavior in the presence of a saint. Such is the nature of much of our experience: the knowing, not the ignorant, consult meaningfully with the expert; the talented, rather than the mediocre, can collaborate with the truly gifted; the strong, not the feeble, can spar with the mighty; the bright, rather than the dull, can converse with the brilliant; the noble, rather than the ordinary, can approach the sublime. Extrapolating from this, it is assumed that, if anything, for communicating with transcendent G-d Himself, only man's most sublime features—only his spiritual faculties—can be of use, whereas his more mundane dimensions must be suppressed and hidden. As it were, if only rungs eight and nine of the ladder are appropriate for communicating with rung ten, it is certain that they are appropriate for communicating with rung one hundred.

But all of this assumes that man and G-d are in fact on the same ladder; that G-d is at the loftier end of the same continuum as man. But as we have seen earlier,[3] a great divide separates all of man's faculties, including his heart and mind, from G-d. It is, as we have seen, even inappropriate to say that G-d cannot be comprehended by the human mind. G-d is separated from man by a chasm, a "quantum leap." Moreover, a great divide separates G-d Himself from even *Divine* wisdom, and kindness—that is, from the very "operating systems" of wisdom and kindness. For all specific features and defined entities, however lofty, are meaningless to G-d Himself as He stands prior to tzimtzum.[4] It follows that the notion that man's mental and emotional endeavors enjoy a *natural* relationship with G-d is mistaken. Human capabilities and G-d are not on the same ladder. Man's loftiest ideas and most sublime sentiments are incomparably further removed from G-d than are a child's intellectual displays from a world authority's thinking; his most refined behavior is further removed than is a crude person's behavior from a saint—for indeed, in the latter cases the distance is relative; in the former it is absolute.

Moreover, upon reflection it can be seen that man's lower and higher faculties are in fact, inherently, equidistant from G-d. Where two arenas exist as totally detached frames of references, the highs and lows in one arena are meaningless in the other. By way of analogy, to a deaf person, there is no difference between particularly pleasing and uplifting harmony, and particularly dissonant and irritating cacophony. An outstanding musical symphony and particularly unpleasant noise will elicit precisely the same response—the same lack of response. Unlike the hard of hearing, the deaf have no access to the world of sound at all. Their exclusion is not relative but absolute, excluded by an unnegotiable chasm; hence, the intense differences the hearing discern and insist on affirming, in the world of sound, not only lose their prominence with regard to the deaf, but lose their values altogether. Similarly (though in reverse), since man is removed from G-d by an *absolute* chasm, since G-d operates on an "operating system" which has no relationship, no channels of discourse with man's "operating system," the human's loftier side and mundane side are equidistant from G-d—they are equally irrelevant and meaningless.

But if man, by his very nature, has no faculties which relate meaningfully to G-d, does this mean that all religious activities lose their inherent value? If man is separated from G-d as the deaf are from sound, if man's lofty side elicits the same response in G-d as does his mundane side—zero—then what is the value of religious endeavor on his part?

Chasidut maintains that, indeed, it is solely the fact that G-d's inscrutable Will calls for a certain form of behavior that imbues this behavior with significance. If not for G-d's command, no form of human behavior would, in fact, be meaningful at all to Him.[5]

It follows, then, that though the criteria of the human frame of reference judge prayer and meditation more lofty and spiritual than physical mitzvot, there is no such preference in terms of G-d. *Prima facie—if* not for G-d's command—both are equally meaningless; if G-d chooses, he can will either, and thereby imbue His desired choice with meaning.

The analogy of the deaf, used differently, further elucidates our position in relation to mitzvot.

A deaf person enters your room where an audio system is blaring out of control. You motion to him to improve it. He goes over, studies the dial and turns it—all the way up! He argues that he's fixed the stereo—the dial *looks* better this way! From his unfortunate point of view he cannot discern the values and preferences at the other side of the chasm. So his attempts to bring satisfaction to the hearing, using the criteria of vision available to him, result in the precise reverse.

Nevertheless, the deaf are in truth able to satisfy the criteria of those fortunate to have access to the world of sound. The hearing can prescribe to them how to act. If the instructions are followed correctly, the deaf will perform in a way that is of value to the world of sound.

In similar fashion, though man's activities cannot relate to G-d along the terms of his own frame of reference, they can be of value to G-d along lines plotted out by Him, on terms man can never apprehend.

This insight, in turn, reinforces the notion that we ought not assert that physical mitzvot are inherently inferior to prayer or meditation. Since G-d's instructions are our only clue to meaningful communication with Him, if G-d declares that physical mitzvot are meaningful to Him, we must acquiesce, as we have no faculties with which to make an alternative assessment. Indeed, if we insist upon offering G-d a prayer when He has requested wearing woolen strings (*tzitzit*), we might be acting no more appropriately than the deaf person who turns the stereo all the way up.

In sum, in light of general Chasidic teachings we dismiss the *a priori* inferiority of physical mitzvot and set them on an inherently equal footing with man's spiritual activities as possible candidates for G-d's instructions. But these insights themselves do not yet ascribe *positive* qualities specific to physical mitzvot. We now return to Dirah Betachtonim where, in a final fleshing out of the basic ideas of the Dirah Betachtonim system, we elaborate upon the dimension of physical mitzvot which in fact justifies and warrants their predominance within Judaism.

Physical Mitzvot and the Essence of G-d

As amply dwelt upon in previous chapters, in addition to the notion that physical mitzvot uniquely express the infinity of G-d and the "infinity" of man's connection with Him (*manifestations*), more importantly, it is in particular they that provide an avenue to the Essence of G-d; whereas prayer and meditation, as lofty as they may seem, give expression only to *manifestations* of man and similarly relate merely to *manifestations* of G-d, but do not touch the essence, the *être*, of man or the Essence of G-d.

Put somewhat differently, more profoundly as well as more radically, "spiritual" religious activities are in a very subtle sense almost an insult to G-d. For they seem to ignore the fact that G-d is greater than humans *absolutely*, as they focus on areas in which man and G-d share. The types of *difference* between the worshiper and He who is worshipped that are at the fore during such forms of worship, as well as the modes of *communication* between the worshiper and the Worshipped that are involved, are not unique to the man-G-d relationship. Take prayer for example. This experience highlights that, unlike man, G-d is "Great, Powerful and Awesome," and that man is the mere beneficiary of all good that emanates from G-d the provider. But amongst human beings, too, there are differences in terms of greatness, power and awe, as well as benefactor-recipient relationships. Similarly, with regard to the mode of communication involved, forms of praise similar to prayer can be utilized in communication even amongst humans, as was, for example, the case with serfs and monarchs of old. Moreover, similar forms of expression, such as passionate, humble or poetic statements, may be suitable in relation to awesome natural wonders or aesthetically overwhelming scenes. Neither the character of the highlighted differences nor the communication experience is uniquely man-G-d oriented.

Thus, these forms of worship are in a subtle sense almost an affront to G-d.[6] For communicating with G-d (only) on wavelengths that are appropriate for non-Divine beings regards Him, by implication, as belonging within the same framework.

More profoundly, it is true that once existence is a fact, there is a continuum of character and quality, ranging, for example, from the lowly to the great, or from the powerless to the mighty. "Spiritual" forms of worship occur along this continuum. Man at the lower end of the continuum of greatness, power and awe communicates with G-d who is at its apex. But this means that here is communication *within* the frame of reference of the existing, addressing *qualities* of things that exist—concerned with *manifestations* of existence—whilst the fact that things exist is taken for granted. This is, in fact, the reason why this experience can be enjoyed by even two non-Divine entities, two *created* beings: the experience is not created-Creator oriented, as it addresses issues that arise once existence is a fact.

Here lies the difficulty in confining man's communication with G-d through a spiritual medium. G-d is implicitly experienced as within the framework of the existing, whereas the deepest mystery of all, the deepest Divinity of all—the plane *unique* to G-d that stands outside this frame of reference, i.e., essence, *being*—is overlooked. It is forgotten here that G-d straddles reality's non-existence and existence, that G-d is the Master of being, that He called all into being (catered for the being of all)—including the frame of reference, existence itself. Relating to G-d's *qualities,* however sublime, with heart and mind via prayer and meditation, is a rejection, as it were, of the Being of G-d that lies beyond.

But worship through physical mitzvot is different. Unlike the mind and heart, the hands, or moreover pieces of leather (*tefillin*), are not vehicles one would naturally choose for prayerful expression or for other forms of devotional experience. Nor are they appealing to the Love or Wisdom of G-d. No emotional quality, no logical idea, is expressed by mere hands or hide. Or, in other words, within the frame of reference of the rational, emotional and devotional these are totally unresponsive, meaningless, zero. Indeed, even the humility felt in prayer before the greatness, power and awesomeness of G-d is not applicable here, as that too is experiential, meaningless in the world of indifferent, hard and fast objects. Thus, when the worshiper does in fact take a piece of leather in his hand, proposing to make it a vehicle for communicating with G-d—no intellectual, emotional or other religiously *meaningful* channels are available. But yet, even this religiously opaque object is part of G-d's world. In which way? Its being, and nothing else. Its being was catered for by G-d; it partakes in the Divine Being; and moreover, its very spiritual indifference represents transparency to and oneness with its core, the in-itself of the Divine *Being.* Hence, when the worshiper attempts to make a connection with G-d, it occurs on the wavelength of Being.

The introduction of physical entities into worship, then, forces the worshiper beyond the continuum, beyond the frame of reference of qualities or features, to that plane unique to G-d—to the mystery of existence itself. Here, as it were, the very frame itself communicates with G-d: essence to Essence. In the absence of meaning and significance, man is brought before the Essence of G-d.

True, then, as it appeared at the very outset, leather, wool or food appear uninspiring; certainly, an initial evaluation of Judaism may find it bogged down with minutiae and restrictions. But it is specifically the dark, finite, restrictive nature of physical mitzvot, maintains Dirah Betachtonim, that frees worship of the qualities that color existence, enabling man's essence as well as the essence of the physical objects involved to be bare of coverings, superimpositions and taintings, and be at one with the Essence of G-d, as it stands uncompromised beyond His most sublime qualities.

Excerpt from Faital Levin, *Heaven on Earth: Reflections on the Theology of the Lubavitcher Rebbe, Rabbi Menachem M. Schneerson* (Brooklyn, N.Y.: Kehot Publication Society, 2002).

Endnotes

1 In, for example, Guide for the Perplexed III, 51 and III, 27.
2 See, inter alia, *Mitzvah* 545.
3 Chapters 2, 6 and 11.
4 Though, as we have seen, the "laser apparition," despite its manifest great difference from light, is *inherently* light.
5 Put differently: Mitzvot are an expression of the Will of G-d. The Will of G-d transcends both human logic and even Divine logic, as it were. And in this transcendence, the *a priori* notion of material mitzvot being inferior to man's spiritual self, or even totally immaterial to G-d, which is ultimately the product of a rational assessment, loses itself. Thus, human acts that are inherently meaningless to G-d assume value—due to His Will. As explained at length in *Chasidut*, human experience provides an analogy: humans, too, can, in a limited way, will things that have no meaning for them when a purely rational or emotional assessment is undertaken—whereupon they assume meaning for them.
6 See *Megillah* 25:a.

INSPIRATION

BY RAFI ROSENBERG

> *A woman, the wife of one of the prophets, cried out to Elisha: "My husband, your servant, has died. . . . and the creditor has come to take my two sons as slaves."*
> *Said Elisha to her: ". . . Tell me, what have you in your home?" And she answered: "Your maidservant has nothing in the house but a cruse of oil."*
> *Said [Elisha]: "Go, borrow vessels . . . from all your neighbors; empty vessels, only that they not be few. . . . And pour [of your oil] into these vessels. . . ."* (II Kings 4:1–4; from the *haftorah* for Parshat Vayeira)

I want to paint a picture. I don't have any specific ideas, but I want to paint. I want to write a story. I don't know what to write, but I feel that I must. So I stand at my easel, canvas, oils and brushes at the ready. Or I sit before my computer and gaze at the screen.

Once upon a time . . . I type a few words. And suddenly a stream. Then a river. A torrent of words rushing from somewhere deep within me. Inspiration.

I unzip the velvet bag that holds my *tefillin*, remove the black leather box and bind it to my arm. I reach into my pocket, dig out a coin and insert it into the slot of the charity box. My movements are sluggish. A thousand times I have done this. Thousands more I will. My actions seem forced and automatic. I do these things because G-d has commanded me to, because I recognize that this constitutes my mission and purpose in life. But the experience feels meaningless.

I am not a robot. I feel things, sometimes deeply. I feel hurt, anger, love and elation. But I do not feel like putting on *tefillin*.

RAFI ROSENBERG

Rabbi Rafi Rosenberg codirects Chabad of Skylake in North Miami Beach, Florida.

The Problem

In the fourth chapter of the second book of Kings, we read of the "miracle of the cruse of oil" performed by the prophet Elisha. An impoverished widow seeks the help of Elisha, crying that her debtors are about to take her two children as slaves, and all she possesses is a single cruse of oil. The prophet tells her to borrow as many empty vessels as she can, and to proceed to fill them with oil from her cruse. Miraculously, the oil keeps on flowing as long as there are vessels to receive it.

Chassidic teaching explains the deeper significance of the widow's quandary and Elisha's advice:

A woman, the wife of one of the prophets, cried out to Elisha. . . . —The soul of fire[1] calls out to G-d.

"My husband, your servant, has died. . . . —My service of You is lifeless, devoid of inspiration. I yearn to fill my deeds with meaning and significance. . . .

. . . and the creditor has come to take my two sons as slaves." —but my animalistic inclinations are monopolizing my emotions. They want me to love the present and revere the temporal. They cloud my vision of Your all-pervading, eternal truth.

Taking Stock

Said Elisha to her: ". . . what have you in your home?" —G-d answers, "What is left of your soul that it can call its own?"

And she answered: "Your maidservant has nothing in the house, but a cruse of oil."—"Nothing but the pristine essence of my soul, the small 'cruse of oil' at her core that remains forever unsullied by the mundanities of life."

The Miracle

Said [Elisha]: ". . . borrow vessels . . . from all your neighbors; empty vessels, only that they not be few. . . . —Act. Continue to do positive and G-dly deeds, many positive and G-dly deeds, even if they seem "borrowed" and empty to you. Remember, deeds are vessels, ready recipients for content and fulfillment. . . .

. . . and pour [of your oil] into these vessels. . . ." —The more vessels you acquire, the more your "oil" will flow from its source and fill your actions with meaning and significance. Without the vessel of deed, there is nothing to provoke the oil of inspiration. Ultimately, if you persist in doing what you know to be just and right, your divine essence will fill your every "empty vessel."

Rafi Rosenberg, "Inspiration," in Yanki Tauber (adaptor, based on the works of the Rebbe, Rabbi Menachem Mendel Schneerson), *The Inside Story* (Brooklyn, N.Y.: Vaad Hanachos Hatmimim, 1997), pp. 267–269.

Endnote

1 Based on the Rebbe's talks on Shabbat Vayeira, 5725 (October 24, 1964) and on other occasions. *Likkutei Sichot*, vol. V, pp. 331–335.

Lesson 3

Depiction of scales of justice (detail, rightmost panel of triptych). Benjamin Senior Godines, c. 1680. (Jewish Museum, London)

A HIGHER PARADIGM

HOW G-D'S PARADIGM INFORMS OUR VALUES

The Torah seems to ignore foundational cornerstones of Western society: it appears to compromise human freedom and tightly govern the way people live, and seemingly does not treat all people equally. Do we want to have a relationship with the Author of this Torah? Are His words relevant? This lesson compares and contrasts the ideological origins of the Torah and modern values, to navigate their differences and clarify their objectives.

Exercise 1

The Clash

Brainstorm aspects of Jewish law and tradition that seem to be socially outdated. Use the categories below to help guide you:

EGALITARIANISM

SOCIAL ROLES

FREEDOM OF CHOICE

TEXT 1

MAGNA CARTA, JUNE 15, 1215

TO ALL FREE MEN OF OUR KINGDOM we have also granted, for us and our heirs forever, all the liberties written out below, to have and to keep for them and their heirs, of us and our heirs. . . .

MAGNA CARTA

The Magna Carta is a charter of English liberties granted by King John in 1215, under threat of civil war. By declaring the sovereign to be subject to the rule of law and documenting the liberties held by "free men," the Magna Carta would provide the foundation for individual rights in Anglo-American jurisprudence.

TEXT 2

U.S. DECLARATION OF INDEPENDENCE, JULY 4, 1776

We hold these truths to be self-evident, that all men are created equal, that they are endowed by their Creator with certain unalienable Rights, that among these are Life, Liberty and the pursuit of Happiness.

U.S. DECLARATION OF INDEPENDENCE

The Declaration of Independence, signed by 56 delegates of the Second Continental Congress on July 4, 1776 in Philadelphia, severed the political connections of the 13 American colonies to Great Britain. The document outlines the reasons why the colonies declared independence from English rule. Notably, the document speaks of the inherent rights of life, liberty, and the pursuit of happiness, which can never be violated by government.

Coin commemorating the 50th anniversary of the enactment of the Civil Rights Act of 1964.

QUESTION FOR DISCUSSION

Both the Magna Carta and the U.S. Declaration of Independence declare the rights of humanity. Is there any significant difference between them?

TEXT 3a

THOMAS PAINE, *COMMON SENSE,* 1776

Some writers have so confounded society with government, as to leave little or no distinction between them; whereas they are not only different, but have different origins. Society is produced by our wants, and government by our wickedness; the former promotes our happiness *positively* by uniting our affections, the latter *negatively* by restraining our vices. . . .

Government, like dress, is the badge of lost innocence; the palaces of kings are built upon the ruins of the bowers of paradise. For were the impulses of conscience clear, uniform and irresistibly obeyed, man would need no other lawgiver.

THOMAS PAINE
1737–1809

American journalist, inventor. Paine authored many influential essays and pamphlets. "Common Sense," Paine's most influential piece, brought his ideas to a vast audience, swaying U.S. public opinion to the view that independence from the British was a necessity.

TEXT 3b

THOMAS PAINE, IBID.

But that not being the case, he finds it necessary to surrender up a part of his property to furnish means for the protection of the rest; and this he is induced to do by the same prudence which in every other cause advises him, out of two evils to choose the least. Wherefore, security being the true design and end of government, it unanswerably follows that whatever form thereof appears most likely to ensure it to us, with the least expense and greatest benefit, is preferable to all others.

Common Sense, pamphlet by Thomas Paine in 1775–76 advocating independence from Great Britain for people in the Thirteen Colonies.

COMMON SENSE;

ADDRESSED TO THE

INHABITANTS

OF

AMERICA,

On the following intereſting

SUBJECTS.

I. Of the Origin and Deſign of Government in general, with conciſe Remarks on the ENGLISH Conſtitution.

II. Of Monarchy and Hereditary Succeſſion.

III. Thoughts on the preſent State of AMERICAN Affairs.

IV. Of the preſent Ability of AMERICA; with ſome miſcellaneous Reflections.

A NEW EDITION, with ſeveral Additions in the Body of the Work. To which is added an APPENDIX; together

TEXT 4a

U.S. DECLARATION OF INDEPENDENCE, JULY 4, 1776

That to secure these rights, Governments are instituted among Men, deriving their just powers from the consent of the governed.

TEXT 4b

IBID.

That whenever any Form of Government becomes destructive of these ends, it is the Right of the People to alter or to abolish it, and to institute new Government, laying its foundation on such principles and organizing its powers in such form, as to them shall seem most likely to effect their Safety and Happiness.

TEXT 5

EXODUS 24:7

וַיִּקַּח סֵפֶר הַבְּרִית וַיִּקְרָא בְּאָזְנֵי הָעָם.
וַיֹּאמְרוּ, "כֹּל אֲשֶׁר דִּבֶּר ה' נַעֲשֶׂה וְנִשְׁמָע".

Moses took the Book of the Covenant and read it to the people.

They said, "All that God has instructed we will follow and we will learn."

Depiction of Mt. Sinai.
Yoram Raanan, 2014.

TEXT 6

EXODUS 19:16–18

> וַיְהִי בַיּוֹם הַשְּׁלִישִׁי בִּהְיֹת הַבֹּקֶר, וַיְהִי קֹלֹת וּבְרָקִים וְעָנָן כָּבֵד עַל הָהָר, וְקֹל
> שֹׁפָר חָזָק מְאֹד; וַיֶּחֱרַד כָּל הָעָם אֲשֶׁר בַּמַּחֲנֶה.
>
> וַיּוֹצֵא מֹשֶׁה אֶת הָעָם לִקְרַאת הָאֱלֹקִים מִן הַמַּחֲנֶה; וַיִּתְיַצְּבוּ
> בְּתַחְתִּית הָהָר.
>
> וְהַר סִינַי עָשַׁן כֻּלּוֹ, מִפְּנֵי אֲשֶׁר יָרַד עָלָיו ה' בָּאֵשׁ; וַיַּעַל עֲשָׁנוֹ כְּעֶשֶׁן
> הַכִּבְשָׁן, וַיֶּחֱרַד כָּל הָהָר מְאֹד.

On the morning of the third day, there were thunder claps and lightning flashes. A thick cloud hovered over the mountain. There was a deafening blast of a shofar. The entire nation that was in the camp shuddered.

Moses led the people out of the camp to meet God. They stood at the bottom of the mountain.

Mount Sinai was completely covered by smoke because God had descended upon it in fire. Its smoke ascended like the smoke of the kiln. The entire mountain quaked violently.

TEXT 7

TALMUD, SHABBAT 88A

> מְלַמֵּד שֶׁכָּפָה הַקָּדוֹשׁ בָּרוּךְ הוּא עֲלֵיהֶם אֶת הָהָר כְּגִיגִית.
>
> וְאָמַר לָהֶם, "אִם אַתֶּם מְקַבְּלִים הַתּוֹרָה, מוּטָב. וְאִם לָאו, שָׁם תְּהֵא קְבוּרַתְכֶם".

These words teach us that God held the mountain over the Jews like a barrel.

God said to them, "If you accept My Torah, then it is good. If you don't, this will be your burial place."

BABYLONIAN TALMUD

A literary work of monumental proportions that draws upon the legal, spiritual, intellectual, ethical, and historical traditions of Judaism. The 37 tractates of the Babylonian Talmud contain the teachings of the Jewish sages from the period after the destruction of the Second Temple through the fifth century CE. It has served as the primary vehicle for the transmission of the Oral Law and the education of Jews over the centuries; it is the entry point for all subsequent legal, ethical, and theological Jewish scholarship.

TEXT 8a

DEUTERONOMY 13:1

אֵת כָּל הַדָּבָר אֲשֶׁר אָנֹכִי מְצַוֶּה אֶתְכֶם, אֹתוֹ תִשְׁמְרוּ לַעֲשׂוֹת; לֹא תֹסֵף
עָלָיו וְלֹא תִגְרַע מִמֶּנּוּ.

Everything that I command you, you shall be careful to do. You shall neither add to it, nor subtract from it.

TEXT 8b

DEUTERONOMY 29:28

וְהַנִּגְלֹת, לָנוּ וּלְבָנֵינוּ עַד עוֹלָם, לַעֲשׂוֹת אֶת כָּל דִּבְרֵי הַתּוֹרָה הַזֹּאת.

The revealed aspects of this Torah [i.e., the laws] are for us and our children to observe forever.

TEXT 9

MAIMONIDES, *MISHNEH TORAH,* LAWS OF THE FOUNDATIONS OF THE TORAH 9:1

דָבָר בָּרוּר וּמְפוֹרָשׁ בַּתּוֹרָה שֶׁהִיא מִצְוָה עוֹמֶדֶת לְעוֹלָם וּלְעוֹלְמֵי עוֹלָמִים. אֵין לָהּ לֹא שִׁינּוּי וְלֹא גֵּרָעוֹן וְלֹא תּוֹסֶפֶת, שֶׁנֶּאֱמַר: "אֵת כָּל הַדָּבָר אֲשֶׁר אָנֹכִי מְצַוֶּה אֶתְכֶם, אוֹתוֹ תִשְׁמְרוּ לַעֲשׂוֹת. לֹא תוֹסֵף עָלָיו וְלֹא תִגְרַע מִמֶּנּוּ".

וְנֶאֱמַר, "וְהַנִּגְלֹת לָנוּ וּלְבָנֵינוּ עַד עוֹלָם, לַעֲשׂוֹת אֶת כָּל דִּבְרֵי הַתּוֹרָה הַזֹּאת".

הָא לָמַדְתָּ, שֶׁכָּל דִּבְרֵי תּוֹרָה מְצוּוִּין אָנוּ לַעֲשׂוֹתָן עַד עוֹלָם.

It is clear and explicit in the Torah that it is [God's] everlasting commandment, and is not subject to change, addition, nor diminishment, as the Torah states: "Everything that I command you, you shall be careful to do. You shall neither add to it, nor subtract from it."

It also states: "The revealed aspects [i.e., laws,] of this Torah are for us and our children to observe forever."

This teaches that we are commanded to fulfill all the Torah's directives forever.

RABBI MOSHE BEN MAIMON (MAIMONIDES, RAMBAM) 1135–1204

Halachist, philosopher, author, and physician. Maimonides was born in Córdoba, Spain. After the conquest of Córdoba by the Almohads, he fled Spain and eventually settled in Cairo, Egypt. There, he became the leader of the Jewish community and served as court physician to the vizier of Egypt. He is most noted for authoring the *Mishneh Torah,* an encyclopedic arrangement of Jewish law, and for his philosophical work, *Guide for the Perplexed.* His rulings on Jewish law are integral to the formation of halachic consensus.

Figure 3.1a

The Two Systems (Practical Differences)

MODERN GOVERNMENT AND LAW	TORAH LAW
Willfully created by its citizens	Imposed by God
Amendable	Immutable
Repealable	Eternal

TEXT 10

RABBI YEHUDAH LOEW, *TIFERET YISRAEL,* CH. 22

מַה שֶׁכָּפָה עֲלֵיהֶם הָהָר, שֶׁלֹּא יֹאמְרוּ יִשְׂרָאֵל: "אֲנַחְנוּ קִבַּלְנוּ הַתּוֹרָה מֵעַצְמֵנוּ, וְאִם לֹא הָיִינוּ רוֹצִים לֹא הָיִינוּ מְקַבְּלִים הַתּוֹרָה".

וְדָבָר זֶה לֹא הָיָה מַעֲלַת הַתּוֹרָה, כִּי הַתּוֹרָה כָּל הָעוֹלָם תָּלוּי בָּהּ, וְאִם לֹא הָיְתָה הַתּוֹרָה, הָיָה הָעוֹלָם חוֹזֵר לְתוֹהוּ וָבֹהוּ.

וּלְפִיכָךְ אֵין רָאוּי שֶׁתִּהְיֶה קַבָּלַת הַתּוֹרָה בִּבְחִירַת יִשְׂרָאֵל,

רַק שֶׁהָיָה הַקָּדוֹשׁ בָּרוּךְ הוּא מְחַיֵּיב וּמַכְרִיחַ אוֹתָם לְקַבֵּל הַתּוֹרָה, שֶׁאִי אֶפְשָׁר זוּלַת זֶה, שֶׁלֹּא יַחֲזוֹר הָעוֹלָם לְתוֹהוּ וָבֹהוּ.

God held the mountain over the Jewish people so that they wouldn't say: "We chose to accept the Torah. Had we not found it appealing, we would have rejected it."

This attitude would have undermined the value of the Torah: The world depends on the Torah. Without it, the world would revert to nothingness.

Therefore, it would be inappropriate for the Torah's acceptance to hinge upon the willingness of the Jewish people.

God forced the Jewish people to accept the Torah because there was no alternative. Otherwise, the world would have reverted to nothingness.

RABBI YEHUDAH LOEW (MAHARAL OF PRAGUE) 1525–1609

Talmudist and philosopher. Maharal rose to prominence as leader of the famed Jewish community of Prague. He is the author of more than a dozen works of original philosophic thought, including *Tiferet Yisrael* and *Netsach Yisrael.* He also authored *Gur Aryeh,* a supercommentary to Rashi's biblical commentary, and a commentary on the nonlegal passages of the Talmud. He is buried in the Old Jewish Cemetery of Prague.

QUESTION FOR DISCUSSION

Considering the proposition of Text 10, what might be the reason for the eternal and immutable nature of Torah law?

TEXT 11

RABBI YOSEF YITSCHAK SCHNEERSOHN, CITED IN *HAYOM YOM,* 22 SHEVAT

עֶס זַיינֶען דָא צְוֵוייעֶרְלֵיי חוּקִים: א) אַ גֶעזֶעץ וָועלְכֶער שַׁאפְט לֶעבֶּען ב) אַ גֶעזֶעץ וָועלְכֶער וֶוערְט בַּאשַׁאפֶען פוּן לֶעבֶּען.

מֶענְשְׁלִיכֶע גֶעזֶעצֶען זַיינֶען גֶעשַׁאפֶען פוּן לֶעבֶּען, דֶערְפַאר זַיינֶען זֵיי אִין יֶעדֶער לַאנְד פַארְשִׁידֶען, לוֹיט דִי תְּנָאִים פוּן לַאנְד.

תּוֹרַת ה', אִיז דֶער גֶ-טְלִיכֶער גֶעזֶעץ וָועלְכֶער שַׁאפְט אַ לֶעבֶּען. תּוֹרַת ה' אִיז תּוֹרַת אֱמֶת, דִי תּוֹרָה אִיז אִין אַלֶע עֶרְטֶער אוּן אִין אַלֶע צַייטֶען גְלַייךְ, תּוֹרָה אִיז נִצְחִית.

There are two types of laws: laws that create life, and laws created by life.

Human laws are created by life. Therefore, they vary in different countries, each according to its circumstances.

[Conversely,] the Almighty's Torah is a Godly law that creates life. God's Torah is the Torah of truth, the same in all places, at all times. The Torah is eternal.

RABBI YOSEF YITSCHAK SCHNEERSOHN (RAYATS, FRIERDIKER REBBE, PREVIOUS REBBE) 1880–1950

Chasidic rebbe, prolific writer, and Jewish activist. Rabbi Yosef Yitschak, the sixth leader of the Chabad movement, actively promoted Jewish religious practice in Soviet Russia and was arrested for these activities. After his release from prison and exile, he settled in Warsaw, Poland, from where he fled Nazi occupation, and arrived in New York in 1940. Settling in Brooklyn, Rabbi Schneersohn worked to revitalize American Jewish life. His son-in-law, Rabbi Menachem Mendel Schneerson, succeeded him as the leader of the Chabad movement.

Figure 3.1b

The Two Systems (Ideological Differences)

	MODERN GOVERNMENT AND LAW	TORAH LAW
Historical Trigger	The denial of people's natural rights	God's vision for humanity
Goal	For people to enjoy their natural rights	For humanity to reach its potential
Function	To ensure the protection of people's natural rights	To guide humanity toward its purpose

Do you see a correlation between Figure 3.1a and Figure 3.1b?

TEXT 12a

HAIM COHN, *HUMAN RIGHTS IN JEWISH LAW* (NEW YORK, N.Y.: KTAV PUBLISHING HOUSE, 1984), PP. 17–18

Speaking of human rights concepts I must say at once that no explicit concept of this kind is to be found in Jewish law. It is not only that the formative sources of Jewish law precede by millennia the first enunciation of such slogans as civil liberties, citizens' rights, or individual freedom; Jewish law is in no way unique or isolated among ancient systems of law or of religion which fail to recognize human rights specifically.

HAIM COHN, PHD
1911–2002

Israeli jurist. Cohn was appointed manager of the legislation department of Israel's Ministry of Justice and later served as *State Attorney*. He was later appointed CEO of the Ministry of Justice and *Attorney General* of Israel. In 1960, he was appointed to the Supreme Court of Israel, a position he held until his retirement in 1981. He published a number of books, including *Human Rights in Jewish Law.*

TEXT 12b

HAIM COHN, IBID., PP. 18–19

It stands to reason that from the duty to assist and maintain the poor a fundamental human right of every human being to his livelihood may reasonably be inferred, as the fundamental right of life may justifiably be inferred from the prohibition of homicide.

Exercise 2

This chart lists six of the Ten Commandments—the ones pertaining to interpersonal conduct. Presuming that all duties imply corresponding rights, what rights do these commandments imply?

THE TORAH'S ARTICULATION: DUTIES	MODERN LAW'S ARTICULATION: RIGHTS
Honor your father and mother.	
You shall not murder.	
You shall not commit adultery.	
You shall not steal.	
You shall not bear false witness against your neighbor.	
You shall not covet your neighbor's house, wife, manservant, maidservant, ox, donkey, or anything that is your neighbor's.	

Exercise 3

Individualism vs. Common Purpose

How well does the law ensure, celebrate, and encourage people's individualism?

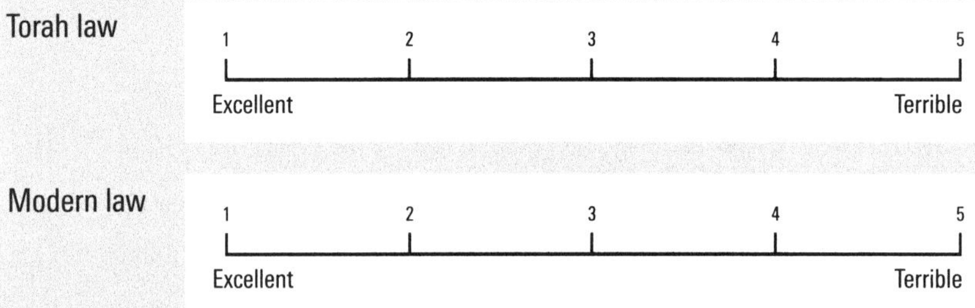

How well does the law, celebrate, and encourage humanity's common purpose?

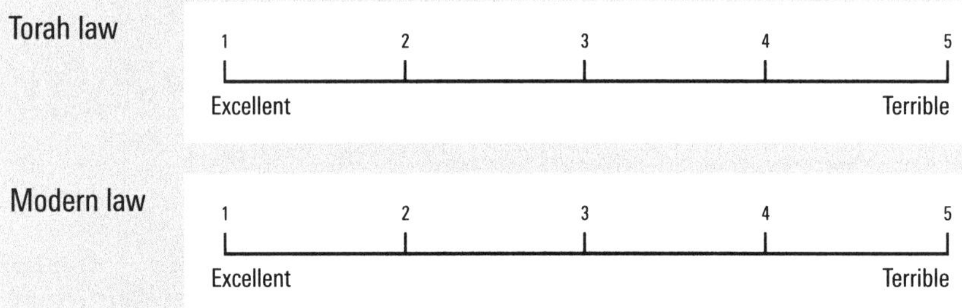

TEXT 13

MISHNAH, SANHEDRIN 4:5

> לְפִיכָךְ נִבְרָא אָדָם יְחִידִי . . .
> לְפִיכָךְ כָּל אֶחָד וְאֶחָד חַיָּב לוֹמַר: בִּשְׁבִילִי נִבְרָא הָעוֹלָם.

It is for the following reason that Adam was created alone. . . .

Every person must say, "The world was created for me."

MISHNAH

The first authoritative work of Jewish law that was codified in writing. The Mishnah contains the oral traditions that were passed down from teacher to student; it supplements, clarifies, and systematizes the commandments of the Torah. Due to the continual persecution of the Jewish people, it became increasingly difficult to guarantee that these traditions would not be forgotten. Rabbi Yehudah Hanasi therefore redacted the Mishnah at the end of the second century. It serves as the foundation for the Talmud.

TEXT 14

TALMUD, KIDUSHIN 82B

> אֲנִי לֹא נִבְרֵאתִי אֶלָּא לְשַׁמֵּשׁ אֶת קוֹנִי.

I was only created to serve my Master.

Figure 3.2

Words with the Hebrew root of ע-ל-ם (A-L-M)

עוֹלָם	הֶעֱלֵם
World	Concealment

TEXT 15

RABBI YOSEF YITSCHAK SCHNEERSOHN, *SEFER HAMAAMARIM KUNTREISIM* 2:738

זֶהוּ שֶׁאָמְרוּ רַבּוֹתֵינוּ זִכְרוֹנָם לִבְרָכָה, "בִּשְׁבִילִי נִבְרָא הָעוֹלָם". כְּלוֹמַר: הַהֶעְלֵם וְהַהֶסְתֵּר נִבְרָא לְמַעֲנִי, כְּדֵי שֶׁאֲבַטֵּל אוֹתוֹ וַאֲגַלֶּה אֶת הָאֱמֶת.

The saying of the sages, "The world was created for me," means as follows: The hiddenness and concealment [of God] were created for me, that I may eradicate it and reveal the truth.

Le Valet De Chambre (The Valet), Chaim Soutine, oil on canvas, c. 1927.

KEY POINTS

1 Government does not and may not assign objectives or purpose to people's lives. Therefore, it is utterly hopeless to rely solely on it for moral direction. In our search for creating a healthy society, we must look beyond rights.

2 In contrast to modern law, the Torah does offer humanity meaning, purpose, guidance, and instruction. Its instruction is essential for humanity to reach its final destination. "Its laws create life."

3 By necessity, the Torah assigns people with roles to play in the journey of humanity. A person's role, with its demands and privileges, is their key to finding meaning and purpose.

4 Shifting our focus from human rights to human purpose is both challenging and rewarding: challenging, because it confronts us to attach substantial weight to our life's choices; and rewarding, because it imbues our lives with utmost significance.

5 In a word: Modern governments protect people. The Torah makes them necessary. Perhaps we can make room for both.

Appendix

TEXT 16

HAIM COHN, *HUMAN RIGHTS IN JEWISH LAW* (NEW YORK, N.Y.: KTAV PUBLISHING HOUSE, 1984) P. 231

Article 29.2 of the Universal Declaration of Human Rights provides that in the exercise of his rights and freedoms, everyone shall be subject only to such limitations as are determined by law solely for the purpose of securing due recognition and respect for the rights and freedoms of others and of meeting the just requirements of morality, public order, and the general welfare in a democratic society.

"Securing due recognition and respect for the rights and freedoms of others" is, indeed, the paramount duty incumbent upon any man who claims any right or freedom for himself. Of Hillel . . . it is reported that a heathen once challenged him to teach him the whole of the law while he was standing on one foot. Hillel said, "Do not do to another what you would not like another to do to you: that is the whole of the law—and everything else is but comment and elaboration" . . . ([TALMUD,] *SHABBAT 31A*). . . . There is some deep meaning in the condensation of the whole of the law into this of all rules. On the one hand, it legitimizes the purely subjective and individualistic value of judgment—what you want or what you do not want to be done to you—as the basis of legal norm-setting; but on the other hand, the only norm it puts on the pedestal of law is the purely prohibitive and altruistic one: do not do to others. All of the law is self-restraint, is practical recognition and implementation of the rights of others; both the motivation and the justification of such self-restraint may be the ultimate recognition of and respect for your own rights. However motivated and justified, the fact remains that almost all normative Jewish law as between man and man is, in orientation and effect, wholly altruistic. If "human rights" can be said to provide a basis or starting point, or perhaps also the ultimate goal, of the norm-creating process, it is the duties, the do and the do-not, the care and respect for the other man, that make for true law.

TEXT 17

FRANS DE WAAL, *GOOD NATURED: THE ORIGINS OF RIGHT AND WRONG IN HUMANS AND OTHER ANIMALS,* (CAMBRIDGE, MASS.: HARVARD UNIVERSITY PRESS, 1996), P. 167

A morality exclusively concerned with individual rights tends to ignore the ties, needs, and interdependencies that have marked our existence from the very beginning. It is a cold morality that puts space between people, assigning each person to his or her own little corner of the universe. How this caricature of a society arose in the minds of eminent thinkers is a mystery.

FRANCISCUS BERNARDUS MARIA "FRANS" DE WAAL, PHD
1948–

A Dutch primatologist and ethologist, Frans de Waal is a professor of primate behavior at the Emory University psychology department, and the director of the Living Links Center at the Yerkes National Primate Research Center. The author of numerous books, his research centers on primate social behavior. He is a member of the United States National Academy of Sciences and the Royal Netherlands Academy of Arts and Sciences.

The Chess Player, Isidor Kaufmann, c. 1900.

Additional Readings

HIGH AND LOW

BY RABBI YANKI TAUBER

> *And [Korach and his following] massed upon Moses and Aaron and said to them: Enough! The entire community* is *holy and G-d* is *amongst them; why do you raise yourselves above the congregation of G-d?!* Numbers 16:3

Korach had a problem with holiness. Why is praying a "holy" act, while plowing a field is not? Why is studying G-d's Torah a "holy" pursuit, while developing the material resources of G-d's world is not? If holiness means proximity to the Divine, then everyone and everything is holy, for G-d dwells in each individual and in every component of His creation. Is Moses atop Mount Sinai, or Aaron offering *korbanot* in the Sanctuary, any "closer" to G-d than the craftsman at his workbench and the laborer at his daily toil?

Whence this dividing line between the spiritual and the material?

Korach's challenge to Moses' and Aaron's leadership followed another tragic mutiny among the Jewish people, that of the Spies. Ten of the twelve tribal leaders sent to scout the land of Canaan returned to dissuade the people from their mission of conquering the land. Here in the desert, they argued, sustained by manna from heaven and shielded from a corporeal and hostile world by the heavenly "clouds of glory," our souls are free to plumb the depths of the divine wisdom in Torah and soar in meditative attachment to G-d; there, we shall be subject to the political and economic mundanities intrinsic to an earth-bound existence. "It is a land that consumes its inhabitants,"[1] they warned the people, reminding them that many a spiritual giant had been corrupted when exposed to the enmeshments of material life. So why abandon our spiritual idyll in the desert for a life of subsisting off the land?[2]

The Spies erred in confining their relationship with G-d to the realm of the spirit, rejecting, in effect, the purpose of the Exodus and the very essence of Israel's mission: to conquer and settle the land of Canaan as the "Holy Land"—to realize the *land's* potential for holiness and sanctity. Korach took the lesson of the Spies' error to the other extreme, contesting the very distinction of spiritual life as something loftier and more desirable than material life. The Spies spurned the mundane; Korach and his followers denied that there was anything mundane about the mundane.

A Hierarchy of Holiness

A most irritating thorn in Korach's ideological side was the *kehunah* ("priesthood") and, particularly, the *matanot kehunah,* the "gifts to the *Kohanim,*" instituted by Moses.[3]

By the command of G-d, Moses had divided the people of Israel into several classes of holiness: "ordinary" Israelites, Levites, *Kohanim* ("Priests") and, at the peak of this pyramid of sanctity, the *Kohen Gadol* ("High Priest"). The Israelites—the farmers, merchants, craftsmen, soldiers and statesmen of Israel—were to pursue the "normal" existence of physical man: a life and vocation that involve the bulk of a person's time and talents in the material world. The tribe of Levi, however, was "distinguished by the G-d of Israel from the community of Israel, to be brought closer to Him,"[4] to serve as spiritual leaders

RABBI YANKI TAUBER, 1965–

Chasidic scholar and author. A native of Brooklyn, NY, Rabbi Tauber is an internationally renowned author who specializes in adapting the teachings of the Lubavitcher Rebbe. He is a member of the JLI curriculum development team, and has written numerous articles and books, including *Once Upon a Chassid* and *Beyond the Letter of the Law.*

and priests, "instructing Your laws to Jacob and Your Torah to Israel; placing incense in Your nostrils and burnt offerings upon Your altar."[5] Within the tribe of Levi itself, Aaron and his descendants were consecrated as *Kohanim* and entrusted with the primary role in serving G-d in the Sanctuary. Aaron himself was appointed *Kohen Gadol,* "the greatest of his brethren"[6] in this hierarchy of holiness.

This apportionment of roles did not, in itself, disturb Korach, who appreciated the need for spirituality and transcendence in man's relationship with his Creator. He was himself a Levite, a spiritual notch above the materially involved Israelite; indeed, in his arguments against Moses he allowed that he coveted the office of *Kohen Gadol* for himself. But Korach, while seeing his own calling as spiritual, was outraged by the elevation of the spirit as the "higher" and "holier" role. Korach saw the material and the spiritual as separate but equal venues of achievement. Both are part of G-d's creation, he argued; both, when properly employed, can equally bring man close to G-d.

Korach also objected to the concept of "higher" and "lower" realms within an individual's life, a division expressed in the institution of *matanot kehunah.* The giving of the *matanot kehunah* was commanded by G-d, but Korach argued that Moses had misinterpreted their function and role.

The tribe of Levi was to be given no allotment in the Land of Israel; "G-d is their lot" and the perfection of the spirit their vocation.[7] Their material needs would therefore be provided by their brethren, in whose stead they serve in the Holy Temple and whose lives they supply with the spiritual dimension of Israel's mission. Hence the tithe of the Jew's produce given to the Levite, and "the twenty-four gifts"[8] given to the *Kohen.* On a deeper level, the *matanot kehunah* represent the resources that each and every individual reserves for the *"Kohen"* within himself—the time, energy and possessions he allots for his own spiritual pursuits.

Here, again, Korach did not object to the *matanot kehunah* per se. But he refused to accept the notion that the bushel of grain that the Israelite farmer reserves for the *Kohen,* or the daily hour or two he devotes for study and prayer, are somehow loftier and "holier" than the rest of his harvest or day. Korach agreed that the materially involved individual ought to designate a certain portion of his life and wealth for matters of the spirit, supporting the men of spirit of his community[9] and setting aside islands of time in his material day for spiritual endeavors of his own. But to see these as the most important aspect of his life? As the ultimate objective of everything he does? It is enough, argued Korach, that we recognize the spiritual as the appropriate avocation for certain individuals, and as a necessary segment of every individual's life. But why, he demanded of Moses and Aaron, do you insist on defining it as the apex of our communal and individual endeavors? The entire community is holy, and G-d is amongst them and in their every positive effort. Why do you raise yourselves, and the spiritual ideal that you—and, indeed, I myself—represent, above the congregation of G-d?

First Things First

In the aftermath of Korach's mutiny, G-d again expressed His choice of Aaron as *Kohen Gadol,* reiterating His rejection of Korach's bid to assume, and redefine, the highest spiritual station in the community of Israel.[10] Soon afterward, in detailing the laws of several of the *matanot kehunah,* G-d again endorsed the elevation of the spiritual over the physical, saying to Aaron: "The choicest of the olive oil, the choicest of the wine and grain . . . the first ripening of all that is in the land, which they shall offer to G-d, shall be given to you."[11]

"The choicest to the *Kohen*" is the Jew's attitude toward his material life. In the words of Maimonides, "Everything that is for the sake of G-d should be of the best and most beautiful. When one builds a house of prayer, it should be more beautiful than his own dwelling. When one feeds the hungry, he should feed him of the best and sweetest of his table. When one clothes the naked, he should clothe him with the finest of his clothes. Whenever one designates something for a holy purpose, he should sanctify the finest of his possessions; as it is written,[12] 'The choicest to G-d.'[13]"

The same applies to that which a person reserves for the *Kohen* within himself. If the schoolday must include both sacred and secular studies, the former should be scheduled for the morning hours when the mind is at its freshest and most receptive. If one's talents are to be divided between two occupations, one whose primary function is to pay the bills and a second which benefits his fellow man, he should devote his keenest abilities to the latter. "The first of your grain-cradle," commands the Torah, "you shall uplift to G-d"[14]: the best years of your life, the prime hours of your day, the freshest of your energies, the choicest of your talents—what is first and uppermost in you—devote to G-dly pursuits.

In "uplifting" the choicest to G-d, a person, in effect, is saying: "Here lies the focus of my life. Quantitatively, this may represent but a small part of what I am and have; but the purpose of everything else I do and possess is to enable this percentile of spirit to rise above my matter-laden life."

As Maimonides points out, in the very first generation of history, G-d demonstrated that He accepts no other delineation of His relationship with man. As the Torah relates, Cain and Abel both made offerings to the Almighty; but G-d rejected Cain's offering and accepted Abel's, because only Abel "brought of the firstborn and choicest of his flocks."[15]

"Lowly" Defined

Korach was correct in his contention that our involvement with the material can be no less G-dly an endeavor than the most transcendent flights of spirit. Indeed, our sages consider man's sanctification of material life the ultimate objective of creation. "G-d desired a dwelling in the lowly realms," states the Midrash;[16] "This," writes Rabbi Schneur Zalman of Liadi in his Tanya, "is what man is all about; [this is] the purpose of his creation, and the creation of all worlds, supernal and terrestrial."[17] But Korach erred in his understanding of the nature of this "dwelling in the lowly realms" that G-d desires, and the manner in which man can indeed fashion a divine home out of his material self and world.

But first we must understand why it is that the material is regarded as "lower" than the spiritual. Should not the focus and objective of G-d's creation be considered its loftiest element? And yet, in the very sentence in which the Midrash states that the Creator's desire lies specifically in the physical existence, it refers to it as "the lowly realms"!

The cardinal law of existence is, "There is none else besides Him."[18] If you have an area one hundred cubic feet in size, and a hundred-cubic-foot object is occupying it, no other object can share this space. If you have an object of infinite size, no other object can possibly occupy any space, anywhere. If we substitute "reality" for "space," it follows that the reality of G-d, which suffers no limits or qualifications, "fills" the entire expanse of reality. This is true not only of the physical parameters of time and space, but also of the conceptual parameters of existence: the very concept "existence" is not "large" enough to contain any additional existences aside from the divine reality. Indeed, "existence" is not large enough to "contain" G-d, who, as the Creator and Definer of existence, cannot be defined by a concept of His creation. The reality of G-d, which overflows the conceptual boundaries of "existence," certainly "fills" the "area" framed by these boundaries, to the exclusion of all else.

Hence the axiom, "There is none else besides Him." Any other existences or realities we may identify—the objects and forces of the physical universe, the axiomatic truths we contemplate, the "I" of our identities—simply have no existential "place" in which to be. We must therefore conclude that either: a) they do not, in truth, exist; or b) they are not existences "besides Him" but expressions of His all-embracing reality.

This explains why the physical reality is the "lowest" element of G-d's creation. The more "existence" a thing possesses, the more presence it presumes, the greater a distortion it is of the divine truth. While spiritual realities also possess definition and existence, these are far more ethereal than the brute tangibility of the physical. More importantly, the spiritual entity is of a "selfless" nature, always expressing and serving a reality greater than itself, while physical matter manifests only the "I am" of its tactual being. An idea or an emotion is always about something else; a stone or tree is ostensibly about itself. A person praying or studying is demonstrably relating to a higher truth; a person dealing or eating is demonstrably affirming his individual being.

So of all the "worlds" and realities created by the Almighty, the physical reality is "the lowest in degree, of which there is none lower—'lowest' in the sense that it most conceals His manifest reality. It is a world of doubled and redoubled darkness, so much so that it even contains 'evil'—elements which oppose the reality of G-d, declaring:

'I[19] am the ultimate.'"[20]

Nevertheless—indeed, because of this—the "lowly realm" of the material world is where G-d's purpose in creation is realized.[21] For G-d wanted more than the spiritual's natural affirmation of His truth. He wanted that the physical world, whose nature is inhospitable—indeed contrary—to the divine truth, be made to "house" Him, to serve and express His all-transcendent, all-pervading reality.

Man achieves this by living a material life, but doing so in the service of a higher, spiritual goal. When a person spends ninety percent of his life earning a living, eating, sleeping, recreating and otherwise attending to his material needs, yet does so in a way that demonstrates that all this is only to enable the ten percent he devotes to prayer, study, charity and other G-dly endeavors, he is transforming the very nature of the physical. The "I exist" of the physical, which so blatantly belies the divine truth, has now become partner to the reality that "There is none else besides Him." It has acknowledged its subservience to that which is greater than itself.

In other words, as long as the material is not made to express its subservience to the spiritual, it remains the element of creation that is "furthest" from its divine source. Yet when the "inferiority" of the material is made manifest, when the materially involved individual orders his priorities so that his every material act is for the sake of the *Kohen* and the *Kohen* within himself, then the "lowliest realm" of creation becomes its G-dliest, its greatest assertion of the divine truth.

A Holy Ambition

This is where Korach's mistake lay. The different levels of spirituality among the various segments of the people, and within each individual's life, *do* take the form of a "hierarchy"—a ladder on which the materially involved individual looks up to his more spiritual brother, and regards his own spiritual moments as the loftiest part of his day. The farmer regards the produce that he gives to the *Kohen* as the holiest part of his yield, for it represents the spiritual focus of all his endeavors. The businessman looks to the scholar as the ideal; he feels trapped and stifled by the demands of his vocation and lives for those few precious moments which he manages to devote to study.

This is not because those who fill the more spiritual roles occupy a more important place in G-d's world. On the contrary—the "lowly realm" of the material is the arena in which the divine purpose in creation is realized. But the specialty of the materially involved individual lies precisely in that he deals with the lowest elements of creation (that is, those which least express the reality of G-d in any manifest way) and, recognizing their lowliness, directs them towards the *higher* purpose of serving his spiritual endeavors and spiritual brethren.

Interestingly enough, although Korach disavowed this "vertical" relationship between matter and spirit, he himself was a prime example of it. Korach's desire for the High Priesthood, his yearning for a rung on the ladder more spiritual than his own, was a positive ambition[22]—and the ultimate refutation of his challenge to Moses.[23]

Excerpt from Rabbi Yanki Tauber (adaptor, based on the works of the Rebbe, Rabbi Menachem Mendel Schneerson), *The Inside Story* (Brooklyn, N.Y.: Vaad Hanachos Hatmimim, 1997), pp. 231–241.

Endnotes

1 Numbers 13:32.
2 See previous essay, *Fallen Angels*, pp. 225-228.
3 See Yalkut Shimoni and other Midrashim on Numbers, ch. 16.
4 Numbers 16:9.
5 Deuteronomy 33:10.
6 Leviticus 21:10.
7 Deuteronomy 18: 1-2; see note 9 below.
8 These include a portion of the harvest *(terumah),* of all baked goods *(challah),* the first ripened fruits *(bikkurim),* certain cuts of meat from every slaughtered animal, the "first shearing" of the season's wool, etc.
9 See Maimonides' Mishneh Torah, *Laws of Shemittah and Yovel* 13:13: "Not only the tribe of Levi, but any man of all the inhabitants

of the earth, whose spirit has moved him and whose mind has given him to understand to set himself aside to stand before G-d to serve Him, to worship Him, to know G-d and walk justly as G-d has created him [justly], and he cast from his neck the yoke of the many calculations that men seek—this man has become sanctified, a holy of holies, and G-d shall be his portion and his lot for ever, and shall merit him his needs in this world, as He has merited the *Kohanim* and the Levites."

10 Numbers 17:15-26.

11 Ibid., 18:12-13.

12 Leviticus 3:16.

13 Mishneh Torah, *Laws of Things Forbidden to Be Brought on the Altar* 7:11.

14 Numbers 15:20.

15 Genesis 4:3-5; Mishneh Torah, loc. cit.

16 Midrash Tanchuma, Nasso 16.

17 Tanya, ch. 36.

18 Deuteronomy 4:35.

19 Isaiah 47:8.

20 Tanya, loc. cit.

21 As Rabbi Schneur Zalman goes on to point out, the very structure of *hishtalshelut* (i.e., the chain of successively less-spiritual worlds which G-d created) indicates that the divine purpose lies with our world, the most physical and least divinely expressive of realities. For if the objective of creation were to be a "spiritual" reality—i.e., a reality which constitutes a lesser concealment of the divine truth then G-d would not have created any world at all, since even the most spiritual of existences is already something of a concealment of His oneness and exclusivity of being. Obviously, then, the objective is concealment, and the chain of consecutively coarsened worlds points to its lowest link as the environment in which G-d's purpose of creation is to be realized.

22 This explains why an entire section of Torah (Numbers 16-18) carries the name "Korach"—the name of an unrepentant sinner. For we are to derive the positive aspect of Korach's deed—his yearning for an existence more spiritual than his own—and apply it to our lives.

23 Based on the talks of the Rebbe, Shabbat Korach 5714 (June 26, 1954) and on other occasions. Likkutei Sichot, vol. II, pp. 326-330, and vol. IV, pp. 1048-1055, et al.

FROM FEMINISM TO CHASIDISM

BY CHANA SHLOUSH

Had I known that the decision to keep kosher and *Shabbat* in 1971 would eventually lead me, many years later, to walking around Brooklyn in a wig and modest clothing, I might have been too paralyzed to have done the first *mitzvah*. There I was, 19 years old and thrilled about being a college student in Boston, exploring all the "isms" of the day: pacifism, socialism, vegetarianism, meditation, feminism, mysticism and Judaism.

My involvement in Torah Judaism came through an Orthodox relative, a woman in her 50s who welcomed me into her home like an adopted child. She was a European refugee like my father, able to fill in blanks about the vanished world I yearned to understand. Particularly in the context of her lifestyle she described much: "This is the tune your grandfather sang for the Grace After Meals. Now you are mixing up the cake your grandmother baked for *Shabbos*. These teacups were a gift to me from your aunt who died in Auschwitz." She was not an intellectual and also had no formal Jewish schooling, so she could not answer my whys about the performance of *mitzvot*, but she did them all with a compelling *joie de vivre*. She was also able to talk a little, in her down-to-earth way, about her relationship with G-d. She obviously had no hangups about that relationship, and she tried to convince me that there was no reason for concern. But Jewish spirituality and mysticism, which greatly interested me, were not part of her vocabulary—she did not radiate them or discuss them. Thus she could not give me some key information I required, and I had no recourse but to work through those issues in my own way. Thankfully, she also accepted me exactly as I was at every step.

My Torah commitment came about after many basic questions about observance and lifestyle had been

CHANA SHLOUSH

Chana Shloush graduated from Brandeis University and then studied at the Pardes Institute in Jerusalem. Shloush lives in Brooklyn, New York, and has worked for various Jewish organizations.

answered. There was a moment when, with an English Bible open to Exodus 20 (the *Shema* prayer), I had an overwhelming inner experience. *Kabbalat ol,* acceptance of the yoke of Heaven, is perhaps the most correct description. One might call it a leap of faith, yet afterward I found myself walking, not in midair, but on very solid ground. I committed myself to *Shabbat* and *kashrut* observance and was determined to eventually keep the rest of the *mitzvot* as well. Months and years actually passed before I had the intellectual knowledge and emotional readiness to take on many other *mitzvot.* I had also been forewarned about doing too much too fast, as there were others who had apparently taken that route and then abandoned their observance.

In 1971 feminism was a brand new, hot issue on campus. Those present at my first Women's Liberation meetings included an editor of the original *Our Bodies, Ourselves* and a woman who later wound up on the FBI's Ten Most Wanted list for bank robbery and murder, committed for the sake of "the revolution." I belonged to a women's literary circle which read and discussed feminist literature. I studied poetry and received personal advice from feminist poet Adrienne Rich. I came to find radical feminism frightening and distasteful because it bespoke such hatred of men. I didn't hate men: I was simply resentful whenever they seemed to get a better deal than women. One day a friend said, "You're interested in Judaism and also in feminism—why not explore the two together?"

My desire to establish a women's *minyan* arose from intense spiritual frustration and doubts about the status of the Jewish woman, based largely on my synagogue experience. At the time, praying in Hebrew was difficult, especially for one who had learned little more than *alef-bet* in Reform Sunday School. Trying concomitantly to pray in, and understand the Hebrew was even harder. Attempting to juggle all this and have a spiritual experience in the women's section of a traditional synagogue caused me terrific problems. When everyone sang spiritedly in unison, I managed well. But usually I sensed an uncomfortable silence, especially among women. I yearned for good concentration, warmth and openness during prayer, from myself and others. Instead I was confronted with furtive whispering or mouthing of the words of prayers. Usually by the end of services the atmosphere warmed up a bit, but then all too soon it was time to leave. I wondered why these women, who were saying the same words as the men, seemed, in my perception, to be lacking something in their self-expectations regarding a personal relationship with G-d. I had been told that women were not second-class citizens, but how could I not begin to have doubts when so many women behaved as if they thought that perhaps they were? My Orthodox relative did not act like a second-class citizen, but then, neither did she intellectualize, so I thought that maybe some wool was being pulled over her eyes without her knowing or caring. If G-d had created a system in which I was a second-class citizen, could I trust Him enough to have a close personal relationship? On the other hand, what about the times when I did have positive spiritual experiences, which certainly occurred without my having any thoughts of feminism? The issue was paradox-laden, and I was confounded. Precisely at the time when I needed a spiritual boost, I found frustration. So I continued praying in a traditional synagogue, meanwhile seeking alternatives. A visit to a *havurah* group proved disillusioning because of the members' lack of consistency in their Jewish commitment. A more intense practice of meditation served temporarily as a satisfying spiritual outlet, but I did not believe that I could ever transform it into a positive Jewish group ritual experience.

The idea to establish the first women's *minyan* in America (to my knowledge) took root in my mind late in 1971, during a lecture at Harvard Hillel by a Conservative rabbi. About ten days later, our "Women's *Minyan*" was born, with seven women in attendance. Our beginnings were tenuous; everyone seemed nervous and self-conscious. I was frustrated, but we plugged on with the group, meeting bi-weekly and having Torah study sessions together on occasion. I was spurred by one of my professors, the late Dr. Pauli Murray, a lawyer who nominated herself to be the first black female Supreme Court justice in the early 1970s, and later entered the Christian clergy. She encouraged me to keep a log of the group's progress. I don't believe there ever really was any progress, despite the fact that women in other places caught wind of the idea and set up similar groups. I didn't give up, though, and our *"minyan"* continued for the remaining year and a half until I graduated. I reasoned that other *mitzvot* had felt awkward and uncomfortable at first and had grown to feel like second nature; I kept hoping that I would eventually experience our group that way as well. However, I never found spiritual satisfaction in our *"minyan"* or any of the other women's *davening* groups I attended sporadically over the course of the next six years.

Not everyone in the *"minyan"* viewed it as I did. The student I recruited to be the co-founder of the "Women's *Minyan*" went on to become a Reform rabbi and made headlines a few years ago as the first female member of the Rabbinical Assembly, the Conservative rabbinical organization. In fact, I helped her draft a letter in 1972 to the chancellor of the Jewish Theological Seminary, requesting an application to Conservative rabbinical school. While I toyed with the idea of becoming a rabbi, I had to reject it, because I knew that the truth I was seeking had to lie somewhere within traditional Judaism. Instinct told me that finding it would involve a search—and I was prepared for a lengthy one if necessary—but not the kind of battle my friend was waging.

Concerned over missing out on important spiritual experiences, I did other kinds of Jewish feminist experimentation at the same time. I made my own *talit,* in beautiful pastel colors, learning from a man how to tie the *tzitzit.* I also created a very feminine headband which I wore for about two years. I thought that wearing the *talit* would help me shut out the external distractions, and sometimes this was the case. However, the *talit* induced other, greater inner distractions: the fact that I knew many pairs of eyes were on me, and the fact that deep down I sometimes enjoyed the attention and notoriety my behavior was bringing me. My initial basic motives were quite sincere. But whatever spiritual highs I experienced started to be clouded by the awareness of such falseness at the root of motivation.

I once put on *tefillin.* The woman who owned them asked for them back after ten minutes: at that point I did not want to take them off. I knew I could have some incredible meditations wearing them. But I was also overcome by immense awe and sensed that *tefillin* were too holy to wear if there were even an iota of an ego trip involved, especially if there were no *mitzvah* for—and some prohibitions against—my wearing them.

I also felt a sense of loss at not being able to come close to the physical Torah, to watch over the shoulder of the *baal koreh* as he *lehned* (read aloud)—or to actually be that *baal koreh.* So I learned the *trup* (cantillation) for Torah, *Haftorah* and the Song of Songs. There was some exhilaration in *lehning,* and it greatly aided my following the Torah reading in synagogue as well as personal learning, but I found the study and memorization of each *parsha* difficult and painstaking. With time, I also came to suspect that a great percentage of the exhilaration was an ego trip.

In retrospect, I believe that my stiff feminist principles became burdensome at a certain point, preventing me from trying out new *mitzvot* or delving deeper into already familiar ones. They also kept me from meeting the kinds of people I needed to encounter in order to gain the knowledge I craved.

A key transitional experience between feminism and Chasidism occurred in 1974. I spent that school year after college graduation in Jerusalem, studying Torah—mainly Talmud—in Hebrew, in an effort to gain the skills for independent text study. A group of Americans would study *Chasidut* one evening a week with a Chasidic rabbi in Meah Shearim. If he had an address, we didn't know it; we knew only which alleys to go down, which courtyards to cross. He spoke no English and taught quietly and patiently in the simplest Hebrew. One warm evening, a friend and I stayed after class to ask questions. His wife appeared with a glass of water which she handed me with a smile. Suddenly I was riveted to the floor. There was something intensely spiritual about the way that woman gave me the glass of water. I didn't want to leave. I wanted to grab her and shake her and beg her to tell me what the secret was, to say that I had been waiting for this moment for years and had to understand. But I couldn't. It seemed to me that the gaps in language and culture were too vast to even attempt it. So I went home that night and, without understanding why, carefully packed away my *talit* in an old footlocker. Today the reason is clear: I could no longer afford the luxury of alienating Torah-observant and Chasidic women who might bear the keys to locked doors I desired to open.

Perhaps the woman was a mystic. Or perhaps she changed my life with very strong *kavanah* (positive intention and concentration) in performing the *mitzvah* of *hachnassat orchim,* serving guests. Had I never put away the *talit,* it is hard to imagine ever having learned of the latter explanation.

Another incident greatly changed my attitude toward Torah study. I was not blessed with the analytical *Gemara Kop* that best absorbs Talmud. However, I was determined—again, partially on the feminist principle of not missing out on anything—to maintain an ongoing study of it. I had picked up an attitude from a number of supposedly learned men, that other parts of Torah were somehow lacking in comparison with "the sea of Talmud," and that one could not attain any respectable level of Torah knowledge without mastering it, much less gain wisdom. After the year in Israel, I moved to New York, where I found a genius of a teacher who taught Talmud to women on weekday evenings. A small group spent as many as six hours a week learning Tractate *Berachot* (Blessings) *b'amkut,* slowly and intensively. Our teacher loved to search within the discussions for deeper generalizations. I recall his spending several weeks on a brief passage in trying to understand the nature of a blessing, and his excitement over his conclusion. A blessing, he found, is like the economic principle of pump priming (my analogy), in which we open up the gates of Heaven so G-d can grant us His blessings.

Several years later, just before moving to Crown Heights, I attended the Bais Chana Women's Institute in Minnesota. Shortly after my arrival we went to wash our hands for bread before lunch. One self-appointed young woman helped everyone wash, as most were newcomers to observance. She was obviously quite new herself. As we waited, I could not help but perk up my ears as she explained to another woman the purpose for the blessing: "*Chasidut* says. . . ." Would the reader like to guess the rest? This was not a case where, as often happens, someone accidentally misquoted a source, since my teacher had worked for weeks to come up with an original explanation. In a manner totally uncharacteristic for me, I viewed that girl as a G-dly messenger. Never again did I force myself on principle to study Talmud. Today I will open a volume of the Talmud if I have a specific reason, but my basic daily Torah study focuses on other works. Perhaps the real inner process of my transition out of feminism becomes clearest with the struggle over the *mechitzah* issue. I had never battled the notion of *mechitzah,* yet neither had I ever really trusted the explanations which I had received. In particular, the protests that those men who led the services weren't really the focus of attention on a community-condoned ego trip smacked of "The Emperor's New Clothes." I accepted the *mechitzah* because it was part of the package deal of Torah, but for many years my mind was not at peace with it.

The eve of Yom Kippur, around 1980. Men and women alike were packed into Lubavitch international headquarters for *Kol Nidre,* somewhat like passengers on a Jerusalem bus during rush hour. The *baal tefillah* took his place to begin the service. I was anticipating an inspiring voice, a poignant melody to sweep me into the mood of the holiday. Instead, a man with an ordinary voice began the prayers with an atonal melody and then broke down in what appeared to be sincere sobs.

He sounded ridiculous. I was annoyed. An instant later, I was forced in all honesty to redefine my emotion as terror. I had no inspiration, no melody to hide behind. The *baal tefillah* was not about to lift me to any spiritual heights. Here was a man leading the prayers for thousands of Jews, including no less a personage than the Lubavitcher Rebbe, yet he was on anything but an ego trip. This meant that I was missing absolutely nothing on the other side of the *mechitzah.* At that moment, the *mechitzah* figuratively came crashing down once and for all, hitting me with what the issue had been in the first place. There were contradictory feelings involved: on one hand, a concern that somehow G-d was present only on the other side of that divider curtain, and on the other, a fear that if He weren't, I wouldn't be able to cope with the confrontation. In a way it had been easy to hide behind my anger. Now that the reality was clear, it would just have to be me and G-d—me facing up to my real self in front of G-d.

I was not able to cast off the women's *minyan, talit,* and the rest—nor was I interested in doing so—until there were other spiritual resources to take their places. A crucial factor in the change process was the study of *Chasidut.* Part of what helped me trust the system was finding that *Chasidut* is replete with feminine imagery. The subject would be interesting and inspiring in itself, but it is beyond the scope of this article.

I did not find Chabad *Chasidut* accessible until I was living in Crown Heights and attended classes, local synagogues where I had role models for proper concentration during prayer, and the Rebbe's *farbrengens* (Chasidic gatherings). With a deepening of study and *mitzvah* observance has come a heightened awareness of what was superficial in the past, and a natural wish to reject it. Hence, the change has mainly come gradually, like casting off clothes which neither fit any longer nor are needed. I suppose I entered into my feminist Jewish experiments with the soul of an innocent child. On one hand there were wide-eyed openness, beauty and wonder, which remain a refreshing source of inspiration when I recall the early days of observance. On the other hand, there was a passivity, as if important spiritual experiences should be conferred upon me from Above simply by virtue of, say, wearing certain accoutrements. I used to assume that G-d was providing all kinds of lovely merry-go round rides for men as they performed their particular *mitzvot.* Hands-on experience, Torah study and discussions with men led me to the conclusion that the men were unlikely to be getting free goodies any more than I ever had. With time came a gradual shift away from initial unrealistic and hence unfulfilling expectations.

There was an acceptance of my responsibility not only to fulfill my requirements in *mitzvah* observance, but to infuse energy and enthusiasm into each *mitzvah.* Originally I had demanded that my role models—including all those women behind the *mechitzah*—be perfect. When I stopped expecting so much from my fellow Jewish women, and had gained enough self-confidence to realize that perhaps I was meant to try to set an example for them, prayers and other *mitzvot* flowed more easily.

It is impossible to minimize the significance of tremendous female role models. I have met human dynamos, whom I believe rank among the spiritual Green Berets of the Jewish people. They have the shortcomings of all of us mortals, but their maximization of potential is astounding. During my early feminist years, the praises in Torah literature of the Jewish woman had sounded like so many platitudes: "A superior wisdom was granted to women," "A woman of valor, who can find?" etc. In meeting women who exemplified these verses, my views had to change radically. Even more, when I married and started a family I began to appreciate that the spiritual fortitude, the *mesirat nefesh*—the total giving of one's best—with which the Torah challenges a Jewish woman, is no less than the highest form of mystical practice I could ever have imagined, as different in form as it might at times appear to be on the surface. I seem to have come around full circle in trying to live up to models like the Meah Shearim woman, and the relative who first inspired me with her *joie de vivre* in *mitzvot.* I am grateful to be connected to a community where, spiritually speaking, the streets are paved with gold. In fact, who knows? Had my eyes been open all those years ago to see that gold, performing the first *mitzvah* might not have been paralyzing at all.

Excerpt from Baila Olidort (ed.), *Feeding Among the Lilies: The Wellsprings Reader* (Brooklyn, N.Y.: Wellsprings Journal, 1999).

Lesson

FINDING COMFORT

SEEING G-D THROUGH THE BLINDING PAIN

Landscape with a bush on fire, scorching the earth.
Fire-Flower, Jong Gu Lee, acrylic on Korean paper, 2006. (Korean Art Museum Association, South Korea)

When tragedy strikes, where is G-d? Our suffering feels like abandonment. We seek relief and assurance of His presence, and instead, we find loneliness and silence. What does Judaism offer as a response to and relief from life's difficulties? How do we relate to a G-d Who appears to be uncaring and feels so distant?

Exercise 1

Common Human Responses to Tragedy

Statement	1	2	3	4	5
When we suffer tragedy, we seek to understand its cause and meaning.	Strongly Disagree				Strongly Agree
Struggling with faith in G-d, due to suffering, results from a lack of belief.	Strongly Disagree				Strongly Agree
When we suffer tragedy, we are prone to feelings of loneliness.	Strongly Disagree				Strongly Agree
The tragedies that we suffer often leave a scar. We never return to our previous selves.	Strongly Disagree				Strongly Agree

TEXT 1

THE REBBE, MENACHEM MENDEL SCHNEERSON, *IGROT KODESH* 33:254

לֹא רַק שֶׁאֲנִי לֹא מַאֲמִין לָזֶה שֶׁאַתְּ כּוֹתֶבֶת שֶׁאֵינָךְ מַאֲמִינָה בֶּאֱלֹקִים חַס וְשָׁלוֹם, אֶלָּא בָּרוּר לִי שֶׁגַּם אַתְּ לֹא מַאֲמִינָה לָזֶה.

וְהַהוֹכָחָה הִיא שֶׁמִּדֵּי רְאוֹתָךְ הֶעְדֵּר הַצֶּדֶק וְהַיּוֹשֶׁר בִּסְבִיבָתֵךְ אוֹ מִדֵּי הַעֲלוֹתָךְ עַל זִכְרוֹנֵךְ עִנְיַן הַשּׁוֹאָה בְּעִקְבוֹת הִיטְלֶר יִמַּח שְׁמוֹ, כְּמוֹ שֶׁמַּזְכִּירָה אַתְּ בְּמִכְתָּבֵךְ, הֲרֵי זֶה מְבַלְבֵּל מְנוּחָתֵךְ. וְאִילוּ הָיְתָה הַמְּצִיאוּת שֶׁאֵין מַנְהִיג וּמְתַכְנֵן, מַהוּ הַפֶּלֶא כְּשֶׁיֵּשׁ מְאוֹרָעוֹת הֵיפֶךְ הַצֶּדֶק וְהַיּוֹשֶׁר וְהַגָּדוֹל מֵחֲבֵרוֹ חַיִּים בּוֹלְעוֹ וְכוּ'?

וְהַשְּׁאֵלָה הִיא לֹא רַק בְּמַמַּדִים גְּדוֹלִים כְּמוֹ הַשּׁוֹאָה הַנִּזְכָּר לְעֵיל, כִּי גַם בְּמַסְלוּל הַחַיִּים הַנִּקְרָאִים "חַיִּים אֲפוּרִים" שֶׁל כָּל יוֹם וָיוֹם רוֹאִים בְּמוּחָשׁ שֶׁכָּל תּוֹפָעָה שֶׁהִיא הֵיפֶךְ הַצֶּדֶק וְהַיּוֹשֶׁר מְבַלְבֶּלֶת מְנוּחַת הַנֶּפֶשׁ וּמַבִּיטִים עַל זֶה כִּמְאוֹרָע שֶׁלֹּא צָרִיךְ הָיָה לִהְיוֹת כֵּן.

וַהֲרֵי בְּוַדַּאי שֶׁחוֹמֶר הַדּוֹמֵם וַאֲפִילוּ בַּעֲלֵי חַיִּים שֶׁבִּסְבִיבָתֵנוּ אֵין הֵם מְצוּוִּים עַל הַצֶּדֶק וְהַיּוֹשֶׁר.

וּבְוַדַּאי שֶׁחוֹסֶר מְנוּחָה הַנִּגְרֶמֶת עַל יְדֵי תּוֹפָעוֹת אֵלּוּ מְקוּשָּׁר בְּמַשֶּׁהוּ שֶׁהוּא לְמַעֲלָה מֵהַדּוֹמֵם צוֹמֵחַ וְחַי, וַאֲפִילוּ לְמַעֲלָה מִן הָאָדָם, וּמַשֶּׁהוּ זֶה נִמְצָא בְּלֵב כָּל אָדָם פְּנִימָה. וּמִזֶּה הַוַּדָּאוּת בְּעֵינֵי כָּל אֶחָד וְאַחַת שֶׁהַצֶּדֶק צָרִיךְ לִהְיוֹת הַשּׁוֹלֵט בָּעוֹלָם, וְהַהַנְהָגָה בִּסְבִיבָתוֹ צְרִיכָה לִהְיוֹת דַּוְקָא עַל פִּי יוֹשֶׁר, שֶׁלָּכֵן אִם נִרְאֶה לָעַיִן מַשֶּׁהוּ שֶׁלֹּא בְּסֵדֶר, מְחַפֵּשׂ הוּא בְּכָל הַמֶּרֶץ וְהַדְּרָכִים לִמְצוֹא אֶת הַגּוֹרֵם שֶׁגָּרַם הַהֵיפֶךְ מִמַּה שֶּׁצָּרִיךְ הָיָה לִהְיוֹת.

RABBI MENACHEM MENDEL SCHNEERSON 1902–1994

The towering Jewish leader of the 20th century, known as "the Lubavitcher Rebbe," or simply as "the Rebbe." Born in southern Ukraine, the Rebbe escaped Nazi-occupied Europe, arriving in the U.S. in June 1941. The Rebbe inspired and guided the revival of traditional Judaism after the European devastation, impacting virtually every Jewish community the world over. The Rebbe often emphasized that the performance of just one additional good deed could usher in the era of Mashiach. The Rebbe's scholarly talks and writings have been printed in more than 200 volumes.

I don't believe your assertion that you don't believe in God. In fact, it is clear to me that even you don't believe it!

The proof is: You write in your letter, that upon perceiving in your world a lack of justice and fairness, and upon recalling the Holocaust caused by Hitler, may his name be erased, you are disturbed. Now, if there were no force conducting and planning [world events], why is it surprising when injustices occur, and the big swallows the small, etc.?

[Note that] this question [of unfairness] is not only regarding world-scale events like the Holocaust. Even regarding simple day-to-day occurrences, we are disturbed by any unfair event and expect things to be different.

Now, the realms of the inanimate and the animal kingdom surely aren't expected to abide by the rules of justice. [Who or what, then, do we expect to act justly?]

We must conclude that the uneasiness caused by these [negative] events must be due to [an awareness of] a force that is beyond the inanimate and animal realms, and even the human realm. The [awareness of this] force is found in the heart of every person. This is what gives rise to the wide-held conviction that justice ought to rule the world and that world events ought to be fair.

Therefore, when something isn't right, we desperately seek the cause for this unnatural state of events.

TEXT 2

GENESIS 18:25

> חָלִלָה לְּךָ מֵעֲשֹׂת כַּדָּבָר הַזֶּה לְהָמִית צַדִּיק עִם רָשָׁע וְהָיָה כַצַּדִּיק כָּרָשָׁע;
> חָלִלָה לָּךְ! הֲשֹׁפֵט כָּל הָאָרֶץ לֹא יַעֲשֶׂה מִשְׁפָּט?

It would be unthinkable for You to do such a thing—to kill the righteous with the wicked, thereby making the righteous and wicked equal. It is unthinkable for You! Will the Judge of the entire world not do what is just?

Landscape with Three Burning Cities: Sodom, Gomorrah and Tyrus (detail), Augustin Hirschvogel, etching, c. 1500. (National Gallery of Art, Washington, D.C.)

TEXT 3

DEUTERONOMY 31:17

הֲלֹא עַל כִּי אֵין אֱלֹקַי בְּקִרְבִּי מְצָאוּנִי הָרָעוֹת הָאֵלֶּה?

Haven't these disasters happened to me because my God isn't with me?

Rachel Mourning her Children, Ludwig Meidner, charcoal and watercolor, c. 1942. (Jewish Museum, Frankfurt)

TEXT 4

EXODUS 3:7–14

וַיֹּאמֶר ה', "רָאֹה רָאִיתִי אֶת עֳנִי עַמִּי אֲשֶׁר בְּמִצְרָיִם, וְאֶת צַעֲקָתָם שָׁמַעְתִּי
מִפְּנֵי נֹגְשָׂיו, כִּי יָדַעְתִּי אֶת מַכְאֹבָיו. וָאֵרֵד לְהַצִּילוֹ מִיַּד מִצְרַיִם וּלְהַעֲלֹתוֹ
מִן הָאָרֶץ הַהִוא, אֶל אֶרֶץ טוֹבָה וּרְחָבָה אֶל אֶרֶץ זָבַת חָלָב וּדְבָשׁ, אֶל מְקוֹם
הַכְּנַעֲנִי וְהַחִתִּי וְהָאֱמֹרִי וְהַפְּרִזִּי וְהַחִוִּי וְהַיְבוּסִי.

"וְעַתָּה, הִנֵּה צַעֲקַת בְּנֵי יִשְׂרָאֵל בָּאָה אֵלָי, וְגַם רָאִיתִי אֶת הַלַּחַץ אֲשֶׁר
מִצְרַיִם לֹחֲצִים אֹתָם. וְעַתָּה, לְכָה וְאֶשְׁלָחֲךָ אֶל פַּרְעֹה, וְהוֹצֵא אֶת עַמִּי
בְנֵי יִשְׂרָאֵל מִמִּצְרָיִם".

וַיֹּאמֶר מֹשֶׁה אֶל הָאֱלֹקִים, "מִי אָנֹכִי כִּי אֵלֵךְ אֶל פַּרְעֹה, וְכִי אוֹצִיא אֶת בְּנֵי
יִשְׂרָאֵל מִמִּצְרָיִם?"

וַיֹּאמֶר, "כִּי אֶהְיֶה עִמָּךְ. וְזֶה לְּךָ הָאוֹת כִּי אָנֹכִי שְׁלַחְתִּיךָ: בְּהוֹצִיאֲךָ אֶת
הָעָם מִמִּצְרַיִם, תַּעַבְדוּן אֶת הָאֱלֹקִים עַל הָהָר הַזֶּה".

וַיֹּאמֶר מֹשֶׁה אֶל הָאֱלֹקִים, "הִנֵּה אָנֹכִי בָא אֶל בְּנֵי יִשְׂרָאֵל, וְאָמַרְתִּי לָהֶם,
'אֱלֹקֵי אֲבוֹתֵיכֶם שְׁלָחַנִי אֲלֵיכֶם', וְאָמְרוּ לִי, 'מַה שְּׁמוֹ?'

"מָה אֹמַר אֲלֵהֶם?"

וַיֹּאמֶר אֱלֹקִים אֶל מֹשֶׁה, "אֶהְיֶה אֲשֶׁר אֶהְיֶה". וַיֹּאמֶר, "כֹּה תֹאמַר לִבְנֵי
יִשְׂרָאֵל, 'אֶהְיֶה שְׁלָחַנִי אֲלֵיכֶם'".

God said, "I have indeed seen the misery of My people who are in Egypt, and I have heard their cries of distress because of their slave drivers, for I am aware of their suffering. I have come down to rescue them from the hands of the Egyptians and to bring them up from that land, to a good and spacious land, to a land flowing with milk and honey, to the place of the Canaanites, the Hittites, the Amorites, the Perizites, the Hivites, and the Jebusites.

"And now, the cry of the Children of Israel has come to Me, and I have also seen how the Egyptians are oppressing them. Now go! I will send you to Pharaoh, and you will take My people, the Children of Israel, out of Egypt."

But Moses said to God, "Who am I that I should go to Pharaoh, and that I should take the Children of Israel out of Egypt?"

He replied, "For I will be with you. And this will be your sign that I sent you: when you take the people out of Egypt, you will serve God on this mountain."

Moses said to God, "I will come to the Children of Israel, and I will say to them, 'The God of your fathers has sent me to you,' and they will say to me, 'What is His name?'

"What shall I respond to them?"

God said to Moses, "*Ehyeh asher ehyeh* [I will be what I will be]." And He said, "Say the following to the Children of Israel, "*Ehyeh* [I will be] has sent me to you."

TEXT 5

THE REBBE, RABBI MENACHEM MENDEL SCHNEERSON, *LIKUTEI SICHOT* 26:23–24

אוּן דָאס אִיז גֶעוֶוען שְׁאֵלָתוֹ שֶׁל מֹשֶׁה: "הִנֵּה אָנֹכִי בָא אֶל בְּנֵי יִשְׂרָאֵל וְאָמַרְתִּי לָהֶם אֱלֹקֵי אֲבוֹתֵיכֶם שְׁלָחַנִי אֲלֵיכֶם (מוּז דָאס אַרוֹיסְרוּפְן) וְאָמְרוּ לִי **מַה שְּׁמוֹ**"–

אִידְן וֶועלְן תֵּיכֶּף פְרֶעגְן: וָואס פַאר אַ "שֵׁם" אוּן הַנְהָגָה אִיז דָאס, וָואס דֶערְלָאזְט אַזַא מַצָּב שֶׁל גָלוּת מְאוּיָּים וּבְמֶשֶׁךְ הַרְבֵּה שָׁנִים, אוּן עֶרְשְׁט נָאך דֶעם וִוי טוֹיזְנְטֶער אוּן טוֹיזְנְטֶער אִידִישֶׁע קִינְדֶער זַיינֶען אוּמְגֶעקוּמֶען, רַחֲמָנָא לִצְלַן, קוּמְט דֶער אָנְזָאג פוּן "צַעֲקָתָם שָׁמַעְתִּי גוֹ' וָאֵרֵד לְהַצִּילוֹ"?

אוּן מֹשֶׁה אִיז מוֹסִיף וּמַדְגִישׁ אַז דָאס אִיז אוֹיךְ בַּא עֶם אַ שְׁאֵלָה-צַעֲקָה –"מָה אוֹמַר אֲלֵיהֶם"?

This was Moses's question: "I will come to the Children of Israel, and I will say to them, 'The God of your fathers has sent me to you.' This will undoubtedly elicit the question: '*What is His name?*'"

The Jews will immediately ask: What kind of "name,"—i.e., behavior—is this: to allow a terrible exile to endure for so many years; and only after thousands upon thousands of Jewish children have been murdered, that's when we are told that "I have heard their cry . . . I will descend to rescue them . . ."?

Moses adds—and emphasizes—that he himself has this question and protest, too: "What should I tell them?"

TEXT 6a

EXODUS 3:14

וַיֹּאמֶר אֱלֹקִים אֶל מֹשֶׁה, "אֶהְיֶה אֲשֶׁר אֶהְיֶה".
וַיֹּאמֶר, "כֹּה תֹאמַר לִבְנֵי יִשְׂרָאֵל, 'אֶהְיֶה שְׁלָחַנִי אֲלֵיכֶם'".

God said to Moses, "*Ehyeh asher ehyeh* [I will be what I will be]."

And He said, "Say the following to the Children of Israel, '*Ehyeh* [I will be] has sent me to you.'"

TEXT 6b

RASHI, AD LOC.

אֶהְיֶה עִמָּם בְּצָרָה זֹאת אֲשֶׁר אֶהְיֶה עִמָּם בְּשִׁעְבּוּד שְׁאָר מַלְכֻיוֹת

"I will be" with them in this trouble, "that I will be" with them in their subjugation by other kingdoms.

RABBI SHLOMO YITSCHAKI (RASHI) 1040–1105

Most noted biblical and Talmudic commentator. Born in Troyes, France, Rashi studied in the famed *yeshivot* of Mainz and Worms. His commentaries on the Pentateuch and the Talmud, which focus on the straightforward meaning of the text, appear in virtually every edition of the Talmud and Bible.

TEXT 7

THE REBBE, RABBI MENACHEM MENDEL SCHNEERSON, *LIKUTEI SICHOT* 26:24

אויף דעם איז געווען דער ענטפער פון אויבערשטן "אֶהְיֶ' אֲשֶׁר אֶהְיֶ'", טייטשט רש"י "אֶהְיֶ' עִמָּם בְּצָרָה זֹאת כו'":

ס'איז ניט חס ושלום אז במשך זמן הגלות "פארקוקט" דער אויבערשטער אויף די צרות פונעם גלות המר, נאר אדרבא – "**אֶהְיֶ' עִמָּם בְּצָרָה זֹאת**", דער אויבערשטער געפינט זיך צוזאמען מיט די אידן "בְּצָרָה זֹאת".

וואס דאס איז מדגיש, אז דער אויבערשטער געפינט זיך מיט אידן ניט בלויז אין דעם זעלבן **מקום**, נאר ער געפינט זיך כביכול **אין דער צרה**, וכמו שנאמר "בְּכָל צָרָתָם **לוֹ צָר**" – בשעת אידן זיינען אין צרה ווערט דערפון, כביכול, דעם אויבערשטנ'ס צרה.

This, then, was the meaning of God's response, "I will be what I will be," as understood by Rashi: I will be with them in both this hardship and in future hardships:

God hadn't ignored the suffering of the Jewish people in their bitter exile. Heaven forbid! On the contrary, "*I will be with them in this hardship*"—God is together with the Jewish people in this hardship.

This doesn't only mean that God is found in *their presence*. Rather, He is found in *their pain*. As the prophet says, "Whenever they are in pain, He, too, is in pain" (ISAIAH 63:9). When the Jewish people suffer, this, so to speak, causes God to suffer, too.

PSALMS 23:1–4

> מִזְמוֹר לְדָוִד:
>
> ה' רֹעִי לֹא אֶחְסָר.
>
> בִּנְאוֹת דֶּשֶׁא יַרְבִּיצֵנִי; עַל מֵי מְנֻחוֹת יְנַהֲלֵנִי.
>
> נַפְשִׁי יְשׁוֹבֵב; יַנְחֵנִי בְמַעְגְּלֵי צֶדֶק, לְמַעַן שְׁמוֹ.
>
> גַּם כִּי אֵלֵךְ בְּגֵיא צַלְמָוֶת לֹא אִירָא רָע כִּי אַתָּה עִמָּדִי.
>
> שִׁבְטְךָ וּמִשְׁעַנְתֶּךָ הֵמָּה יְנַחֲמֻנִי.

A song of David:

God is my shepherd; I lack nothing.

He lays me down in green pastures. He leads me beside peaceful waters.

He restores my energy; He guides me in paths of righteousness for His name's sake.

Though I walk in the valley of the shadow of death, I will fear no harm for You are with me.

Your rod and Your staff—they comfort me.

TEXT 9

JAY LITVIN, "FROM UNDER THE COVERS," CHABAD.ORG

During this time of my illness, I have sought to connect what is happening in my life within the context of my religious observance and my personal relationship with G-d. From the intensity of my current condition, I find myself in a surprisingly intimate and direct alliance with the Almighty, though in a way I would not have predicted. . . .

Beneath it all, there is this quiet awareness of G-d, there is the foundation of His presence, there is a silent recognition that I can always call Home when I need to and that Someone will show up if it's raining too hard and I've forgotten my umbrella. . . .

G-d is not asking me to place Him out there somewhere and talk to Him, pray and meditate on His Glory and his Kingdom. Instead, during this time, He has come with the incredible opportunity to find Him in every detail of the daily challenge before me. . . .

No, G-d has not left me in the dark. He sits in a chair at my bedside watching over me. And rather than needing to call out in my moments of fear, I simply need to slip my hand from under the covers to reach out and take His hand in mine for only the moment it takes to reassure me of His presence.

JAY LITVIN
1944–2004

Chicago-born Litvin moved to Israel in 1993 to serve as medical liaison for Chabad's Children of Chernobyl program, and he took a leading role in airlifting children from the areas contaminated by the Chernobyl nuclear disaster. He also founded and directed Chabad's Terror Victims program in Israel. He passed away in April of 2004 after a valiant four-year battle with non-Hodgkin's lymphoma.

Figure 4.1a

Tracking God's Presence

	SUFFERER'S QUESTION	GOD'S RESPONSE
Spoken question	Suffering is due to God's lack of care. If God is truly present, how could He watch me suffer?	God never leaves a sufferer's side. On the contrary, He suffers with them. He is hidden in the unknowable purpose of suffering.
Underlying Beliefs	a. The world is full of chaos. b. Tragedy is the unfortunate result of random causes. c. Suffering is a frighteningly lonely experience.	a. b. c. A sufferer is always in God's company.

TEXT 10

RABBI JOSEPH B. SOLOVEITCHIK, *KOL DODI DOFEK,* TR. BY DAVID Z. GORDON; ED. BY JEFFREY WOOLF (NEW YORK, N.Y.: YESHIVA UNIVERSITY, AND HOBOKEN, N.J.: KTAV PUBLISHING HOUSE, 2006), PP. 4-5

Evil is a fact that cannot be denied. There is evil in the world. There are suffering and agony, and death pangs. He who would deceive himself by ignoring the split in existence and by romanticizing life is but a fool and a fabricator of illusions. It is impossible to conquer monstrous evil with philosophical-speculative thought. . . .

Certainly, the testimony of the Torah regarding creation—that "it is very good" (GENESIS 1:31) — is true. However, this is only stated from the unbounded perspective of the Creator. In man's finite, limited view, the absolute good in creation is not apparent. The contrast is striking and undeniable. . . .

To what might this situation be compared? To a person who views a beautiful tapestry, the work of a fine artisan, which contains, woven into it on its front, a representation dazzling to the eye. To our great sorrow, we see this image [i.e., the world] from the obverse side. Can such a sight become a sublime esthetic experience? Thus, we are incapable of comprehending the panorama of reality without which one cannot uncover God's master plan—the essence of the works of the Holy One.

RABBI JOSEPH B. SOLOVEITCHIK
1903–1993

Talmudist and philosopher. A scion of a famous Lithuanian rabbinical family, Rabbi Soloveitchik was one of the most influential Jewish personalities, leaders, and thinkers of the 20th century. In 1941, he became professor of Talmud at RIETS—Yeshiva University; in this capacity, he ordained more rabbis than anyone else in Jewish history. Among his published works are *Halakhic Man* and *Lonely Man of Faith.*

TEXT 11

JEREMIAH 12:1

צַדִּיק אַתָּה ה' כִּי אָרִיב אֵלֶיךָ, אַךְ מִשְׁפָּטִים אֲדַבֵּר אוֹתָךְ. מַדּוּעַ דֶּרֶךְ
רְשָׁעִים צָלֵחָה, שָׁלוּ כָּל בֹּגְדֵי בָגֶד?

God, You are always right when I contend with You, yet I will still argue with You. Why does the way of the wicked prosper, and all who deal with treachery enjoy tranquility?

Meus Avos (My Grandparents), Lasar Segall, 1921. (Museu Lasar Segall, São Paulo)

Figure 4.1b

Tracking God's Presence—Hidden God

	SUFFERER'S QUESTION	GOD'S RESPONSE
Spoken question	Suffering is due to God's lack of care. If God is truly present, how could He watch me suffer?	God never leaves a sufferer's side. On the contrary, He suffers with them. He is hidden in the unknowable purpose of suffering.
Underlying Beliefs	a. The world is full of chaos.	a. The world runs with perfect order.
	b. Tragedy is the unfortunate result of random causes.	b. Tragedy is humanity's perception of God's unknowable order.
	c. Suffering is a frighteningly lonely experience.	c. A sufferer is always in God's company.

TEXT 12a

PSALMS 22:2

אֵ-לִי אֵ-לִי לָמָה עֲזַבְתָּנִי?
רָחוֹק מִישׁוּעָתִי דִּבְרֵי שַׁאֲגָתִי.

My God, my God, why have You forsaken me?

[You are] far from my salvation [and] my outcry.

TEXT 12b

RABBI SAMSON RAPHAEL HIRSCH, PSALMS, PSALM 22:2

לָמָה (מִלְרַע)–לְשֵׁם אֵיזֶה מַטָּרָה, וְלֹא לָמָה (מִלְעֵיל)–מֵאֵיזוֹ סִיבָּה.

Instead of reading the word as ***LA**-mah*, meaning "for what reason," read the word as *la-**MAH***, meaning "for what purpose."

RABBI SAMSON RAPHAEL HIRSCH
1808–1888

Born in Hamburg, Germany; rabbi and educator; intellectual founder of the *Torah Im Derech Eretz* school of Orthodox Judaism, which advocates combining Torah with secular education. Beginning in 1830, Hirsch served as chief rabbi in several prominent German cities. During this period, he wrote his *Nineteen Letters on Judaism*, under the pseudonym of Ben Uziel. His work helped preserve traditional Judaism during the era of the German Enlightenment. He is buried in Frankfurt am Main.

TEXT 13

RABBI JOSEPH B. SOLOVEITCHIK, *KOL DODI DOFEK,* TR. BY DAVID Z. GORDON, ED. BY JEFFREY WOOLF (NEW YORK, N.Y.: YESHIVA UNIVERSITY AND HOBOKEN, N.J.: KTAV PUBLISHING HOUSE, 2006), PP. 6-8

According to Judaism, man's mission in this world is to turn fate into destiny—an existence that is passive and influenced into an existence that is active and influential; an existence of compulsion, perplexity, and speechlessness into an existence full of will, vision, and initiative. . . .

Destiny bestows on man a new status in God's world. It bestows upon man a royal crown, and thus he becomes God's partner in the work of creation. . . .

The question of questions is: What does suffering obligate man to do? This problem was important to Judaism, which placed it at the center of its *Weltanschauung*. . . .

We do not wonder about the ineffable ways of the Holy One, but instead ponder the paths man must take when evil leaps up at him. We ask not about the reason for evil and its purpose, but rather about its rectification and uplifting. How should a man react in a time of distress? What should a person do so as not to rot in his affliction?

TEXT 14

JAY LITVIN, "GRIEF," CHABAD.ORG

A colleague wrote me about her grief and sorrow at the loss of a friend who was killed. . . .

At the end of my letter I wrote a strange line to my friend. I was surprised when I read the words as I typed them. "May G-d comfort you when the time is right for comfort," I said, "and until then, may the grief enter into the core of your heart, and in its breaking, bring you closer to G-d."

And when I reread this line, I knew I was speaking to myself, writing words to another that were intended for me to hear. . . .

What if my heart would break, time and time again, each time revealing a new depth of feeling and connection, causing a new sensitivity, a new vulnerability and penetrability, a new sense of faith and source of strength, the strength that comes from knowing that I can feel the fullness of my love and sorrow and still survive; that I can not only survive, but grow to be a source of comfort as well, and a testament to those we have lost.

I cannot undo the acts of G-d. I cannot undo the horror and loss of life. But I can respond to it with my most human and G-dly self. I can open my heart to the pain and loss. I can allow my heart to break with the knowledge that it will heal and grow larger. And in so doing, I can come closer to the soul that binds us one to the other, closer to G-d and the Jewish people.

Homage to Michelangelo: Loneliness, Ali Talib, 1994.

Figure 4.1c

Tracking God's Presence—Our Response

<table>
<tr><th></th><th>SUFFERER'S QUESTION</th><th>GOD'S RESPONSE</th><th>OUR RESPONSE</th></tr>
<tr><td>Spoken question</td><td>Suffering is due to God's lack of care. If God is truly present, how could He watch me suffer?</td><td>God never leaves a sufferer's side. On the contrary, He suffers with them.
He is hidden in the unknowable purpose of suffering.</td><td rowspan="2">• We are not helpless victims of fate. We are capable of shaping our future.
• Viewing suffering as an impetus for growth enables us to imbue it with meaning.
• God is waiting for our response. What will it be?</td></tr>
<tr><td>Underlying Beliefs</td><td>a. The world is full of chaos.
b. Tragedy is the unfortunate result of random causes.
c. Suffering is a frighteningly lonely experience.</td><td>a. The world runs with perfect order.
b. Tragedy is humanity's perception of God's unknowable order.
c. A sufferer is always in God's company.</td></tr>
</table>

Exercise 2

Imagine If...

Imagine that you had the wisdom of foresight. Upon becoming aware of inevitable unfortunate circumstances in your future life, you had the opportunity to write a letter to your future—struggling—self. Among other things, you would advise your future self of the most effective way to respond to your negative situation.

What would you write?

KEY POINTS

1 We shouldn't confuse our tragedy for God's disinterest in our well-being. He is with us in our hardest times and shares in our pain. We are never alone.

2 Responding to tragedy with confusion and outrage is religiously legitimate, and even sanctioned. It is unreasonable and impossible for humans to defend the mysterious ways of God, since we aren't capable of understanding His ways.

3 God has endowed humanity with creative capacities. He wants us to partner with Him in creating the story of life. We are not the victims of fate. We are the authors of destiny.

4 Although we can't control our circumstances, we can control our responses to them. With enough hope and courage, we can respond to tragedy with personal growth. This is the ultimate challenge.

Appendix

TEXT 15a

PROVERBS 15:3

בְּכָל מָקוֹם עֵינֵי ה', צֹפוֹת רָעִים וטוֹבִים.

The eyes of God are everywhere, observing the bad and the good.

TEXT 15b

GENESIS 18:14

הֲיִפָּלֵא מֵה' דָבָר?

Is anything impossible for God?

TEXT 15c

PSALMS 145:9, 17

טוֹב ה׳ לַכֹּל, וְרַחֲמָיו עַל כָּל מַעֲשָׂיו . . .
צַדִּיק ה׳ בְּכָל דְּרָכָיו, וְחָסִיד בְּכָל מַעֲשָׂיו.

God is good to all, and His compassion is upon all His creations. . . .

God is righteous in all His ways, and benevolent in all His deeds.

Figure 4.2

God's Name Count

NAME OF GOD	APPEARANCES IN SCRIPTURE
Havaye (the Tetragrammaton)	6,639
Elokim	2,000+
Kel	235
Shakai	48
Ehyeh	3

TEXT 16a

RABBEINU BECHAYE, EXODUS 3:13

הָיָה רָאוּי שֶׁיֹּאמַר מַה אוֹת,

כִּי הָאִישׁ הַמִּתְנַבֵּא אֶל עַם בִּדְבַר ה', אֵין מַחֲזִיקִין אוֹתוֹ כְּנָבִיא וְלֹא יַאֲמִינוּ בִּדְבָרָיו עַד שֶׁיִּתֵּן לָהֶם אוֹת בֶּעָתִיד, וּבָא הָאוֹת וְהַמּוֹפֵת כַּאֲשֶׁר דִּבֶּר, וְכָל שֶׁכֵּן שֶׁלֹּא יִשְׁמְעוּ אֵלָיו לָלֶכֶת אַחֲרָיו.

וּמַה שֶּׁאָמַר מֹשֶׁה, "וְאָמְרוּ לִי מַה שְּׁמוֹ?" יָדוּעַ, כִּי זְכִירַת שֵׁם אֶחָד מִשְּׁמוֹתָיו הַקְּדוֹשִׁים שֶׁל הַקָּבָּ"ה אֵינֶנּוּ אוֹת לְיִשְׂרָאֵל כְּלַל, כִּי אִם יָדְעוּ יִשְׂרָאֵל אוֹתוֹ שֵׁם, גַּם מֹשֶׁה אֶפְשָׁר לוֹ שֶׁיָּדַעְנוּ כָּהֶם, וּמַה הָרְאָיָה בְּהַגִּידוֹ אוֹתוֹ לָהֶם? וְאִם לֹא יְדָעוּהוּ וְלֹא שְׁמָעוּהוּ מֵעוֹלָם מַה הָרְאָיָה וְהַמּוֹפֵת בִּזְכִירַת הַשֵּׁם שֶׁיַּאֲמִין בּוֹ עַתָּה מִי שֶׁלֹּא הָיָה מַאֲמִין בּוֹ מִתְּחִלָּה?

וַהֲרֵי אָנוּ רוֹאִים כִּי מֹשֶׁה אַחֲרֵי שֶׁהוֹדִיעַ הַקָּבָּ"ה הַשֵּׁם הַהוּא, אָמַר וְהֵן לֹא יַאֲמִינוּ לִי, וְהוּצְרַךְ הַקָּבָּ"ה לָתֵת לוֹ אוֹתוֹת.

It would have made more sense for Moses to [have anticipated that the Jewish people would] ask, "What prophetic sign do you have?"

Whenever a person presents himself to a nation as a prophet of God, he is not considered a legitimate prophet, nor are his words believed, until he provides a future prophetic sign and it materializes. He is certainly not listened to or obeyed [without this].

[Considering this,] why did Moses say, "They will ask me, 'What is His name?'" He should have known that simply mentioning one of God's holy names would not be a sufficient sign for the Jewish people: If they were familiar with that name, Moses could have known it as well, so mentioning it would not have been proof; and

RABBEINU BECHAYE BEN ASHER
C. 1265–1340

Biblical commentator. Rabbeinu Bechaye lived in Spain and was a disciple of Rabbi Shlomo ben Aderet, known as Rashba. He is best known for his multifaceted commentary on the Torah, which interprets the text on literal, midrashic, philosophical, and kabbalistic levels. Rabbeinu Bechaye also wrote *Kad Hakemach*, a work on philosophy and ethics.

if they were not familiar with it and had never heard of it, what proof would there be in mentioning it? Would someone who hadn't previously believed in God now believe in Him?

Indeed, [even] after God told Moses His name, Moses further pressed, "They will not believe me." God was then required to provide him with prophetic signs.

TEXT 16b

NACHMANIDES, AD LOC.

וְדֶרֶךְ שְׁאֵלָה בִּקֵּשׁ שֶׁיוֹדִיעֵהוּ מִי הַשּׁוֹלֵחַ אוֹתוֹ, כְּלוֹמַר בְּאֵי זוֹ מִדָּה הוּא שָׁלוּחַ אֲלֵיהֶם . . .

וְהִנֵּה אָמַר, "יִשְׁאָלוּנִי עַל שְׁלִיחוּתִי אִם הִיא בְּמִדַּת אֵ-ל שַׁדַ-י הִיא שֶׁעָמְדָה לָאָבוֹת, אוֹ בְּמִדַּת רַחֲמִים עֶלְיוֹנִית שֶׁתֵּעָשֶׂה בָּהּ אוֹתוֹת וּמוֹפְתִים מְחוּדָּשִׁים בַּיְצִירָה".

Moses was inquiring as to Who, i.e., which attribute of God, was backing his mission. . . .

Moses was saying to God, "The Jewish people will ask me regarding [the nature of] my mission: Is it charged with the energy of *Shakai*, which stood by [i.e., intervened for] the forefathers? Or, is it charged with the sublime energy of *rachamim,* which is capable of completely changing the order of creation?

RABBI MOSHE BEN NACHMAN (NACHMANIDES, RAMBAN) 1194–1270

Scholar, philosopher, author, and physician. Nachmanides was born in Spain and served as leader of Iberian Jewry. In 1263, he was summoned by King James of Aragon to a public disputation with Pablo Cristiani, a Jewish apostate. Though Nachmanides was the clear victor of the debate, he had to flee Spain because of the resulting persecution. He moved to Israel and helped reestablish communal life in Jerusalem. He authored a classic commentary on the Pentateuch and a commentary on the Talmud.

TEXT 17a

THE REBBE, RABBI MENACHEM MENDEL SCHNEERSON, *IGROT KODESH* 23:371

> אִיךְ גְלוֹיבּ, אַז אִיר וֶועט מִיט מִיר מַסְכִּים זַיין, אַז עֶס [אִיז] נִיט גֶעוֶוען סְתַּם אַ צוּפַאל דָאס וָואס דִי אַלֶע אוֹיטֶענְטִישֶׁע פְּרֶעגֶער זַיינֶען גֶעבְּלִיבְּן בַּא זֵייעֶר אֶמוּנָה; נָאר אַז עֶס הָאט גָאר אַנְדֶערְשׁ נִיט גֶעקֶענְט זַיין.

I believe that you will agree with me that it is no coincidence that all the authentic questioners remained in their faith; indeed, it could not have been otherwise.

TEXT 17b

THE REBBE, RABBI MENACHEM MENDEL SCHNEERSON, IBID.

> אִיז דָאךְ פַארְשְׁטֶענְדְלֶעךְ, אַז אַזַא טִיפֶער גֶעפִיל קֶען קוּמֶען נָאר פוּן דֶער אִיבֶּערְצַייגוּנְג, אַז דֶער אֶמֶת'עֶר צֶדֶק אִיז דֶער צֶדֶק וָואס שְׁטַאמְט פוּן אַן **אִיבֶּער**מֶענְטְשְׁלֶעכְן מָקוֹר, דָאס הֵייסְט, וָואס אִיז הֶעכֶער סַיי פוּן דֶעם מֶענְטְשְׁלֶעכְן שֵׂכֶל אוּן סַיי פוּנֶם מֶענְטְשְׁלֶעכְן גֶעפִיל. דֶערְפַאר רִירְט דִי קַשְׁיָא אָן נִיט נָאר רֶגֶשׁ אוּן שֵׂכֶל, נָאר אוֹיךְ זַיין פְּנִימִיּוּת אוּן עֶצֶם מְצִיאוּת.

It is self-understood that such a deep feeling can only come from the conviction that true justice flows from a suprahuman source—i.e., a source that is higher than both human understanding and human feeling. Indeed, for this reason, the question agitates not only the emotions and the intellect, but also one's inner self and the very essence of one's being.

TEXT 17C

THE REBBE, RABBI MENACHEM MENDEL SCHNEERSON, IBID.

> אָבֶּער נָאךְ דֶעם עֶרְשְׁטְן שְׁטוּרְמִישְׁן אַרוֹיסְטְרִיט, מוּז עֶר זִיךְ כַּאפְּן אַז דֶער גַאנְצֶער צוּגַאנְג פוּן שְׁטֶעלְן דִי קַשְׁיָא אוּן פוּן וֶועלְן פַארְשְׁטֵיין מִיטְן שֵׂכֶל דָאס וָואס אִיז הֶעכֶער פוּן שֵׂכֶל, הָאט קֵיין אָרְט נִיט. דֶערִיבֶּער מוּז עֶר - נָאךְ אַ דֶערְשִׁיטֶערְנְדֶען אַמְפֶּערְן זִיךְ אוּן דוּרְכְוֵוייטִיקְן - סוֹף כָּל סוֹף קוּמֶען צוּם אוֹיסְפִיר - "עִם כָּל זֶה אֲנִי מַאֲמִין!" אַדְרַבָּא - נָאךְ שְׁטַארְקֶער.

But after the initial passionate reaction, the [believing questioner] will inevitably realize that the entire premise—that one can seek to understand that which is higher than the intellect by using the intellect—has no place. Therefore, after a tumultuous and painful inner debate, he must in the end conclude that, "Despite all that, I believe!"—and, furthermore, more strongly than before.

TEXT 18

JAY LITVIN, "ME AND MY BODY," CHABAD.ORG

I often relate to my illness as something that has brought much good in my life—deeper understanding, improvements in my relationships, a closer connection to G-d. This is why I say that it comes from G-d, from the goodness of G-d, because it has clearly brought good into my life. I don't mean to belittle the "bad," nor do I wish to invite the cancer into my life for any longer than it need be here. And I would be glad to see it go once and for all (Get outta here!). But there has been unbelievable good that has come from it as well. Clearly it is something that I must have "needed" or fits into my destiny. Something that is real in my life. . . .

It takes me from being an opponent to being a partner. It redefines healing. It allows for acceptance.

Additional Readings

WHY BAD THINGS HAPPEN TO GOOD PEOPLE

BY RABBI ABRAHAM J. TWERSKI

We have previously alluded to the problem of suffering and its potential impact on self-esteem. There is yet another concept in Torah related to human suffering that deserves mention.

G-d appeared in a vision to the patriarch Abraham and said to him, "You must know that your children will be strangers in a foreign land, and they will be enslaved and tortured for four hundred years . . . and then they will emerge with great wealth" (Genesis 15 :13). It is clear that the wealth which G-d is referring to is not the booty acquired at the Exodus from Egypt, because this was certainly not worth the indescribable suffering of the Egyptian captivity. The wealth to which G-d was referring was the spiritual wealth of the acquisition of the Torah at Sinai after the deliverance from Egypt. It is thus evident that G-d considered the Egyptian experience to be a prerequisite for receiving the Torah.

The theme of suffering as a necessary precondition for acquiring spiritual fulfillment is found elsewhere in Torah. "Three gifts were given to Israel, all of which were acquired through suffering: the Torah, the land of Israel, and Paradise" (Berachos 5a).

Our minds cannot fathom this. Why could we not receive spiritual gifts without painful ordeals? Why was it necessary to endure centuries of spirit-crushing and back-breaking enslavement to merit the spiritual wealth of the Torah?

The answer is provided in the Torah, and although it may not satisfy us because it is beyond our logical understanding, it is the answer nevertheless. Moses tells us that "G-d delivered you from the *purifying furnace* of Egypt" (Exodus 4:20). The Egyptian ordeal of suffering, much like a furnace where the iron is melted and extracted from the impurities of the ore, was a purification process.

Why, however, did we need purification? What were the impurities from which we needed to be cleansed? And in any event, how does suffering cleanse? Occasionally we are given some insight, as when the Midrash states that the Egyptian ordeal atoned for the sale of Joseph into slavery by his brothers. People so dominated by envy that they can sell a brother into slavery are not worthy of Torah. People who are enslaved develop a sense of consideration and responsibility for one another, and the common suffering serves as a bond which amalgamates them into one unit. The metaphor of the "purifying furnace" is thus well-chosen, for whereas the lumps of iron ore are separate and distinct, the molten iron solidifies into a single mass. Perhaps this union through suffering is what enabled the two million Jews of the Exodus to stand at the foot of Sinai with unanimity of thought and will. "And the people all answered together as one, 'All that G-d commands we will do'" (Exodus 19:8). They were "like one person, with one heart" (Rashi, Exodus 19:20).

My deep dislike and disapproval of suffering, however does not permit me to logically accept the means as justified by the end. But here, as elsewhere, the Torah Jew is obligated to defer his logical understanding to Divine wisdom. He may not understand the

RABBI ABRAHAM J. TWERSKI, M.D., 1930–

Psychiatrist and noted author. Rabbi Twerski is a scion of the Chernobil Chasidic dynasty and a well-known expert in the field of substance abuse. He has authored more than 50 books on self-help and Judaism, and has served as a pioneer in heightening awareness of the dangers of addiction, spousal abuse, and low self-esteem. He served as medical director of the Gateway Rehabilitation Center in Pittsburgh and as associate professor of psychiatry at the University of Pittsburgh School of Medicine.

purpose, yet trusts that the suffering is not without a purpose.

I was privileged to hear an address by a woman who had recovered after a long siege of addiction to alcohol. Following the narration of her biography, wherein she related the multiple traumas and repeated losses she had sustained during the years of drinking, she was asked how she managed to survive all her losses.

The woman's answer was a revelation to me. "When I lost my marriage and my job, I thought my world had come to an end. I felt terrible pain, and because I was hurting, I became rebellious and defiant. I did not really believe in G-d except as the object of all my anger and bitterness. Why are You doing this to me? What is it that You want from me?

"Only now, after eight years of sobriety, can I see that G-d was taking from me those things that I did not have the good judgment to get rid of by myself. Looking back with a clear mind, I can see that the marriage was not in my best interest, nor was the job. I have now gone back to school and am getting my master's degree, which I never would have done otherwise. I am now happily remarried, with a relationship that is far healthier than the one I lost could ever have been.

"Things are not always easy for me now. I still have my disappointments. But the wisdom I have gained from my previous experiences helps me to realize that just as I had been unable to see the ultimate good in what were then terrible happenings, so perhaps I am now misinterpreting as losses what I will someday realize to be in my best interests."

Although I had often heard recovered alcoholics attest that they never could have achieved their personality growth and maturation without going through the torment of alcoholism, I had never been so profoundly moved as by this woman's statement.

The concept that suffering is a growth and maturation process nevertheless falls short of satisfying my understanding for its existence. Can there not be an alternate method for achieving personality growth?

Yes, if I had designed the world I would have sought a painless method for growth. But the fact is that I did *not* design the world and G-d *did*. My belief in the infinite wisdom and the benevolence of G-d compels me to conclude that for reasons completely beyond my capacity to understand, there is no other way to achieve such personality growth. Indeed, this was G-d's response to Job's complaints about his suffering. "Where were you when I created the universe?" (Job 38:4). I believe that G-d's benevolence far surpasses my own, and as I try to treat my patients with the least painful effective treatment, certainly G-d would provide a painless alternative, if this were possible according to His infinite wisdom.

It is not expected that awareness of suffering as a growth process will significantly diminish pain for most people, nor may it eliminate the anger and the bitterness which suffering evokes. The Talmud states, "A person is not culpable for the feelings he has when he is suffering" (Baba Basra 16b). G-d does not find fault with those who are unable to endure suffering with equanimity. Rather, what is expected is that after the acute, severe pain subsides, we should be able to apply our faith and trust and accept our past suffering as necessary to our spiritual growth.

The Talmud and the ethical works refer to a concept of a "descent in the interest of ascent" [*Tanya*, ch. 31]. A setback may occur with the ultimate purpose of enabling a person to rise to even greater spiritual heights. Again and again the ethical works stress that a person should not allow suffering to separate him from a close relationship with G-d. The *sitra achra* will use every opportunity available to interfere with a person's spiritual growth, and when suffering occurs, will exploit it to drive a wedge between man and G-d, and cast man into paralyzing depression. The Torah concept of suffering must be adhered to tenaciously to avoid this pitfall. At all times, in distress as in comfort, our self-esteem and sense of worthiness must be preserved.

Excerpt from Abraham J. Twerski, *Let Us Make Man: Self-Esteem through Jewishness* (Lakewood, N.J.: CIS Publishers Inc., 1987).

WHY DOES G-D ALLOW SUFFERING?

BY RABBI SHMUEL POLLEN

Everyone reading this has experienced suffering. So has the one writing it. Sometimes the most pious among us seem to suffer the most. And sometimes the ones who hurt others the most live best. So it's only human to ask, "Why does a good G-d allow bad things to happen to good people?"

Rabbis don't like answering this question. Not because they can't. Because of the risk. If your brother's pain makes sense, it might not bother you the same way. In that case, it would be better to have no answer at all. So if you want to understand "why," you must promise me one thing. That in the face of others' pain, you will forget every explanation and just be silent. Just look into their eyes. Into the pain. And don't stop until they know for certain that you share in it. Until they know they're not alone.

Also know, the true answer to any suffering can only come from the One who gave it, which is G-d. He will reveal the true answers Himself one day in the Messianic era. Today, all we can do is learn the Torah He gave us, to gain a glimpse into His view of the world, as opposed to only seeing our own. Because when we start to dissolve those differences between ourselves and our Father in Heaven, we will surely find comfort.

Let's begin.

A group of boys decide to play a game of basketball. One boy doesn't hear so well. A ball is handed to him, so he puts it on the floor and kicks it hard to the other side of the court. The other kids turn to him angrily and say, "What the heck are you doing?"

He says, "What do you mean? I just scored a goal."

They say, "No, you didn't. You scored nothing, got us a penalty, and gave the other team control of the ball."

The boy is confused and dejected. The issue? He was playing soccer. They were playing basketball. I call this problem "playing the wrong game." And "playing the wrong game" is the biggest mistake you can make in life.

Whatever you face now, whether it be debt, hunger, addiction or disabilities, that's how G-d "kicked the ball." You get angry and think something must be wrong with Him. Or with you. In truth, the only problem is the two of you are playing different games. Let's introduce them.

You are playing a game called "My Perfect Life." Every day, you strive to have perfect health, perfect finances and the perfect marriage. Or as close as you can get to them. When suffering occurs, you're angry because that means your game is being ruined.

What game is G-d playing? It's called "The Perfect *Story*." G-d wants to tell the greatest story ever told. He unfolds His story (history) like acts in a play. The story is full of drama. Heroes and villains. Victory and catastrophe. Sadness and joy. And we are told that it's all being recorded "above" like one big 7,000-year-long movie.

So where are you in this game? You're on camera! You're an actor and He's the director. You've been in this movie the whole time. The problem is, you don't realize you're in it. You're playing the other game, so the director's instructions don't seem relevant. Meanwhile, there is no one who can play your role, and that's ruining *this* game. Until one day, you decide to listen. The words you hear affect you to the very core of your being. You begin to feel like you've awakened from a bad dream. You aren't who you thought you were. And your life isn't what you thought it was. Things begin to come into focus.

This is what the Director said: "My child, I chose you for this specific role for a reason. I waited a long time for you to turn to Me and find out what it was. So I will tell you what it is. Your role was never to have

RABBI SHMUEL POLLEN

Rabbi Shmuel Pollen received a law degree from Benjamin N. Cardozo School of Law, and resides in Rockaway, New Jersey. He is the founder of Bnei Noah, a nonprofit organization that provides food and medicine to the needy of Gujarat, India, and eastern Ukraine. Bnei Noah also educates non-Jews about the seven Noahide Laws.

the perfect life for yourself. Your role is to find a way to be a hero for someone else. What's a hero? Anyone who is willing to go beyond himself for the greater good. Anyone who is willing to put his personal desires aside, to fulfill My wishes for him.

"What do I wish? I wish you would uplift others who have fallen, with a kind word or a small act of charity. I wish you would feel grateful for all of the good that surrounds you, and that you would humbly accept the challenge to overcome the rest. I wish you would fight every day to defeat the demons I gave you, be they greed, lust, laziness or anything else.

"Because I want you to know: buried underneath the jagged rocks I've put in front of you is hidden gold. It is in those darkest moments, when you see no way out, that all the souls who have passed, 'the great audience in heaven,' will be glued to the screen, crying for you, praying for you, waiting to see what you'll do and who you'll become.

"And where will I be? Not behind the camera like any other director. I will be with you in that moment of pain. Experiencing it just as you do. Because we are not separate. We are one. And you will never be alone. I want you to hear My instructions, and listen to them, because I know that's what's best for you. I know because I created you. But even if you ignore everything I say, the love I have for you will be the same. You are my daughter. You are my son. Always."

Upon hearing these words, you look back at everything you've been through. And say, "Yes, I've been cut. Yes, I've been bruised. Yes, actors I loved have had their roles cut short far too soon. Unfair? Imperfect? Yes. But maybe the goal never was perfection. Maybe the goal was the story itself. And stories never die. I feel inner joy behind all that pain. Because I know that no matter what happens, every day I'm being chosen to have a small part in the Great Production. And I get to work with, and for, the Almighty Creative Director."

The challenges will be there. They aren't torture. They are the Director's way of saying, "I believe in you. I have a lesson that I need to teach the audience, and I think you can do it like no one else in the world." When a challenge seems too big to handle, that just means the Director sees a power in you that you didn't know you had. He wants you to see it too. Distress isn't a cause for anger or despair. No. That's your moment. Do something with it that's worth watching. Something that makes the Director smile.

The best part about this game? You can never lose. Because the failures are worth just as many points as the successes. The story needs those failures. If you can't see how, just wait. In time, He'll show you how the whole production would have fallen apart without them.

What's your role now, right now? Here it is: You're in a scene in which the world has been encompassed by darkness for thousands of years. Everyone has forgotten what light even is. Everyone has a single match, but they don't know what to do with it. You strike your match on a rock, and others are amazed at what they see. They start to do the same. Soon thereafter, candles all over the globe light up the world.

The Director's instructions are the Torah and its mitzvahs. Your match is your actions. Your soul is your fire. And when you hit a rock, instead of losing faith, strike the match. It can change everything. The day is coming when only good things will happen to good people, and justice will be served to the rest. And together with Moshiach, we will create "*Our* Perfect Life." I bless you all to be heroes who don't need any challenges to become great.

Now go and play.

DISGUISED BLESSINGS

BY RACHEL HOLZKENNER

My friend Aviva came to visit Chaya Mushka and me in the hospital. Just four weeks earlier, my daughter was diagnosed with Trisomy 18, a chromosomal disorder. Only 5 percent to 10 percent of babies with this condition survive their first year.

"I just don't understand why this would happen to you," she said to me. We sat facing one another in the NICU. I held Chaya Mushka and kicked the rocking chair into motion. "You and Sholom Meir seem to be such good people. . . ."

"But what if we were chosen to host her? What if her soul selected us as her parents for its short mission on earth, then to return 'home,' unscathed and pristine?" The words slipped from my lips, still unprocessed: "What if she's our blessing?"

"But if you don't listen to Me," says G-d, "I will direct upon you panic, inflammation, fever, disease and anguish. You will sow your seed in vain, and [if it does sprout,] your enemies will eat it. . . ." (Leviticus 26:14, 16).

Harsh!

And that's not it. The Torah continues with close to another 30 verses filled with promises of retribution—they're actually difficult to read.

Surprisingly, Rabbi Schneur Zalman of Liadi makes the following comment about the Torah's harsh words: "In truth, they are nothing but blessings!"

Blessings?!

He then proceeds to explain many of the verses as blessings. For example, "Ten women will bake bread in one oven" (ibid., verse 26). In its simplest sense, this verse is referring to the extreme poverty that will afflict us if we abandon G-d's ways. But Rabbi Schneur Zalman interprets the verse as follows: We will meditate on the oneness of G-d (the oven of "one") with such intensity, that all our 10 soul-powers will be consumed with a fiery love for Him. Then our Torah study (Torah is often referred to in the Scriptures as "bread") will "bake" and marinate in this love.

Rabbi Schneur Zalman uncovers the hidden blessings hidden behind the guise of misfortune. To him, it was obvious and apparent that the curses must be taken beyond face value.

Interestingly, Rabbi Schneur Zalman wasn't the first person to see through apparently unkind wording. The Talmud (Moed Katan 9a) tells us the story of Rabbi Shimon bar Yochai, famed Mishnaic sage and author of the Zohar, who sent his son Elazar to receive blessings from two of his students, Rabbi Yonatan and Rabbi Yehudah. But instead of hearing from them blessings, he heard curses. "May it be G-d's will that you will sow and not reap!" they proclaimed, and then continued with a litany of unpleasant wishes.

An astonished Elazar repeated to his father the rabbis' curses.

"Curses?" responded Rabbi Shimon. "Those were all blessings!

"'You will sow and not reap' means that you will have children and they will not die. . . ." And Rabbi Shimon proceeded to decode all the "curses," patiently explaining to his son the blessings inherent within them.

It was certainly quite clever for Rabbi Shimon to decode the riddles and expose the blessings. But why did the sages speak in such a roundabout way? Why didn't they bless him in language that he could understand?

Rabbi Schneur Zalman's grandson, Rabbi Menachem Mendel of Lubavitch, asks just this question. He concludes that the sages' blessings were of such a lofty and sublime nature that they couldn't be expressed directly. They had to go through the medium of "bad" before they could be exposed as good.

ROCHEL HOLZKENNER

Rochel Holzkenner is a mother of four children and the codirector of Chabad of Las Olas, Florida, serving a community of young professionals. She is a high school teacher and a freelance writer, and also lectures on the topics of kabbalah and feminism, and their application to everyday life.

If G-d is good and He orchestrates our lives with purpose and meaning, then there can be only two types of experiences that He generates: a) good things that we perceive as good; b) good things that we perceive as bad.

And here's the part that seems completely counterintuitive (or maybe not): the good that's perceived as bad is in fact a more potent good.[1]

Compare your personal journal to your published autobiography. The autobiography probably makes a lot more sense to an audience of readers. But your journal is so raw and genuine, so *you*.

When G-d communicates with us from a place closer to His essence, we don't understand Him clearly. Was that a hug? 'Cause it felt like a slap in the face. . . .

In fact, the Talmud (Yoma 23a) tells us that people who are able to remain happy despite their suffering will merit to see G-d in His full glory during the messianic era. These resilient people don't let frustration and disappointment erode their belief that everything that comes from G-d is good. Since they embrace all of G-d—the part they understand, and the part they don't—they eventually experience the totality of G-d's light. They've proven that they can embrace even the most raw and intense parts of G-d.

So, how do we expose the sweet good that's entangled in a bad wrap? The Chassidic masters teach that by merely trusting that there is a potent kernel of good hidden in the pain, we begin to disassemble the screen that veils it.

"Why did this happen to me?" There are two ways to ask this same question. One is rhetorical, a proclamation: "This is wrong and shouldn't have happened to me." The second is authentic: "I wonder why this is happening to me. How can this be good for me?" And just exploring the possibility of good draws it to the surface.

To ask the second type of question, we need to train ourselves to look through the external trappings of an experience and capture its depth.

Rabbi Shimon bar Yochai was clearly a man of unparalleled depth. He authored the Zohar, the primary book of Jewish mysticism. That's why it was so natural for him to see the curse as a blessing. He didn't need to reconcile the shell of the words with their inner meaning—to him the shell was completely transparent.

Rabbi Schneur Zalman authored the *Tanya*, the primary work of Chassidic philosophy. Like Rabbi Shimon, he saw everything with profundity, plumbing the depths of any notion. That's why Rabbi Schneur Zalman read the verses of admonition and immediately entered into their innermost understanding, where all is good, and where what we perceive as bad is in truth the higher expression of G-d's kindness. Like Rabbi Shimon, he didn't have to train himself to see bad as good; to him it was as clear as the sun is bright.

Studying Chassidic teachings, the depth of the Torah's wisdom, trains our eyes with incredible depth perception, and sensitizes us to see the good even when we're disappointed.[2]

And nevertheless, let's bless each other that we all be recipients of only good—and good that we perceive as good!

Endnotes

1 In Kabbalistic language, the good that feels bad comes from the loftier first two letters of G-d's name (the Tetragrammaton), the *yud* and the *hei*, while the good that feels good comes from the second two letters of His name; the *vav* and the (second) *hei* (see *Tanya*, part 1, chapter 26).

2 Based on a talk by the Rebbe, recorded in *Likkutei Sichot*, end of vol. 1.

WHY DID G-D GIVE ME MENTAL ILLNESS?

BY RABBI ARON MOSS

Question:
Can you tell me why G-d gave me a mental illness? Why has he made me suffer? I am not a bad person.

Answer:
Every soul journeys down into this world with two suitcases. One is full of the challenges the soul has to face during its lifetime. The other is full of the talents and strengths necessary to withstand those challenges. The first suitcase is opened for you; the second you have to open yourself.

Your soul's challenge is mental illness. Your mission is to use your talents to turn the pain and frustration into a positive force.

Because of your openness and willingness to share your experiences, you can be an inspiration to others who have mental illnesses. You can bring hope and light to those who are not as strong as you, by showing them just how much they can achieve if they focus on their abilities.

You can also bring understanding and insight to those who have not themselves experienced the pain of mental illness. I for one have learnt an invaluable lesson from speaking to you.

Do you remember our conversation, when I asked you what the hardest thing was about having a mental illness? You said it was the silence; when people discover that you suffer from mental illness, they don't know what to say, and the conversation comes to an abrupt and awkward end.

So I asked you, "What would you like them to say?" Your answer amazed me.

You said, "I wish they would ask me questions about my illness. I wish they would show an interest to understand what I am going through. I wish they would give me the chance to share what I am experiencing, rather than let me suffer alone."

I'm sure not everyone is as willing to talk as you are, but I suspect that for many the stigma of mental illness hurts more than anything else. Thank you for letting me see it from your perspective. I promise to pass on the lesson.

G-d has presented your soul with a challenge, but He has also given you a bright and warm personality and a strength of character that can stand up to the challenges you face. This is a gift that I hope you will share with the world.

RABBI ARON MOSS

Rabbi and author. Rabbi Moss is a teacher of kabbalah, Talmud, and practical Judaism in Sydney, Australia. He serves as rabbi of the Nefesh Synagogue and authors a popular weekly syndicated article on modern Jewish thought.

Lesson 5

BRIDGING THE DIVIDE

G-D'S TORAH AND G-D'S SCIENCE

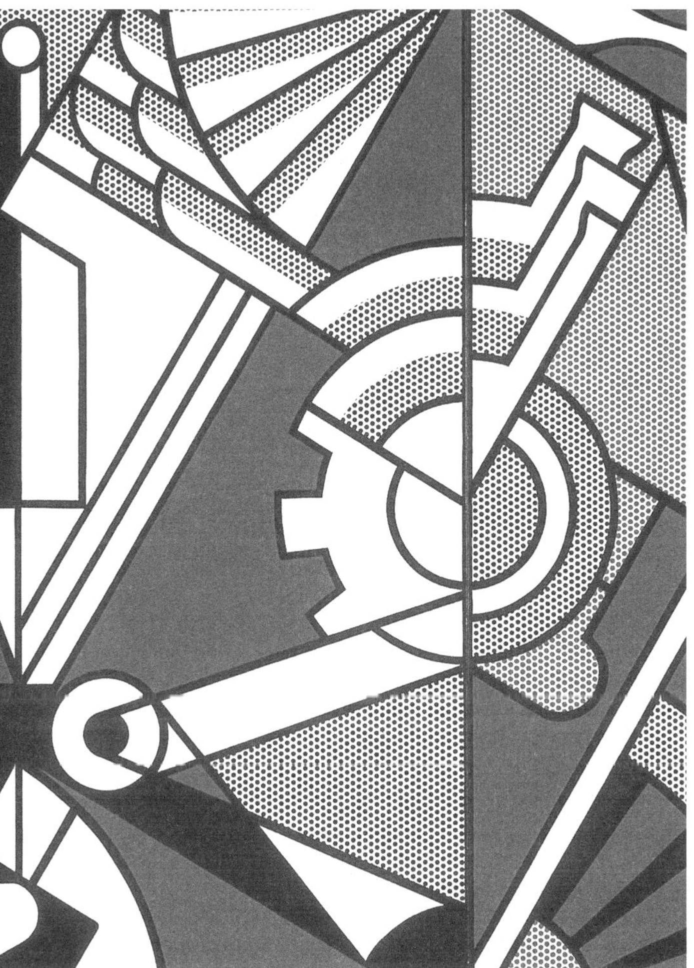

Peace Through Chemistry I (detail), Roy Lichtenstein, five-color lithograph and silkscreen, 1970. (Estate of Roy Lichtenstein)

The scientific universe is inhabited by labs, theories, research, experiments, and cause and effect. But there's a parallel universe: one inhabited by faith, the supernatural, cosmic meaning, and divine purpose. Are these two worlds—seemingly so distant from each other—relevant to each other? Can G-d and science coexist?

Exercise 1

Which of the following choices did you make after extensive research and carefully considering your various options?

1 Your choice of career

2 Your choice of spouse

3 Your choice of home

4 Your choice of school(s) for your child(ren)

5 Your choice of religion

QUESTIONS FOR DISCUSSION

1 Why do we need the Torah?

2 Why do we need science?

3 Does the Torah need science?

4 Does science need the Torah?

Albert Einstein (L.) visiting Mt. Wilson Observatory, undated. (Photo credit: Life Magazine)

Exercise 2a

List three types of injuries that are survivable and three types of injuries that are fatal.

SURVIVABLE	FATAL

Please indicate which field of science you drew on to answer this question.

Exercise 2b

Under what conditions does metal expand, and under what conditions does it contract?

Please indicate which field of science you drew on to answer this question.

Exercise 2c

If you draw a circle around a 30-inch diameter, how large will the circumference be? Use a calculator if necessary.

Please indicate which field of science you drew on to answer this question.

Figure 5.1

Convergence of Torah and Science

SCIENCE	TORAH RELEVANCE
Medicine	The mitzvah to heal the ill When we may violate the laws of Shabbat for a sick person
Zoology, botany, and biology	The species of plants and animals that are subject to the prohibition of crossbreeding
Algebra, geometry, and math	Measuring distances for Shabbat and other halachic purposes
Astronomy	Formulating the Jewish calendar
Linguistics (including syntax and grammar)	Interpreting the Torah and Talmud
Music	Punctuation of the Torah text
Chemistry	Determining ingredients of kosher food

TEXT 1

MAIMONIDES, *MISHNEH TORAH*, LAWS OF THE FOUNDATIONS OF THE TORAH 2:2

בְּשָׁעָה שֶׁיִּתְבּוֹנֵן הָאָדָם בְּמַעֲשָׂיו וּבְרוּאָיו הַנִּפְלָאִים הַגְּדוֹלִים, וְיִרְאֶה מֵהֶם חָכְמָתוֹ שֶׁאֵין לָהּ עֵרֶךְ וְלֹא קֵץ - מִיָּד הוּא אוֹהֵב וּמְשַׁבֵּחַ וּמְפָאֵר וּמִתְאַוֶּה תַּאֲוָה גְדוֹלָה לֵידַע הַשֵּׁם הַגָּדוֹל, כְּמוֹ שֶׁאָמַר דָּוִד "צָמְאָה נַפְשִׁי לֵאלֹקִים לְאֵ-ל חָי" (תהילים מב, ג).

וּכְשֶׁמְּחַשֵּׁב בַּדְּבָרִים הָאֵלּוּ עַצְמָן, מִיָּד הוּא נִרְתָּע לַאֲחוֹרָיו, וְיִירָא וְיִפְחַד וְיֵדַע שֶׁהוּא בְּרִיָּה קְטַנָּה שְׁפָלָה אֲפֵלָה, עוֹמֵד בְּדַעַת קַלָּה מְעוּטָה לִפְנֵי תְּמִים דֵּעוֹת, כְּמוֹ שֶׁאָמַר דָּוִד "כִּי אֶרְאֶה שָׁמֶיךָ... מָה אֱנוֹשׁ כִּי תִזְכְּרֶנּוּ" (תהילים ח, ד-ה).

One who contemplates God's wondrous great deeds and creations and appreciates His infinite wisdom, that surpasses all comparison, will immediately love, praise, and glorify God, yearning with tremendous desire to know God's great name, as David stated: "My soul thirsts for God, for the living God" (PSALMS 42:3).

Those who continue to reflect on these very matters will immediately recoil in awe and reverence, appreciating that they are small, humble, and obtuse creatures with flimsy limited wisdom compared to God, Who is of perfect knowledge, as David stated: "When I see Your heavens, the work of Your fingers . . . I wonder, *What is man that You should consider Him?*" (PSALMS 8:4–5).

RABBI MOSHE BEN MAIMON (MAIMONIDES, RAMBAM) 1135–1204

Halachist, philosopher, author, and physician. Maimonides was born in Córdoba, Spain. After the conquest of Córdoba by the Almohads, he fled Spain and eventually settled in Cairo, Egypt. There, he became the leader of the Jewish community and served as court physician to the vizier of Egypt. He is most noted for authoring the *Mishneh Torah*, an encyclopedic arrangement of Jewish law, and for his philosophical work, *Guide for the Perplexed*. His rulings on Jewish law are integral to the formation of halachic consensus.

TEXT 2

RABBI JONATHAN SACKS, *THE GREAT PARTNERSHIP: SCIENCE, RELIGION, AND THE SEARCH FOR MEANING* (NEW YORK: SCHOCKEN BOOKS, 2012), PP. 29–30

Take a game like football. Some hypothetical visitor from a land to which football has not yet penetrated wants to understand this strange ritual which excites so much passion. You explain the rules of the game, what counts as a foul, what constitutes a goal, and so on. “Fine,” says the visitor, “I now understand the game. What I don’t understand is why you get so excited about it.” Here you might have to launch into some larger reflection about games as ritualised conflict, and the role of play in rehearsing skills needed in actual conflict. You might even suggest that ritualised conflict reduces the need for actual conflict: the football pitch as a substitute for the battlefield.

There is an internal logic of the system—the rules of football—but the meaning of the system lies elsewhere, and it can only be understood through some sense of the wider human context in which it is set. To do this you have to step outside the system and see why it was brought into being. There is no way of understanding the meaning of football by merely knowing its rules. They tell you how to play the game, but not why people do so and why they invest in it the passions they do. The

RABBI LORD JONATHAN SACKS, PHD
1948–

Former chief rabbi of the United Kingdom. Rabbi Sacks attended Cambridge University and received his doctorate from King’s College, London. A prolific and influential author, his books include *Will We Have Jewish Grandchildren?* and *The Dignity of Difference*. He received the Jerusalem Prize in 1995 for his contributions to enhancing Jewish life in the Diaspora, was knighted and made a life peer in 2005, and became Baron Sacks of Aldridge in 2009.

internal workings of a system do not explain the place the system holds in human lives.

The meaning of the system lies outside the system. Therefore, the meaning of the universe lies outside the universe. That was the revolution of Abrahamic monotheism.

The same is true for science, whose subject is the interrelationship of things within the natural world. . . . Nature is sublimely indifferent to who we are and what we deserve. There is nothing moral about it; it carries no meaning within it. Science tell[s] us how the parts are related. But [it] cannot tell us what the totality means.

Only something or someone outside the universe can give meaning to the universe. Only belief in a transcendental G-d can render human existence other than tragic. Individual lives, even within a tragically configured universe, may have meaning, but life as a whole does not.

TEXT 3

LUDWIG WITTGENSTEIN, *TRACTATUS LOGICO-PHILOSOPHICUS* (NEW YORK: HARCOURT, BRACE, AND CO., 1922) 6.41 (P. 183)

The sense of the world must lie outside the world. In the world, everything is as it is, and happens as it does happen. In it there is no value—and if there were, it would be of no value. If there is a value which is of value, it must lie outside all happening and being-so. For all happening and being-so is accidental.

What makes it non-accidental cannot lie in the world, for otherwise this would again be accidental. It must lie outside the world.

LUDWIG JOSEF JOHANN WITTGENSTEIN 1889–1951

Philosopher. Wittgenstein was born in Vienna, Austria. He is known for his philosophical work *Tractatus Logico-Philosophicus* (Latin for Logical-Philosophical Treatise). He was professor of philosophy at the University of Cambridge from 1939 until 1947.

Quotable Quotes

Torah Gives Us the Why

To know an answer to the question, "What is the meaning of human life?" means to be religious.

ALBERT EINSTEIN, *THE WORLD AS I SEE IT*.
(NEW YORK, N.Y.: PHILOSOPHICAL LIBRARY, 1949)

The idea of life having a purpose stands and falls with the religious system.

SIGMUND FREUD, *CIVILIZATION AND ITS DISCONTENTS, STANDARD EDITION*. (LONDON, U.K.: HOGARTH PRESS, 1930/1962)

To believe in God means to understand the question about the meaning of life.
To believe in God means to see that the facts of the world are not the end of the matter.
To believe in God means to see that life has a meaning.

LUDWIG WITTGENSTEIN, *NOTEBOOKS 1914-1916*, EDITED BY G. H. VON WRIGHT AND G. E. M. ANSCOMBE (TRANSLATED BY ANSCOMBE) (NEW YORK, N.Y.: HARPER AND ROW, 1961)

When we have found all the mysteries and lost all the meaning, we will be alone, on an empty shore.

TOM STOPPARD, *ARCADIA*, ACT 2, SCENE 7

TEXT 4

ETHAN SIEGEL, "SCIENTIFIC PROOF IS A MYTH," *FORBES*, NOVEMBER 22, 2017

You've heard of our greatest scientific theories: the theory of evolution, the Big Bang theory, the theory of gravity. You've also heard of the concept of a proof, and the claims that certain pieces of evidence prove the validities of these theories. . . . Except that's a complete lie. While they provide very strong evidence for those theories, they aren't proof. In fact, when it comes to science, proving anything is an impossibility.

Reality is a complicated place. All we have to guide us, from an empirical point of view, are the quantities we can measure and observe. Even at that, those quantities are only as good as the tools and equipment we use to make those observations and measurements. . . . No matter how good our measurements and observations are, there's a limit to how good they are.

We also can't observe or measure everything. . . . At some point, we have to extrapolate. This is incredibly powerful and incredibly useful, but it's also incredibly limiting. . . . You never know when your assumptions will suddenly become invalid. You never know whether the rules you successfully applied for situations A, B, and C will successfully apply for situation D. It's a leap of faith to assume that it will. . . . And that's why everything we

ETHAN SIEGEL, PHD
1978–

Astrophysicist. Siegel was a professor of physics and astronomy at Lewis and Clark College and is a science blogger. He has written for *Forbes*, *Scientific American*, *NASA Space Place*, and many other print and online publications.

do in science, no matter how well it gets tested, is always preliminary. . . .

Every scientific theory will someday fail, and when it does, that will herald a new era of scientific inquiry and discovery.

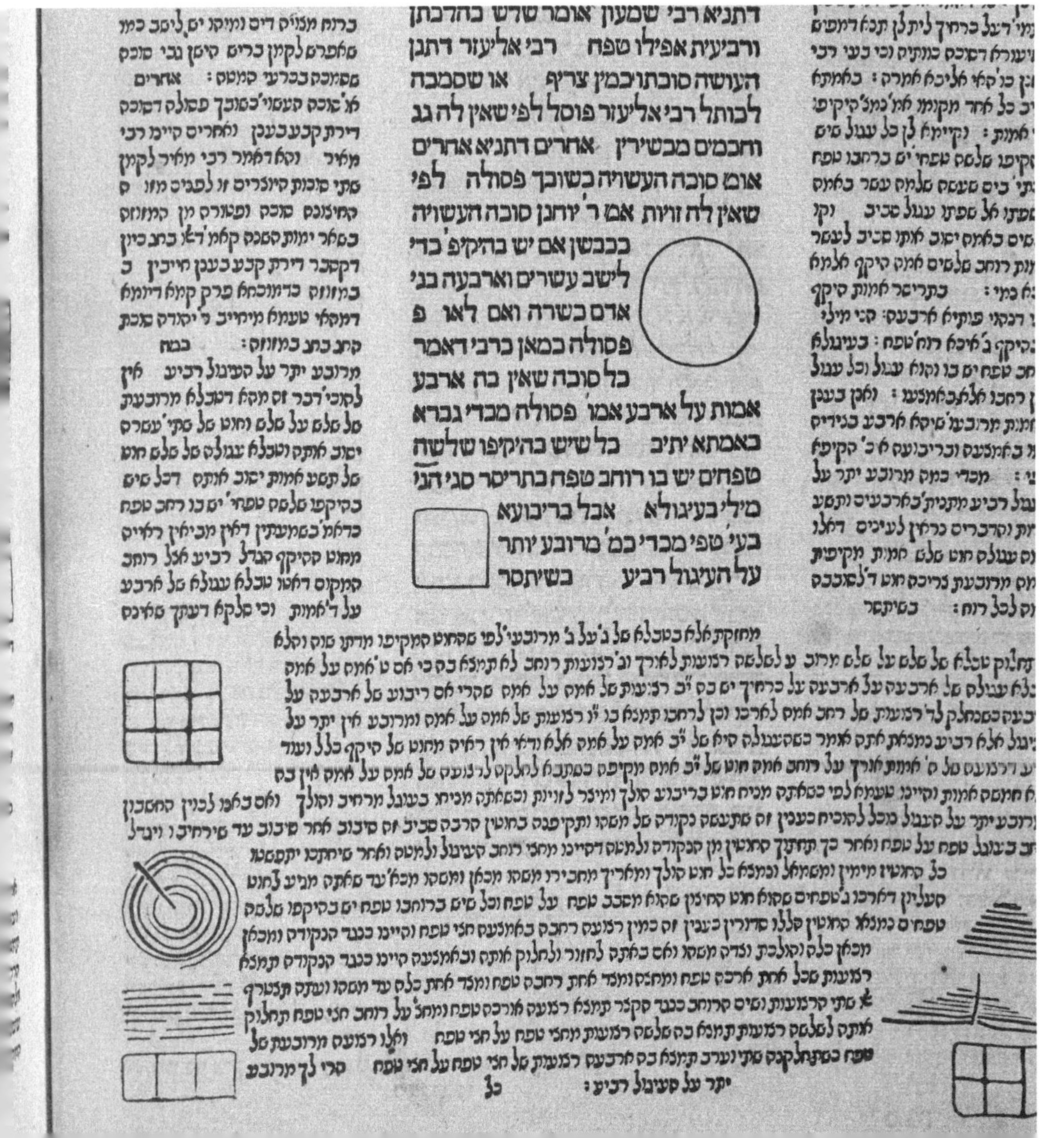

From Tractate Sukkah, Soncino Talmud. Pesaro, c. 1515.

TEXT 5

ALBERT EINSTEIN, CITED IN HELEN DUKAS AND BANESH HOFFMANN, *ALBERT EINSTEIN: THE HUMAN SIDE* (PRINCETON, N.J.: PRINCETON UNIVERSITY PRESS, 1979), P. 18

The scientific theorist is not to be envied. For Nature, or more precisely experiment, is an inexorable and not very friendly judge of his work. It never says "Yes" to a theory. In the most favorable cases it says "Maybe," and in the great majority of cases simply "No." If an experiment agrees with a theory it means for the latter "Maybe," and if it does not agree it means "No." Probably every theory will someday experience its "No"—most theories, soon after conception.

ALBERT EINSTEIN
1879–1955

Mathematician, physicist. A Jewish scientist originally from Germany, Einstein is generally considered the most influential physicist of the 20th century. His work had a major impact on the development of atomic energy. He developed the special and general theories of relativity, and in 1921, he won the Nobel Prize in physics for his explanation of the photoelectric effect. He escaped the Nazis, immigrating to the U.S. in 1933.

TEXT 6

DR. YAAKOV BRAWER, "SOMETHING FROM NOTHING,"
B'OR HATORAH: 8 (1993), PP. 133–139

"Something from something" is the assumption of cause and effect. Everything has an antecedent cause to which it can be directly related. The antecedent to a chicken is an egg. The antecedent to a house is lumber. . . . Every thing and every event is the product of a progressive developmental sequence of causes. Everything comes from an identifiable something; hence the process of "something from something." . . .

The concept that everything comes from something seems obvious, logical, and pragmatic. . . . Everything has a history of which it is the product. On this basis, one can interpret the past and predict, and hence respond to, events in the future. Thus, the process of "something from something" serves as the rationale for diagnosing and treating disease, playing the stock market, or negotiating a treaty with a foreign government. . . .

Since the universe consists of a vast number of entities with measurable physical properties organized in a unique way, its ultimate source must likewise, in some way, be bound by physical characteristics and dimensions. . . . For example, animals, including humans, are made out of chemicals. It follows, then, that the origin(s) of all animal species must be simpler, less processed

DR. YAAKOV BRAWER

Scientist and professor. Dr. Yaakov Brawer is professor emeritus on the Faculty of Medicine at McGill University in Montreal. He lectures on neuroendocrinology and Chasidism. He has authored two books on Chasidic philosophy, *Something from Nothing* and *Eyes that See.*

collections of chemicals, which developed in a stepwise, sequential fashion into what they are at the moment. . . . No matter how far you extrapolate back on the chain of cause and effect, there is a prior cause which shares the same fundamental limitations as its progeny (i.e., it is defined by physical properties).

Illustration from *Our Friend the Atom*, written by Heinz Haber and illustrated by Walt Disney Studios, 1957.

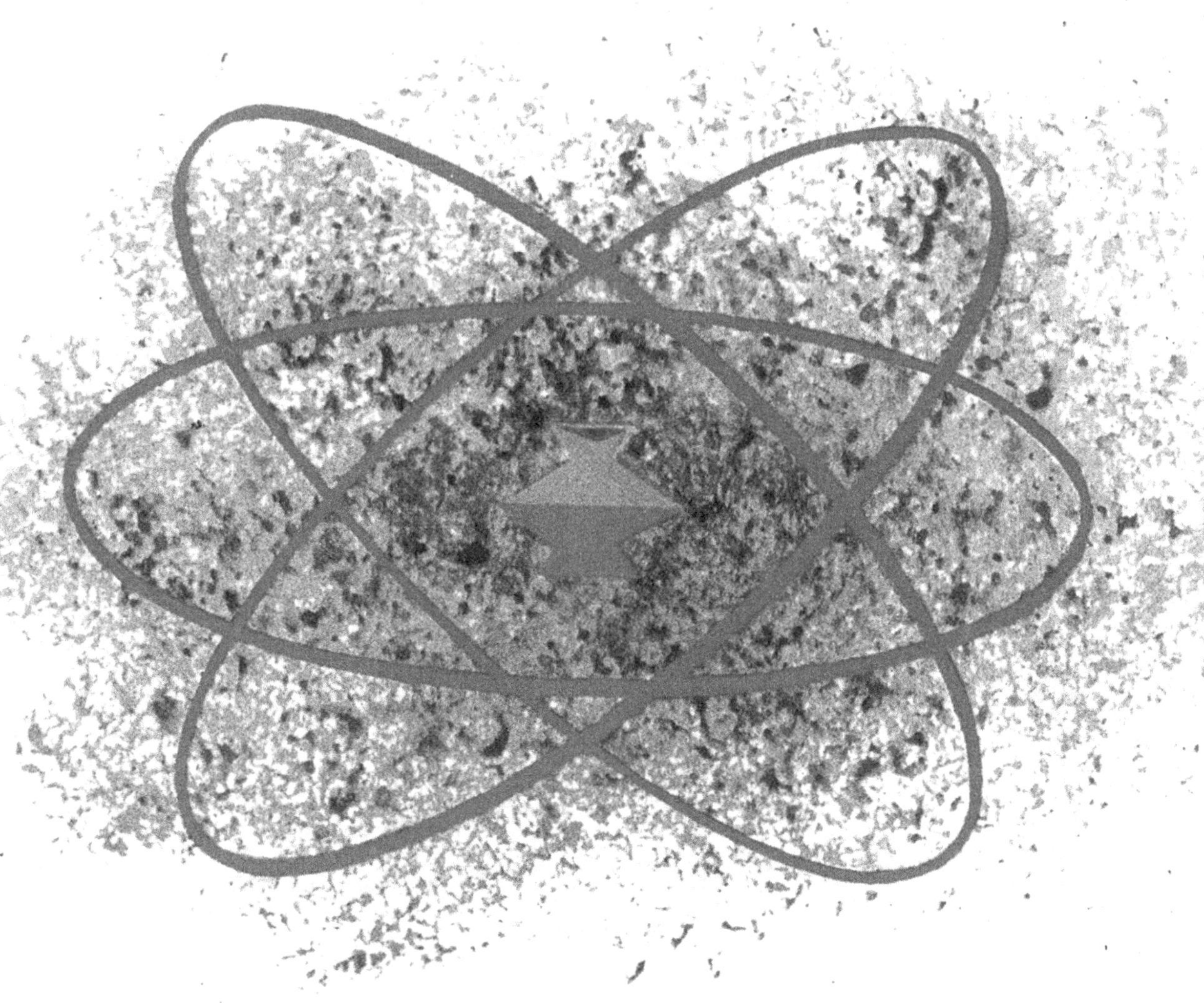

TEXT 7

NACHMANIDES, GENESIS 1:1

הַקָּדוֹשׁ בָּרוּךְ הוּא בָּרָא כָּל הַנִּבְרָאִים מֵאֲפִיסָה מוּחְלֶטֶת.

God created everything from absolute nothingness.

RABBI MOSHE BEN NACHMAN (NACHMANIDES, RAMBAN) 1194–1270

Scholar, philosopher, author, and physician. Nachmanides was born in Spain and served as leader of Iberian Jewry. In 1263, he was summoned by King James of Aragon to a public disputation with Pablo Cristiani, a Jewish apostate. Though Nachmanides was the clear victor of the debate, he had to flee Spain because of the resulting persecution. He moved to Israel and helped reestablish communal life in Jerusalem. He authored a classic commentary on the Pentateuch and a commentary on the Talmud.

Creation of the World: Fifth and Sixth Days, Marc Chagall, stained glass windows, c. 1970. (Museum of Nice, France)

TEXT 8

THE REBBE, RABBI MENACHEM MENDEL SCHNEERSON, *LIKUTEI SICHOT* 15:47

וִויבַּאלְד דִי אֱמֶתֶ'ע מְצִיאוּת פוּן וֶועלְט אִיז דִי אַחְדוּת הַפְּשׁוּטָה פוּן אֱלֹקוּת, דֶערְפַאר דְרִיקְט זִיךְ אוֹיס אָט דִי אַחְדוּת אוֹיךְ אִין דֶער מְצִיאוּת פוּן וֶועלְט גוּפָא, אַז אִין וֶועלְט גוּפָא אִיז דָא דֶער עִנְיָן הָאַחְדוּת.

אוּן דֶער עִנְיָן, דִי אַחְדוּת וָואס אִיז פַארַאן אִין וֶועלְט, וָואס בִּפְנִימִיוּתָה אִיז עֶס דִי אַחְדוּת הַפְּשׁוּטָה פוּן אֱלֹקוּת, וֶוערְט מֶער אוּן מֶער נִתְגַלֶה מִיט דֶער הִתְפַּתְּחוּת פוּן חָכְמוֹת הָעוֹלָם.

אַמָאל הָאט מֶען גֶעמֵיינְט אַז יֶעדֶערֶער פוּן דִי טֶבַע-כּוֹחוֹת אִיז אַ כֹּחַ נִפְרָד בִּפְנֵי עַצְמוֹ, אוּן אַז דֶער חוֹמֶר פוּן יֶעדֶער מְצִיאוּת אִין וֶועלְט אִיז צוּנוֹיפ-גֶעשְׁטֶעלְט פוּן **מֶערֶערֶע פַארְשִׁידֶענֶע** יְסוֹדוֹת (עֶלֶעמֶענְטְן). אָבֶּער וָואס מֶער עֶס שְׁטַייגְט דִי אַנְטְוִויקְלוּנְג פוּן דִי חָכְמוֹת הָעוֹלָם, אַלְץ מֶער קוּמְט מֶען צוּ דֶער הַכָּרָה אַז אָט דֶער רִיבּוּי אוּן פִירוּד אִין בַּאשְׁטַאנְד פוּן דִי יְסוֹדוֹת, אִיז נָאר אַן עִנְיָן חִיצוֹנִי, דֶער אוֹפֶן הַצִירוּף פוּן חֲלָקִים, צִמְצוּם וְהִתְפַּשְּׁטוּת שֶׁלָהֶם וְכוּ'. אוּן מְ'אִיז אַלְץ מֶער מְמַעֵט זֵייעֶר סְכוּם בִּיז צוּ אַנֶערְקֶענֶען אַז דִי נְקוּדַת הַמְצִיאוּת פוּן וֶועלְט בַּאשְׁטֵייט פוּן דֶער פַארְאֵיינִיקוּנְג פוּן דִי צְוֵויי עִנְיָנִים כַּמוּת אוּן אֵיכוּת, חוֹמֶר נוֹשֵׂא הַכֹּחַ אוּן דֶער כֹּחַ.

Because everything that exists is in truth part of God's absolute oneness, one can discern a theme of unity in the universe itself.

The unity in the universe, which is a reflection of God, is becoming more and more pronounced as our scientific understanding of the world progresses.

It was once thought that every force of nature is an isolated force and that the matter of all things is comprised of many diverse elements. However, the more scientists

RABBI MENACHEM MENDEL SCHNEERSON 1902–1994

The towering Jewish leader of the 20th century, known as "the Lubavitcher Rebbe," or simply as "the Rebbe." Born in southern Ukraine, the Rebbe escaped Nazi-occupied Europe, arriving in the U.S. in June 1941. The Rebbe inspired and guided the revival of traditional Judaism after the European devastation, impacting virtually every Jewish community the world over. The Rebbe often emphasized that the performance of just one additional good deed could usher in the era of Mashiach. The Rebbe's scholarly talks and writings have been printed in more than 200 volumes.

study the universe, the more they realize that the seeming multitude and diversity of forces and elements are superficial, related to their synthesis of parts, their contraction and expansion, etc. With time, the basic elements were further reduced, until it was realized that the universe is essentially a union of two components, quality and quantity, or matter and energy.

Abstract image of the internal components of the Large Hadron Collider. *Super Collider v.13*, Timothy Tompkins, enamel on aluminum, 2014. (Embassy of the United States, Bern, Switzerland)

1 Science helps us formulate many points of Jewish law, including the Jewish calendar. It also allows us to better appreciate the greatness of the Creator.

2 The Torah lends meaning, direction, and purpose to an otherwise random and meaningless universe.

3 Science operates using a "something from something" model in which every effect has a cause. The Torah operates on a "something from nothing" model.

4 When you create something from nothing, you begin at the point that is relevant to you. God thus started Creation with a universe that is capable of hosting human life.

5 Because science is the study of God's Creation, it helps us understand the Torah's teachings about God that in the past had to be taken on faith.

Appendix

TEXT 9

TALMUD, SHABBAT 75A

אָמַר רַב זוּטְרָא בַּר טוּבְיָה אָמַר רַב . . . וְהַיּוֹדֵעַ לְחַשֵּׁב תְּקוּפוֹת וּמַזָּלוֹת וְאֵינוֹ חוֹשֵׁב, אָסוּר לְסַפֵּר הֵימֶנּוּ . . .

אָמַר רַב יְהוֹשֻׁעַ בֶּן לֵוִי מִשּׁוּם בַּר קַפָּרָא, כָּל הַיּוֹדֵעַ לְחַשֵּׁב בִּתְקוּפוֹת וּמַזָּלוֹת וְאֵינוֹ חוֹשֵׁב, עָלָיו הַכָּתוּב אוֹמֵר, "וְאֵת פֹּעַל ה' לֹא יַבִּיטוּ וּמַעֲשֵׂה יָדָיו לֹא רָאוּ" (יְשַׁעְיָהוּ ה, יב).

אָמַר רַב שְׁמוּאֵל בַּר נַחֲמֵנִי אָמַר רַב יוֹחָנָן, מִנַּיִן שֶׁמִּצְוָה עַל הָאָדָם לְחַשֵּׁב תְּקוּפוֹת וּמַזָּלוֹת, שֶׁנֶּאֱמַר, "וּשְׁמַרְתֶּם וַעֲשִׂיתֶם כִּי הִוא חָכְמַתְכֶם וּבִינַתְכֶם לְעֵינֵי הָעַמִּים (דְּבָרִים ד, ו)." אֵיזוֹ חָכְמָה וּבִינָה שֶׁהִיא לְעֵינֵי הָעַמִּים? הֱוֵי אוֹמֵר זֶה חִישּׁוּב תְּקוּפוֹת וּמַזָּלוֹת".

Rabbi Zutra the son of Tuvyah said in the name of Rav, . . . "One may not hold conversation with one who knows how to calculate the cycles and planetary courses and refuses to do so." . . .

Rabbi Yehoshua the son of Levi said in the name of Bar Kapara, "Those who know how to calculate the cycles and planetary courses, but fail to do so, of them the Torah proclaims, 'The work of God they do not regard and the deed of His hands they do not see'" (ISAIAH 5:12).

Rabbi Shmuel the son of Nachmeni said in the name of Rabbi Yochanan, "How do we know that it is a mitzvah to calculate the cycles and the planetary courses? For it is written, 'You shall keep them and do them, for that

BABYLONIAN TALMUD

A literary work of monumental proportions that draws upon the legal, spiritual, intellectual, ethical, and historical traditions of Judaism. The 37 tractates of the Babylonian Talmud contain the teachings of the Jewish sages from the period after the destruction of the Second Temple through the fifth century CE. It has served as the primary vehicle for the transmission of the Oral Law and the education of Jews over the centuries; it is the entry point for all subsequent legal, ethical, and theological Jewish scholarship.

is your wisdom and your understanding in the eyes of the people' (DEUTERONOMY 4:6). Which wisdom and understanding are visible to all people? The sciences of the cycles and the planetary courses."

Additional Readings

HOW SCIENTIFIC IS TORAH?

BY RABBI TZVI FREEMAN

Question:
So we hear all the time about how Torah and science don't really contradict. But can you give me at least one or two examples where they actually coincide?

Answer:

- The most outstanding example: For millennia, we were ridiculed for believing the world began. Only in the latter half of the 20th century did the evidence come out overwhelmingly on our side. As Dr. Arno Penzias (one of the three who received a Nobel Prize for identifying the "background radiation" that became one of the pillars of the current Big Bang cosmology) writes, "Creation is supported by all the data so far."[1]
- Abraham was a maverick for believing that all the forces of the cosmos are really a single force. This is the contention of science for the past 100 years and the driving force behind the search for the Unified Field Theory.[2]
- The Torah's account of Creation and of events that defy the laws of physics—and even defy logic—implies that the laws of logic are not absolute—i.e., it is not impossible for those laws to have been created otherwise, and even now, the Creator could adjust them or supersede them at whim. An inkling of this kind of thinking opened the way for modern mathematics, breaking away from the Euclidian view that the axioms of geometry are absolute "self-evident truths," and laying the ground for Einstein's relativity. Indeed, later attempts to demonstrate that mathematics is based on logic have all failed. Thinkers today question the absoluteness of logic itself.[3]
- Torah, by presenting the concept of Divine Providence within nature, requires a universe that is only loosely linear, rejecting the determinist concept that cause and effect are inherently linked. This is an outcome of the Principle of Uncertainty, first enunciated by Heisenberg in 1928.[4] Over the past 30 years, experimentation has repeatedly affirmed this concept.
- Torah does not talk in terms of matter as a self-contained substance, but as an event, a 'word.' Today we understand matter as simply a dynamic of concentrated energy, as in the familiar formula $E=mc^2$. Or, in physicist David Bohm's definition, "That which unfolds, whatever the medium."[5]
- Torah relies on witnesses and observation over intuition. Today we call this objective empiricism. It is what distinguishes the scientist from the Hellenist or medieval philosopher.
- Torah recognizes the role of human consciousness as an active, rather than passive, participant in forming reality.[6] This outcome of the standard model of quantum mechanics was first enunciated by John von Neumann in 1932.[7]
- Torah consistently relies on the concept of synergy: The whole is greater than the sum of its parts. This has become an essential principle in many modern disciplines, from sociology to chemistry.
- Torah, in many halachic applications, relies on "quantum"—smallest possible increments of change within space and time. This was the

RABBI TZVI FREEMAN (1955–)

Rabbi, computer scientist, and writer. A published expert, consultant, and lecturer in the field of educational technology, Rabbi Freeman held posts at the University of British Columbia and the Digipen School of Computer Gaming. Rabbi Freeman is the author of *Bringing Heaven Down to Earth* and *Men, Women and Kabbalah*. He is a senior editor at Chabad.org.

postulate of Max Planck that opened the field of quantum mechanics.

- The Torah describes all of humankind as descending from a single man and—earlier—a single woman.[8] The overwhelming genetic evidence concurs, although the dating is still somewhat skewed. They're still catching up.
- Torah understands the human psyche as being multilayered and multifaceted—there isn't just one person inside. Welcome to modern psychology.
- Torah describes planet earth and the entire cosmos in holistic terms. Science today is moving sharply in this direction, in life sciences and in physics and cosmology.
- Torah provides inference to many of the customs, beliefs, politics, technologies, etc. of ancient times at which historians once balked and archeologists have only recently confirmed.
- Torah presents and rigorously develops the *chazakah*: An event must occur repeatedly under identical conditions to be considered the most likely outcome in the future (such as the case of the consistently goring ox). This is the basis of the scientific method.[9]
- Torah prescribes public education, popular involvement and constitutional governance. Sociologists describe how these elements generate stability and productivity in a society.
- Torah prescribes a responsible stewardship of our environment. Today we have demonstrated that such an approach is the only one possible for sustainable life on the planet.

Many of these examples may seem obvious and trite. However none of them were accepted as such until recently. I'm sure there are more—if you think of some, please fire them over.

Acknowledgement is due to Dr. Moshe Genuth for his valuable suggestions and assistance with this article.

Endnotes

1 See his "Creation is Supported by All the Data So Far," page 78 in Margenau and Varghese, *Cosmos, Bios, Theos*, Open Court, 1992.

2 As the Lubavitcher Rebbe once put it to a group of scientists, "So let's just say we already know there is a Unified Field Theory and we'll call it G-d."

3 See Tzvi Saks, "On the Nature of Truth in Mathematics," in *B'Or HaTorah*, vol. 9, pp. 95–103. In the inimitable style of George Burns (playing G-d), "Mathematics! Another one of my mistakes!"

4 For an intelligent exposition of this concept for the rest of us, see John Gribbin, *In Search of Schrodinger's Cat,* Bantam, 1979. Gribbin dismisses the common misconception that Heisenberg, et al. are talking about our inability to measure precisely. Rather, this is an inherent characteristic of the universe, that there are no perfectly knowable ("discrete") states. As Heisenberg himself put it to the philosophers of his time: Without discrete causes, there are no predetermined effects—and determinism is out the window.

5 In *Wholeness and the Implicate Order,* Routledge & Kegan Paul, 1980

6 See Tzvi Freeman, *Knowledge and Reality*, Chabad.org., 2001

7 In *Mathematical Foundations of Quantum Mechanics.* Eugene Wigner later became the major proponent of this idea, the only coherent competition being the "Multiple Worlds Model." That's not so original, either.

8 Men (Y chromosome) from Noah. Women (mitochondrial DNA) from Eve. The women on the ark were from various families, while the men were from a single father and mother.

9 See responsum of Rabenu Asher ("the Rosh" 1250–1328) 68:23 for a very modern exposition of this concept.

LET'S TALK:
HOW CAN YOU REALLY BELIEVE IN SIX DAYS OF CREATION?

RABBI JOSHUA A. KRISCH

It has been a core belief of the Jewish people for more than three millennia that the world was created in six days, and that the universe is coming up on its 6,000th birthday. So, when my students ask me about the age of the earth, I tell them it's about 6,000 years old. I don't fudge the text or rely on non-literal readings of Genesis, which constitute either minority opinions or outright rejections of our faith.

Trust me, I know how it sounds. I know that many scientists and college students think me an ignorant, Darwin-burning creationist. Even my most respectful students want to know why I am so "anti-science."

So, I ask them if they believe that G-d split the sea.

Many Jews, whether observant or not, believe that G-d split the Sea of Reeds so that the Israelites could escape the Egyptians. And even those who don't believe in the Exodus are not terribly bothered by the fact that I do. Jews believe all kinds of irrational things. Ten Plagues. Talking bushes.

Of course, the entire story is scientifically impossible and, dare I say, "anti-science." Everything we know about chemistry and physics tells us that a sea cannot split opportunistically, allowing one nation to pass through and then closing on its tormentors. In fact, the miracles recorded in the Torah violate scientific norms by their very definitions. Manna falling from heaven. The voice of G-d at Mount Sinai. An angel convincing Abraham not to sacrifice his son. How do we reconcile these miracles with modern science?

The answer is that science defines the world in its steady state, by measuring the laws of nature. The Torah describes cases in which those laws have been broken. I can believe that G-d broke the laws of nature to split the sea without believing that everything we know about hydrogen bonding is hokum. And I can believe that G-d broke the law of nature to create the world in six days, without rejecting geoscience.

Because when science calculates the age of the universe, what they are really calculating (absent a G-d or some other immeasurable factor) is how long it would have taken for this world to come into being spontaneously. Science has solved this. It would have taken 4.5 billion years, give or take. Scientific studies will reflect this because it is true—our universe is indeed the work of 4.5 billion years. But that is simply not how G-d did it. The Torah tells us that G-d (the same Omnipotent being who suspended the laws of physics to split the sea) suspended the natural order to perform a 4.5-billion-year job in six days.

This approach may share passing similarities with creationism, but it is more authentic. For one, it doesn't force us to conclude that G-d created the universe in six non-literal "days"—a problematic approach, especially since the Torah (Genesis 31:15) commands us to celebrate Shabbat once per week as an eternal sign that in "six days, G-d created the heavens and the earth." And an approach made even more problematic by the fact that even if we allow the word "day" to mean millions or billions of years, it would have to represent vastly different quantities of time across adjacent verses. On day four G-d created the sun, on day five He created fish, and on day six He created animals. Scientifically speaking, that means that day four lasted four billion years, day five, 100 million years, and day six, 400 million years. The term

RABBI JOSHUA A. KRISCH

Rabbi Joshua A. Krisch and his wife Andi are Chabad emissaries at Ithaca College in upstate New York. Rabbi Krisch studied biology and conducted cancer research at Yeshiva University, completed graduate work in health sciences at Cornell University, and holds a master's degree in science journalism from New York University. Krisch's work has been published in *The New York Times, Scientific American, VICE Media, The Atlantic,* and other major publications. He is currently the staff science editor at *Fatherly*.

"day" would be rendered meaningless even as a non-literal placeholder.

This approach allows us to celebrate modern science without compromising our beliefs. It's worth studying how the world could have spontaneously come into existence, because the underlying numbers help us identify rising sea levels, speculate about life on Mars, or date ancient potsherds. Studying how the earth that G-d created in six days would have happened absent an active G-d is still a worthy enterprise. Belief in miracles doesn't render science irrelevant.

We can support chemistry without supporting its contention that seas don't split opportunistically. We can support geoscience without supporting its contention that the world was not created by G-d in six days. Because for the thinking Jew, science is what the world does when G-d isn't doing miracles, and how the world would have developed had G-d not created it miraculously fast.

Let's be clear. This argument will not convince my students that the universe is 6,000 years old. For one, it raises as many questions as it answers. What about dinosaurs? How could vegetation exist before sunlight, as claimed in Genesis? Why does radiometric dating suggest that different layers of rock are vastly different ages, when all rock was presumably created on the same day? But that is okay. Belief in the truth of the Torah is a complex philosophical adventure that requires faith and intense study.

Besides, my goal is not for my students to agree with me. The point is to demonstrate that belief in a literal Genesis, an inescapable Torah value, is not remotely "anti-science." When your rabbi tells you that he believes the world is 6,000 years old, he's not saying that he rejects contemporary research. He's saying that he believes in a G-d who is capable of upending nature with miracles, and who did just that to create the world. His position is no more controversial or "anti-science" than belief in G-d Himself.

Fortunately, my students know that I respect science, and suspect that I believe in G-d too.

Joshua A. Krisch, "Let's Talk: How Can You Really Believe in Six Days of Creation?" *Lubavitch International*, Vol. 7, Issue 1, February–March, 2018, p. 22.

CORRESPONDENCE OF THE LUBAVITCHER REBBE
EVOLUTION AND THE AGE OF THE UNIVERSE

BY THE LUBAVITCHER REBBE, RABBI MENACHEM MENDEL SCHNEERSON

By the Grace of G-d
18th of Teveth, 5722 [December 25, 1961]
Brooklyn, NY

Greeting and Blessing:

After not having heard from you for a long time, I was pleased to receive regards from you through the young men of Chabad who visited your community recently in connection with the public lecture. I was gratified to hear that you participated in the discussion, but it was quite a surprise to me to learn that you are still troubled by the problem of the age of the world as suggested by various scientific theories that cannot be reconciled with the Torah view that the world is 5722 years old. I underlined the word *theories*, for it is necessary to bear in mind, first of all, that science formulates and deals with theories and hypotheses while the Torah deals with absolute truths. These are two different disciplines, where reconciliation is entirely out of place.

It was especially surprising to me that, according to the report, the said problem is bothering you to the extent that it has trespassed upon your daily life as a Jew, interfering with the actual fulfillment of the daily *mitzvoth*. I sincerely hope that the impression conveyed to me is an erroneous one. For, as you know, the basic Jewish principle of *na'aseh* (first) and *v'nishmah* (afterwards) makes it mandatory upon the Jew to fulfill G-d's commandments regardless of the degree of understanding, and obedience to the Divine Law can never be conditioned upon human approval. In other words, lack of understanding, and even the existence of "legitimate" doubts, can never justify disobedience to the Divine Commandments; how much less, when the doubts are illegitimate, in the sense that they have no real or logical basis, such as the problem in question.

Apparently, our discussion which took place a long time ago, and which, as I was pleased to learn, has not been forgotten by you, has nevertheless not cleared up this matter in your mind. I will attempt to do so now, in writing, which imposes both brevity and other limitations. I trust, however, that the following remarks will serve our purpose.

Basically the problem has its roots in a misconception of the scientific method or, simply, of what science is. We must distinguish between empirical or experimental science dealing with, and confined to, describing and classifying observable phenomena; and speculative science, dealing with unknown phenomena, sometimes phenomena that cannot be duplicated in the laboratory. Scientific speculation is actually a terminological incongruity; for science, strictly speaking, means knowledge, while no speculation can be called knowledge in the strict sense of the word. At best, science can only speak in terms of theories inferred from certain known facts and applied in the realm of the unknown. Here, science has two general methods of inference:

(a) The method of interpolation (as distinguished from extrapolation), whereby, knowing the reaction under two extremes, we attempt to infer what the reaction might be at any point between the two.

(b) The method of extrapolation, whereby inferences are made beyond a known range, on the basis of

RABBI MENACHEM MENDEL SCHNEERSON, 1902–1994

The towering Jewish leader of the 20th century, known as "the Lubavitcher Rebbe," or simply as "the Rebbe." Born in southern Ukraine, the Rebbe escaped Nazi-occupied Europe, arriving in the U.S. in June 1941. The Rebbe inspired and guided the revival of traditional Judaism after the European devastation, impacting virtually every Jewish community the world over. The Rebbe often emphasized that the performance of just one additional good deed could usher in the era of Mashiach. The Rebbe's scholarly talks and writings have been printed in more than 200 volumes.

certain variables within the known range. For example, suppose we know the variables of a certain element within a temperature range of 0 to 100, and on the basis of this we estimate what the reaction might be at 101, 200, or 2000.

Of the two methods, the second (extrapolation) is clearly the more uncertain. Moreover, the uncertainty increases with the distance away from the known range and with the decrease of this range. Thus, if the known range is between 0 and 100, our inference at 101 has a greater probability than at 1001.

Let us note, at once, that all speculation regarding the origin and age of the world comes within the second and weaker method, that of extrapolation. The weakness becomes more apparent if we bear in mind that a generalization inferred from a known consequent to an unknown antecedent is more speculative than an inference from an antecedent to a consequent.

That an inference from consequent to antecedent is more speculative than an inference from antecedent to consequent can be demonstrated very simply:

Four divided by two equals two. Here the antecedent is represented by the divided and divisor, and the consequent by the quotient. Knowing the antecedent in this case, gives us one possible result—the quotient (the number 2).

However, if we know only the end result, namely, the number 2, and we ask ourselves how we can arrive at the number 2, the answer permits several possibilities, arrived at by means of different methods:

(a) 1 plus 1 equals 2;
(b) 4 - 2 equals 2;
(c) 1 x 2 equals 2;
(d) 4 divided by 2 equals 2.

Note that if other numbers are to come into play, the number of possibilities giving us the same result is infinite (since 5 - 3 also equals 2; 6 divided by 3 equals 2, etc., ad infinitum). Add to this another difficulty, which is prevalent in all methods of induction.

Conclusions based on certain known data, when they are ampliative in nature—i.e., when they are extended to unknown areas—can have any validity at all on the assumption of everything else being equal, that is to say on an identity of prevailing conditions, and their action and counteraction upon each other. If we cannot be sure that the variations or changes would bear at least a close relationship to the existing variables in degree; if we cannot be sure that the changes would bear any resemblance in kind; if, furthermore, we cannot be sure that there were not other factors involved—such conclusions of inferences are absolutely valueless!

For further illustration, I will refer to one of the points which I believe I mentioned during our conversation. In a chemical reaction, whether fissional or fusional, the introduction of a new catalyzer into the process, however minute the quantity of this new catalyzer may be, may change the whole tempo and form of the chemical process, or start an entirely new process.

We are not yet through with the difficulties inherent in all so-called scientific theories concerning the origin of the world. Let us remember that the whole structure of science is based on observances of reactions and processes in the behavior of atoms in their present state, as they now exist in nature. Scientists deal with conglomerations of billions of atoms as these are already bound together, and as these relate to other existing conglomerations of atoms. Scientists know very little of the atoms in their pristine state—of how one single atom may react on another single atom in a state of separateness—much less of how parts of a single atom may react on other parts of the same or other atoms. One thing science considers certain—to the extent that any science can be certain—is that the reactions of single atoms upon each other is totally different from the reactions of one conglomeration of atoms to another.

We may now summarize the weaknesses, nay, hopelessness, of all so-called scientific theories regarding the origin and age of our universe:

(a) These theories have been advanced on the basis of observable data during a relatively short period of time, of only a number of decades, and at any rate not more than a couple of centuries.
(b) On the basis of such a relatively small range of known (though by no means *perfectly* known) data, scientists venture to build theories by the

weak method of extrapolation, and from the consequent to the antecedent, extending to many thousands (according to them, to millions and billions) of years!

(c) In advancing such theories, they blithely disregard factors universally admitted by all scientists, namely, that in the initial period of the birth of the universe, conditions of temperature, atmospheric pressure, radioactivity, and a host of other cataclystic factors were totally different from those existing in the present state of the universe.

(d) The consensus of scientific opinion is that there must have been many radioactive elements in the initial stage that now no longer exist, or that exist only in minimal quantities; some of them elements about which the cataclystic potency is known even in minimal doses.

(e) The formation of the world, if we are to accept these theories, began with a process of colligation (of binding together) of single atoms or the components of the atom and their conglomeration and consolidation, involving totally unknown processes and variables.

In short, of all the weak scientific theories, those that deal with the origin of the cosmos and with its dating are (admittedly by the scientists themselves) the weakest of the weak.

It is small wonder (and this, incidentally, is one of the obvious refutations of these theories) that the various scientific theories concerning the age of the universe not only contradict each other, but some of them are quite incompatible and mutually exclusive, since the maximum date of one theory is less than the minimum date of another.

If anyone accepts such a theory uncritically, it can only lead him into fallacious and inconsequential reasoning.

Consider, for example, the so-called evolutionary theory of the origin of the world. This theory is based on the assumption that the universe evolved out of existing atomic and subatomic particles which, by an evolutionary process, combined to form the physical universe and our planet, on which organic life somehow developed also by an evolutionary process, until homo sapiens emerged. It is hard to understand why one should readily accept the creation of atomic and subatomic particles in a state that is admittedly unknowable and inconceivable, yet should be reluctant to accept the creation of planets, or organisms, or a human being, as we know these to exist.

The argument from the discovery of the fossils is by no means conclusive evidence of the great antiquity of the Earth, for the following reasons:

(a) In view of the unknown conditions that existed in "prehistoric" times, conditions of atmospheric pressures, temperatures, radioactivity, unknown catalyzers, etc., as already mentioned—conditions, that is, that could have caused reactions and changes of an entirely different nature and tempo from those known under the present-day orderly processes of nature—one cannot exclude the possibility that dinosaurs existed 5722 years ago, and became fossilized under terrific natural cataclysms in the course of a few years rather than in millions of years; since we have no conceivable measurements or criteria of calculations under those unknown conditions.

(b) Even assuming that the period of time that the Torah allows for the age of the world is definitely too short for fossilization (although I do not see how one can be so categorical), we can still readily accept the possibility that G-d created ready fossils, bones or skeletons (for reasons best known to Him), just as he could create ready living organisms, a complete man, and such ready products as oil, coal or diamonds, without any evolutionary process.

As for the question, if it be true as above (b), why did G-d have to create fossils in the first place? The answer is simple: We cannot know the reason why G-d chose this manner of creation in preference to another, and whatever theory of creation is accepted, the question will remain unanswered.

The question, "Why create a fossil?" is no more valid than the question, "Why create an atom?" Certainly, such a question cannot serve as a sound argument, much less as a logical basis, for the evolutionary theory.

What scientific basis is there for limiting the creative process to an evolutionary process only, starting with atomic and subatomic particles—a theory full of unexplained gaps and complications—while excluding the possibility of creation as given by the Biblical account?

For, if the latter possibility would be admitted, everything falls neatly into a pattern, and all speculation regarding the origin and age of the world becomes unnecessary and irrelevant. It is surely no argument to question this possibility by saying, "Why should the Creator create a finished universe, when it would have been sufficient for Him to create an adequate number of atoms or subatomic particles with the power of colligation and evolution to develop into the present cosmic order?"

The absurdity of this argument becomes even more obvious when it is made the basis of a flimsy theory, as if it were based on solid and irrefutable arguments overriding all other possibilities.

The question may be asked: If the theories attempting to explain the origin and age of the world are so weak, how could they have been advanced in the first place?

The answer is simple. It is a matter of human nature to seek an explanation for everything in the environment, and any theory, however far-fetched, is better than none, at least until a more feasible explanation can be devised.

You may now ask, "In the absence of a sounder theory, why then isn't the Biblical account of creation accepted by these scientists?" The answer, again, is to be found in human nature. It is a natural human ambition to be inventive and original. To accept the Biblical account deprives one of the opportunity to show one's analytic and inductive ingenuity. Hence, disregarding the Biblical account, the scientist must devise reasons to justify his doing so, and he takes refuge in classifying it with ancient and primitive mythology and the like, since he cannot really argue against it on scientific grounds.

If you are still troubled by the theory of evolution, I can tell you without fear of contradiction that it has not a shred of evidence to support it. On the contrary, during the years of research and investigation since the theory was first advanced, it has been possible to observe certain species of animal and plant life of a short life-span over thousands of generations, yet it has never been possible to establish a transmutation from one species into another, much less to turn a plant into an animal. Hence such a theory can have no place in the arsenal of empirical science.

The theory of evolution, to which reference has been made, actually has no bearing on the Torah account of Creation. For even if the theory of evolution were substantiated today, and the mutation of species were proven in laboratory tests, this would still not contradict the possibility of the world having been created as stated in the Torah, rather than through the evolutionary process. The main purpose of citing the evolutionary theory was to illustrate how a highly speculative and scientifically unsound theory can capture the imagination of the uncritical, so much so that it is even offered as a "scientific" explanation of the mystery of Creation, despite the fact that the theory of evolution itself has not been substantiated scientifically and is devoid of any real scientific basis.

Needless to say, it is not my intent to cast aspersions on science or to discredit the scientific method. Science cannot operate except by accepting certain working theories or hypotheses, even if they cannot be verified, though some theories die hard even when they are scientifically refuted or discredited. (The evolutionary theory is a case in point.) No technical progress would be possible unless certain physical laws are accepted, even though there is no guarantee that the law will repeat itself.

However, I do wish to emphasize, as already mentioned, that science has to do only with theories, but not with certainties.

All scientific conclusions, or generalizations, can only be probable in a greater or lesser degree according to the precautions taken in the use of the available evidence, and the degree of probability necessarily decreases with the distance from the empirical facts, or with the increase of the unknown variables, etc., as already indicated.

If you will bear this in mind, you will readily realize that there can be no real conflict between any scientific theory and the Torah.

My above remarks have turned out somewhat lengthier than intended, but they are still all too brief in relation to the misconception and confusion prevailing in many minds. Moreover, my remarks had to be confined to general observations, as this is hardly the medium to go into greater detail. If you have any further questions, do not hesitate to write to me.

To conclude on a note touched upon in our conversation:

The Mitzvah of putting on Tefillin every weekday, on the hand facing the heart, and on the head—the seat of the intellect—indicates, among other things, the true Jewish approach: performance first (hand), with sincerity and wholeheartedness, followed by intellectual comprehension (head); i.e., *na'aseh* first, then *v'nishmah*.

May this spirit permeate your intellect and arouse your emotive powers, and find expression in every aspect of your daily life, for the essential thing is the deed.

With blessing,
M. Schneerson

CORRESPONDENCE OF THE LUBAVITCHER REBBE
ON THE ANALYSIS OF GEOCHRONOLOGY

BY THE LUBAVITCHER REBBE, RABBI MENACHEM MENDEL SCHNEERSON

By the Grace of G-d
17th Cheshvan, 5723
[November 14, 1962]
Brooklyn, N.Y.

Greeting and Blessing:

My secretary, Dr. Nissan Mindel, has brought your letter of October 23rd to my attention, and I am pleased to note that you took time out to review my letter of the 18th of Teveth, 5722, and to put down in writing your observations thereon. Many thanks.

In reply, I can either follow the order of my letter in the light of your remarks, or take up your remarks as they appear in your letter. I will choose the latter method.

In any case I trust that our views will be reconciled, since, as you indicate in the introductory paragraph of your letter, you are in full sympathy with the aims of my said letter, namely, to resolve any doubts that science presents a challenge to the commandments of our Torah.

I must begin with two prefatory remarks:

(a) It should be self-evident that my letter did not imply a negation or rejection of science or of the scientific method. In fact, I stated so explicitly towards the end of my said letter. I hope that I will not be suspected of trying to belittle the accomplishments of science, especially as in certain areas the Torah view accords science even more credit than science itself claims; hence many laws in Halacha are geared to scientific conclusions (as, e.g., in medicine), assigning to them the validity of objective reality.

(b) A remark has been attributed to you to the effect that just as rabbinic problems should be dealt with by someone who studies rabbinics, so should scientific problems be left to those who studied science. I do not know how accurate this report is, but I feel I should not ignore it nevertheless, since I agree with this principle.
I studied science on the university level from 1928–1932 in Berlin, and from 1934–1938 in Paris, and I have tried to follow scientific developments in certain areas ever since.

Now to your letter:

(1) I quite agree, of course, that for the aim mentioned above, scientific theories must be judged by the standards and criteria set up by the scientific method itself. This is precisely the principle I followed in my letter. Hence, I purposely omitted from my discussion any references to the scriptures or the Talmud, etc.

(2) You wrote that you can heartily applaud my emphasis that scientific theories never pretend to give the ultimate truths. But I went further than that. The point was not that science is not (now) in a position to offer ultimate truths, but that modern science itself sets its own limits, declaring that its predictions are—and will always be, and in every case—merely most probable but not certain; it speaks only in terms of theories.
Herein, as you know probably better than I, lies a basic difference of concept between science today and 19th-century sciences: where in the past, scientific conclusions were considered as natural "laws" in the strict sense of the term, i.e., determined and certain, modern science no longer holds this view. Parenthetically, this view is at variance with the concept of nature and our own knowledge of it (science) as espoused by the Torah, since the idea of miracles implies a change in a fixed order and not the occurrence of a least probable event.
Acknowledging the limitations of science, set by science itself, as above, is sufficient to resolve any doubt that science might present a challenge to

Torah. The rest of the discussion in my said letter was mainly my way of further emphasis, but also because, as already mentioned, according to the Torah, i.e., in the realm of faith and not that of science, it is admissible for the conclusions of science to have the validity of "natural law."

(3) Next, you deplore what you consider a gratuitous attack on the personal motives of scientists. But no such general attack will be found in my letter. I specifically referred to a certain segment of scientists in a certain area of scientific research, namely those who produce hypotheses about what actually occurred thousands upon thousands of years ago, such as the evolutionary theory of the world, hypotheses which contain no significance for present-day research (see in my said letter the paragraph immediately following the paragraph you cite); hypotheses which are not only highly speculative, but not strictly scientific, and are indeed replete with internal weaknesses. Yet lacking any firm basis, these scientists nevertheless reject absolutely any other explanation (including the Torah narrative): it is the motives of these scientists that I attempted to analyze, since their attitude cannot be equated with a desire to promote the truth, or to promote technological advancement, scientific research, etc.

I did not want to accuse them of antireligious bias, especially as some of them, including some of the originators of the theory, were religious. I therefore attempted to explain their attitude by a common human trait, the quest for accomplishment and distinction. Incidentally, this natural trait has its positive aspects and is also basic in our religion, since without the incentive of accomplishment, nothing would be accomplished.

(4) Your remark about the misuse of the terms *fission* and *fusion* in relation to chemical reactions is, of course, valid and well taken. I trust, however, that the meaning was not unduly affected thereby, since it was twice indicated in that paragraph that the subject was chemical reactions. Undoubtedly, the terms *combination* and *decomposition* should have been used. Actually, I believe, the different usage of these terms in nuclear and chemical reactions is more conventional than basic. Nevertheless, I should have been mindful of the standard terminology.

Here, a word of explanation regarding the terminology of my letter is in order. If the terms or expressions used are not always the standard ones, this is due to (a) the fact that I do not usually dictate my letters in English, and while I subsequently check the translation, the perusal may not always preclude an oversight, as the present instance is a case in point; and (b) the fact that I received my scientific training, as already mentioned, in German and French, and previously in Russian, which may also account for some of the variations.

(5) You refer to my statement that scientists know very little about interactions of isolated atoms and subatomic particles, and also question its relevance to the theories about the dating of the world.

The relevance is this: The evolutionary theory—as it applies to the origin of our solar system and planet Earth, from which the dating is inferred—presumes (at least in the case of most of the hypotheses) that in the beginning there were atoms and subatomic particles in some pristine state, which then condensed, combined together, etc.

I am aware of the fact that a major part of physics research in this century has been concerned with interactions of individual units ranging from atoms to the most elementary particles known. But as late as 1931, of the subatomic particles only protons and electrons were known and explored. The bubble chamber was constructed only in 1952, and a field ion microscope (by Dr. Muller of Penn State University?), reaching into the realm of the atom and subatomic particles—only in 1962.

We have good reason to believe, I think, that just as scientific knowledge was enriched with the introduction of the first microscope, we may expect a similar measure of advancement with the aid of the latest (though it had been preceded by the electronic microscope). Therefore, it is safe to assume that all we have learned in the field of nucleonics in the last few decades is very little by comparison with what we can confidently expect to learn in the next few decades.

(6) You object to my statement that conditions of pressure, temperature, radioactivity, etc. must have been totally different in the early stages supposed by some evolutionists from those existing today, and you assert that those environmental conditions have, for the most part, either been duplicated in the laboratory or observed in natural phenomena.

Here, with all due respect, I beg to differ, and I believe the study of the sources will confirm my assertion.

(7) You state that there is no evidence that any radioactive element produces cataclysmic changes, and go on to note that there is a lack of clear distinction in my letter between cosmogony and geochronology.

The reason for the lack of such a distinction in my letter is that it is irrelevant to our discussion. The subject matter of my letter is the theory of evolution as it contradicts the account of Creation in the Torah. According to the Torah, the creation of the whole universe was ex nihilo, including the Earth, the sun, etc. The theory of evolution presents, instead, a different explanation of the appearance of the universe, solar system, and our planet Earth.

Now, in evaluating this theory, I have in mind that the strength of a chain is measured by its weakest link, and in my letter I attempted to point out some of the weakest links in both areas, cosmology and geochronology. With regard to geology and the changes and upheavals that may have occurred at a time when the whole universe is supposed to have been in a state of violent atomic instability, with worlds in collision, etc., cataclysmic changes cannot be ruled out; such nuclear reactions should have caused changes which would void any evolutionary calculations. Similarly, in the evolution of vegetable, animal and human life on the Earth, radioactive processes of such magnitude should have produced sudden changes and transmutations which would normally take long periods of time.

(8) You state, finally, that the crucial point to consider in regard to geochronology is the existence of objects and geological formations in and on the crust of the Earth which serve as physically observable clocks, etc. But I have already pointed out in my said letter that such criteria are valid only as of now and for the future, but cannot be applied either scientifically or logically to a primordial state.

By way of illustration, though you do not identify any of the objects you are referring to, let us examine radiocarbon dating, since most of the letters and questions I received on this subject pointed to it. This method assumes that the average cosmic-ray intensity has remained constant for the whole period of the dating, and that atmospheric mixing is rapid compared to the lifetime of ${}_{6}C^{14}$.

Now to mention but one flaw in the criterion: it requires that the shielding power (density, etc.) remain constant. But the evolution theory is built on the premise that there had been most radical changes.

Incidentally, in most recent years geologists in South Africa discovered such a disorder in geological formations in that part of the world that contradicted all the accepted theories of geology. The discovery was publicized at that time, but I do not have the informational media at hand, and I mention this in passing only. I suggest another look in my letter, p. 5, par. beg. The theory of evolution . . .

Should you wish to continue the discussion, please do not hesitate to write me.

With esteem and blessing,
M. Schneerson

P.S. I have just been able to trace and borrow one of your books, *The Attenuation of Gamma Rays and Neutrons in Reactor Shields*. May I say that I was greatly impressed with the effort, material and clarity of presentation. Incidentally, I noted in it your observations about the discrepancies between theory and experimentation which I found more than once in your book. Such a statement as "Not only is the simplest organism an incredibly complicated entity *whose chemistry and physics are barely glimpsed at* (the italics are mine), but the classical scientific pattern of experimentation *is necessarily not available* (ditto) in studying radiation efforts" is very significant and has a direct bearing on the theory of evolution which involves an age of unimaginable radioactivity both in the universe and our planet Earth.

Lesson 6

Seated Man Contemplating Heart, Gilbert Luján, acrylic, foam, cardboard, mixed media, c. 1980. (University Art Galleries, University of California, Irvine)

FOR THE LOVE OF G-D

FINDING CLOSENESS WITH A G-D YOU CANNOT TOUCH

Judaism is a holistic religion: it demands the engagement of the body, mind, and heart. We cannot reduce G-d to a set of mindless rituals; He is supposed to be a meaningful part of our lives. But can I love someone I've never met? Can I be in awe of something I've never seen? This lesson explores the possibility of having a relationship with Him—whether I can, why it's vital, and how to do it.

TEXT 1

KI ANU AMECHA, YOM KIPPUR LITURGY

כִּי אָנוּ עַמֶּךָ וְאַתָּה אֱלֹקֵינוּ, אָנוּ בָנֶיךָ וְאַתָּה אָבִינוּ.
אָנוּ עֲבָדֶיךָ וְאַתָּה אֲדוֹנֵנוּ, אָנוּ קְהָלֶךָ וְאַתָּה חֶלְקֵנוּ.
אָנוּ נַחֲלָתֶךָ וְאַתָּה גוֹרָלֵנוּ, אָנוּ צֹאנֶךָ וְאַתָּה רוֹעֵנוּ.
אָנוּ כַרְמֶךָ וְאַתָּה נוֹטְרֵנוּ, אָנוּ פְעֻלָּתֶךָ וְאַתָּה יוֹצְרֵנוּ.
אָנוּ רַעְיָתֶךָ וְאַתָּה דוֹדֵנוּ, אָנוּ סְגֻלָּתֶךָ וְאַתָּה אֱלֹקֵינוּ.
אָנוּ עַמֶּךָ וְאַתָּה מַלְכֵּנוּ, אָנוּ מַאֲמִירֶיךָ וְאַתָּה מַאֲמִירֵנוּ.

For we are Your people and You are our God;
we are Your children and You are our Father.

We are Your servants and You are our Master;
we are Your congregation and You are our Portion.

We are Your inheritance and You are our Lot;
we are Your flock and You are our Shepherd.

We are Your vineyard and You are our Watchman;
we are Your handiwork and You are our Creator.

We are Your beloved ones and You are our Beloved;
we are Your treasure and You are our God.

We are Your people and You are our King;
we are Your chosen ones and You are our Chosen One.

QUESTIONS FOR DISCUSSION

1 Which of these metaphors best describe your relationship with God?

2 Do you find any of the metaphors used to describe our relationship with God to be unusual, surprising, or even troubling? If yes, which one(s)?

3 Why is there a need for so many different metaphors to describe the relationship?

Ketubah (Marriage contract) (detail), Shalom Italia, hand-colored etching, Holland, 1648. (Israel Museum, Jerusalem)

TEXT 2

MAIMONIDES, *MISHNEH TORAH*, LAWS OF REPENTANCE 10:3

וְכֵיצַד הִיא הָאַהֲבָה הָרְאוּיָה? הוּא שֶׁיֶּאֱהַב אֶת ה' אַהֲבָה גְדוֹלָה יְתֵירָה עַזָּה מְאוֹד, עַד שֶׁתְּהֵא נַפְשׁוֹ קְשׁוּרָה בְּאַהֲבַת ה' וְנִמְצָא שׁוֹגֶה בָּהּ תָּמִיד. כְּאִלּוּ חוֹלֶה חוֹלִי הָאַהֲבָה שֶׁאֵין דַּעְתּוֹ פְּנוּיָה מֵאַהֲבַת אוֹתָהּ אִשָּׁה וְהוּא שׁוֹגֶה בָּהּ תָּמִיד, בֵּין בְּשִׁבְתּוֹ בֵּין בְּקוּמוֹ בֵּין בְּשָׁעָה שֶׁהוּא אוֹכֵל וְשׁוֹתֶה, יֶתֶר מִזֶּה תִּהְיֶה אַהֲבַת ה' בְּלֵב אוֹהֲבָיו שׁוֹגִים בָּהּ תָּמִיד, כְּמוֹ שֶׁצִּוָּנוּ, "בְּכָל לְבָבְךָ וּבְכָל נַפְשְׁךָ" (דְּבָרִים ו, ה).

וְהוּא שֶׁשְּׁלֹמֹה אָמַר דֶּרֶךְ מָשָׁל, "כִּי חוֹלַת אַהֲבָה אָנִי" (מִשְׁלֵי ב, ה). וְכָל שִׁיר הַשִּׁירִים מָשָׁל הוּא לְעִנְיָן זֶה.

What is the proper degree of love that we ought to have for God? Our love for Him should be powerful and intense to the point that the entirety of our being is consumed with this love, such that it is constantly on our mind. Imagine a man who falls deeply in love with a woman, to the point that he cannot remove her from his thoughts—he thinks of her when he sits, when he stands up, when he eats and drinks, [etc.]. One's love for God ought to exceed this love! Thus we are commanded: "[You shall love your God] with all your heart and with all your soul" (DEUTERONOMY 6:5).

King Solomon referred to this degree of love for God when he exclaimed, "I am lovesick" (SONG OF SONGS 2:5). Indeed, the entire Song of Songs is a parable that describes this intense love.

RABBI MOSHE BEN MAIMON (MAIMONIDES, RAMBAM) 1135–1204

Halachist, philosopher, author, and physician. Maimonides was born in Córdoba, Spain. After the conquest of Córdoba by the Almohads, he fled Spain and eventually settled in Cairo, Egypt. There, he became the leader of the Jewish community and served as court physician to the vizier of Egypt. He is most noted for authoring the *Mishneh Torah*, an encyclopedic arrangement of Jewish law, and for his philosophical work, *Guide for the Perplexed*. His rulings on Jewish law are integral to the formation of halachic consensus.

TEXT 3

SONG OF SONGS 5:2–8

אֲנִי יְשֵׁנָה וְלִבִּי עֵר, קוֹל דּוֹדִי דוֹפֵק, פִּתְחִי לִי אֲחֹתִי רַעְיָתִי יוֹנָתִי תַמָּתִי, שֶׁרֹּאשִׁי נִמְלָא טָל, קְוֻצּוֹתַי רְסִיסֵי לָיְלָה.

פָּשַׁטְתִּי אֶת כֻּתָּנְתִּי, אֵיכָכָה אֶלְבָּשֶׁנָּה? רָחַצְתִּי אֶת רַגְלַי, אֵיכָכָה אֲטַנְּפֵם?

דּוֹדִי שָׁלַח יָדוֹ מִן הַחֹר, וּמֵעַי הָמוּ עָלָיו.

קַמְתִּי אֲנִי לִפְתֹּחַ לְדוֹדִי, וְיָדַי נָטְפוּ מוֹר וְאֶצְבְּעֹתַי מוֹר עֹבֵר עַל כַּפּוֹת הַמַּנְעוּל.

פָּתַחְתִּי אֲנִי לְדוֹדִי, וְדוֹדִי חָמַק עָבָר, נַפְשִׁי יָצְאָה בְדַבְּרוֹ,

בִּקַּשְׁתִּיהוּ וְלֹא מְצָאתִיהוּ, קְרָאתִיו וְלֹא עָנָנִי.

מְצָאֻנִי הַשֹּׁמְרִים, הַסֹּבְבִים בָּעִיר, הִכּוּנִי, פְצָעוּנִי, נָשְׂאוּ אֶת רְדִידִי מֵעָלַי, שֹׁמְרֵי הַחֹמוֹת.

הִשְׁבַּעְתִּי אֶתְכֶם בְּנוֹת יְרוּשָׁלָםִ: אִם תִּמְצְאוּ אֶת דּוֹדִי, מַה תַּגִּידוּ לוֹ? שֶׁחוֹלַת אַהֲבָה אָנִי.

I was asleep, although my heart was awake, when I heard the sound of my beloved knocking on the door: "Open for me, my sister, my beloved, my dove, my perfect one. [Open quickly, for] my head is drenched with dew and my hair is soaked by the rains of the night."

[But I declined to get up to open the door. I responded:] "I have taken off my robe; must I put it back on? I have washed my feet; must I soil them again?"

My beloved extended his hand through a hole [near the door. Upon seeing his hand,] my feelings for him were aroused.

I arose to open the door for my beloved. [I scented myself;] my hands dripped with myrrh; myrrh flowed from my fingers onto the handle of the door lock.

I opened for my beloved, but my beloved turned and was gone. My soul nearly departed from me because of his [harsh] words [with which he left me].

I [wandered the city streets and] searched for him, but did not find him; I called for him, but he did not answer me.

The watchmen who patrol the city found me. They beat me and wounded me; the watchmen of the walls took my jewelry off me.

O daughters of Jerusalem, if you find my beloved, what will you tell him? Swear to me that you will tell him that I am lovesick.

TEXT 4

RABBI BACHYA IBN PAKUDA, *DUTIES OF THE HEART*, GATES OF INTROSPECTION

וְדַע כִּי הַמִּילוֹת תִּהְיֶינָה בַּלָּשׁוֹן, וְהָעִיּוּן בַּלֵּב. וְהַמִּילוֹת כְּגוּף לַתְּפִילָּה, וְהָעִיּוּן כְּרוּחַ.

וּכְשֶׁיִּתְפַּלֵּל הַמִּתְפַּלֵּל בִּלְשׁוֹנוֹ, וְלִיבּוֹ טָרוּד בְּזוּלַת עִנְיַן הַתְּפִילָּה, תִּהְיֶה תְּפִילָּתוֹ גוּף בְּלֹא רוּחַ, וּקְלִיפָּה בְּלֹא לֵב.

Know that words are associated with the [physical] tongue, while thoughts are the domain of the [feelings of the] heart. The words of prayer are the body, and the thought its spirit.

When one prays with the tongue while the heart is preoccupied with something other than the prayer, the prayer is like a body without a spirit, a husk without a heart.

RABBI BACHYA IBN PAKUDA
11TH CENTURY

Moral philosopher and author. Ibn Pakuda lived in Muslim Spain, but little else is known about his life. *Chovot Halevavot* (*Duties of the Heart*), his major work, was intended to be a guide for attaining spiritual perfection. Originally written in Judeo-Arabic and published in 1080, it was later translated into Hebrew and published in 1161 by Judah ibn Tibbon, a scion of the famous family of translators. Ibn Pakuda had a strong influence on Jewish pietistic literature.

TEXT 5

RABBI SHNE'UR ZALMAN OF LIADI, *TANYA*, CHAPTER 4

הָאַהֲבָה הִיא שֹׁרֶשׁ כָּל רַמַ"ח מִצְוֹת עֲשֵׂה, וּמִמֶּנָּה הֵן נִמְשָׁכוֹת, וּבִלְעָדָהּ אֵין לָהֶן קִיּוּם אֲמִתִּי. כִּי הַמְקַיְּמָן בֶּאֱמֶת, הוּא הָאוֹהֵב אֶת שֵׁם ה' וְחָפֵץ לְדָבְקָה בּוֹ בֶּאֱמֶת . . .

וְהַיִּרְאָה הִיא שֹׁרֶשׁ לְשַׁסַ"ה לֹא תַעֲשֶׂה, כִּי יָרֵא לִמְרֹד בְּמֶלֶךְ מַלְכֵי הַמְּלָכִים הַקָּדוֹשׁ בָּרוּךְ הוּא. אוֹ יִרְאָה פְּנִימִית מִזּוֹ, שֶׁמִּתְבַּיֵּשׁ מִגְּדֻלָּתוֹ לַמְרוֹת עֵינֵי כְבוֹדוֹ וְלַעֲשׂוֹת הָרַע בְּעֵינָיו.

Love of God motivates us to fulfill the 248 commandments of the Torah. Also, without this love, our mitzvah observance is deficient. To truly fulfill the *mitzvot,* one must love God and truly desire to cleave to Him. . . .

Awe and the fear of God ensure that we not transgress the 365 prohibitions of the Torah. Because one [who] fears to rebel against the supreme King of Kings, the Holy One, blessed be He, [will abstain from wrongdoing]. A greater level of awe derives from a keen awareness of God's greatness. One with this awareness would be ashamed to defy God by doing what is evil in His eyes.

RABBI SHNE'UR ZALMAN OF LIADI (ALTER REBBE) 1745–1812

Chasidic rebbe, halachic authority, and founder of the Chabad movement. The Alter Rebbe was born in Liozna, Belarus, and was among the principal students of the Magid of Mezeritch. His numerous works include the *Tanya*, an early classic containing the fundamentals of Chabad Chasidism, and *Shulchan Aruch HaRav,* an expanded and reworked code of Jewish law.

TEXT 6

GEORGE STEINER, *IN BLUEBEARD'S CASTLE: SOME NOTES TOWARDS THE REDEFINITION OF CULTURE* (NEW HAVEN, CONN.: YALE UNIVERSITY PRESS, 1971), PP. 36–37

The immensity of the [introduction of monotheism], its occurrence in real time, are certain, and reverberate still. . . . What we must recapture to mind, as nakedly as we can, is the singularity, the brain-hammering strangeness, of the monotheistic idea. Historians of religion tell us that the emergence of the concept of the Mosaic God is a unique fact in human experience, that a genuinely comparable notion sprang up at no other place or time. The abruptness of the Mosaic revelation, the finality of the creed at Sinai, tore up the human psyche by its most ancient roots. The break has never really knit.

The demands made of the mind are, like God's name, unspeakable. Brain and conscience are commanded to vest belief, obedience, love in an abstraction purer, more inaccessible to ordinary sense than is the highest of mathematics. The God of the Torah not only prohibits the making of images to represent Him. He does not allow imagining.

GEORGE STEINER
1929–

Philosopher, author. Born and raised in France to Jewish-Viennese parents, Steiner fled to New York City with his family less than a month before the Nazis occupied Paris. He has held many academic positions over his distinguished career. His books pose philosophical questions about the humanities. In Steiner's view, totalitarianism and the Holocaust have destroyed the assumption that literary culture results in humane values. Steiner resides in England, where he serves on the faculty of the University of Cambridge.

TEXT 7

RABBI YOSEF YITSCHAK SCHNEERSOHN, CITED IN *HAYOM YOM*, 8 CHESHVAN

מִצְוָה לָשׁוֹן צַוְותָא וְחִבּוּר. וְהָעוֹשֶׂה מִצְוָה מִתְחַבֵּר עִם הָעַצְמוּת בָּרוּךְ הוּא, שֶׁהוּא הַמְצַוֶּה אֶת הַצִּיוּוּי הַהוּא.

וְזֶהוּ "שְׂכַר מִצְוָה מִצְוָה" (אָבוֹת ד, ב), דְזֶה מַה שֶׁנִתְחַבֵּר עִם עַצְמוּת אוֹר אֵין סוֹף מְצַוֶּה הַצִּיוּוּי, זֶהוּ שְׂכָרוֹ.

וְיוּבָן בְּמָשָׁל גַשְׁמִי: אִישׁ פָּשׁוּט בְּיוֹתֵר יֵשׁ לוֹ בִּטּוּל פְּנִימִי אֶל הַחָכְמָה וּמַעֲלַת חָכָם, בְּבִטּוּל דְהֶעְדֵר תְּפִיסַת מָקוֹם לְגַמְרֵי. וְכֵן גַם בְּהֶרְגֵשׁ הֶחָכָם הֲרֵי אִישׁ הַפָּשׁוּט אֵינוֹ נִכְנַס אֶצְלוֹ בְּגֶדֶר אֱנוּשִׁי כְּלַל - וְאֵין זֶה דְמְבַטְלוֹ וְדוֹחֶה אוֹתוֹ, חַס וְשָׁלוֹם, דְזֶהוּ מִדָּה רָעָה - וְנֶחְשַׁב בְּעֵינָיו שֶׁאֵין לוֹ קֶשֶׁר שֶׁל יַחַס עִמּוֹ כְּלָל.

וְהָיָה כַּאֲשֶׁר הֶחָכָם יְצַוֶּה לָאִישׁ הַפָּשׁוּט לַעֲשׂוֹת אֵיזֶה דָבָר בִּשְׁבִילוֹ, הִנֵּה בְּצִיּוּי זֶה נוֹלַד מְצִיאוּתוֹ שֶׁל הָאִישׁ הַפָּשׁוּט, הֵן לְעַצְמוֹ שֶׁמַרְגִישׁ מְצִיאוּתוֹ אֲשֶׁר הוּא יָכוֹל לְקַיֵּים מִצְוַת הֶחָכָם וְלוֹ צִיוָּה הֶחָכָם לַעֲשׂוֹת דָבָר, וְהֵן בְּעֵינֵי הֶחָכָם נֶחְשַׁב לִמְצִיאוּת אֲשֶׁר אֵלָיו יְדַבֵּר וִיצַוֶּה, וּלְבַד זֹאת, הֲרֵי צִיוּוּי זֶה מְאַחֵד הֶחָכָם הָרָם וְנַעֲלֶה עִם הָאִישׁ הַפָּשׁוּט בְּיוֹתֵר. וְהַנִמְשָׁל מוּבָן.

וּמוּבָן גַם כֵּן אֲשֶׁר בְּיַחַס לְהַנִזְכַּר לְעֵיל אֵין הֶבְדֵל כְּלַל בַּמֶה יִהְיֶה הַצִּיוּוּי, אִם דָבָר גָדוֹל וְנַעֲלֶה אוֹ קָטָן וּפָשׁוּט.

RABBI YOSEF YITSCHAK SCHNEERSOHN (RAYATS, FRIERDIKER REBBE, PREVIOUS REBBE) 1880–1950

Chasidic rebbe, prolific writer, and Jewish activist. Rabbi Yosef Yitschak, the sixth leader of the Chabad movement, actively promoted Jewish religious practice in Soviet Russia and was arrested for these activities. After his release from prison and exile, he settled in Warsaw, Poland, from where he fled Nazi occupation, and arrived in New York in 1940. Settling in Brooklyn, Rabbi Schneersohn worked to revitalize American Jewish life. His son-in-law, Rabbi Menachem Mendel Schneerson, succeeded him as the leader of the Chabad movement.

The word *mitzvah* is related to the [Aramaic] word *tsaveta*, which means *connection*. One who performs a mitzvah connects with God, the issuer of the commandment.

This is the meaning of [the Mishnaic phrase,] "The reward of a mitzvah is the mitzvah" (ETHICS OF THE FATHERS 2:4): the reward of the mitzvah is the connection (mitzvah, *tsaveta*) it generates with God Who issued the commandment.

This can be understood by way of an analogy from the physical world: A simpleton has an inner sense of *bitul* (nullity) before wisdom and the greatness of a sage, to the extent that, in comparison, he senses himself to be an utter nonentity. Similarly, in the sage's estimation, the simpleton is hardly human. Not that the scholar dismisses or rejects the simpleton, God forbid, for that would be bad manners; but he simply sees no connection or relationship whatsoever.

Now, when the sage instructs the simpleton to do something for him, that command brings the simpleton "into being." In the simpleton's own self-perception, he is no longer a nonentity; he has assumed a status unto himself in that he is able to carry out an order of the sage and it is him that the sage addressed and instructed. In the eyes of the sage, too, the simpleton now "exists"; he is someone to whom the sage can speak and instruct. What is more, the command actually unites the lofty, exalted sage with the simpleton. The analogue is obvious.

It is understood that in the above analogy it makes no difference whether the instruction regards a great and lofty matter or a simple and trivial one.

TEXT 8

RABBI SHNE'UR ZALMAN OF LIADI, *TANYA*, CHAPTER 40

וּבָזֶה יוּבַן הֵיטֵב הָא דִדְחִילוּ וּרְחִימוּ נִקְרָאִים גַדְפִּין, דֶּרֶךְ מָשָׁל . . . וּבְתִקּוּנִים פֵּרֵשׁ, שֶׁהָעוֹסְקִים בַּתּוֹרָה וּמִצְווֹת בִּדְחִילוּ וּרְחִימוּ - נִקְרָאִים בָּנִים, וְאִם לָאו - נִקְרָאִים אֶפְרוֹחִים, דְלָא יָכְלִין לְפַרְחָא.

כִּי כְּמוֹ שֶׁכַּנְפֵי הָעוֹף אֵינָם עִקָּר הָעוֹף, וְאֵין חַיּוּתוֹ תָּלוּי בָּהֶם כְּלַל, כְּדִתְנַן, "נִטְלוּ אֲגָפֶיהָ - כְּשֵׁרָה", וְהָעִיקָּר הוּא רֹאשׁוֹ וְכָל גּוּפוֹ, וְהַכְּנָפַיִם אֵינָם רַק מְשַׁמְּשִׁים לְרֹאשׁוֹ וְגוּפוֹ לְפַרְחָא בְּהוֹן. וְכַךְ דֶּרֶךְ מָשָׁל, הַתּוֹרָה וּמִצְווֹת הֵן עִקַּר הַיִּחוּד הָעֶלְיוֹן, עַל יְדֵי גִילּוּי רָצוֹן הָעֶלְיוֹן הַמִּתְגַּלֶּה עַל יְדֵיהֶן; וְהַדְּחִילוּ וּרְחִימוּ הֵם מַעֲלִים אוֹתָן לְמָקוֹם שֶׁיִּתְגַּלֶּה בּוֹ הָרָצוֹן, אוֹר אֵין סוֹף בָּרוּךְ הוּא, וְהַיִּחוּד, שֶׁהֵן יְצִירָה וּבְרִיאָה.

Awe and love are figuratively called "wings." . . . *Tikunei Zohar* explains that those who study the Torah and perform *mitzvot* out of awe and love are called "children [of God]"; otherwise they are called "fledglings" that cannot fly.

Just as the wings of a bird are not essential parts of the body; its life does not depend upon them, as we learned, "If its wings were removed, it is kosher." The essential parts of the bird are its head and body, while the wings merely serve the head and body, enabling the bird to fly. So, too, by way of example, the Torah and *mitzvot* effect the essential unity with God, because of God's will that is present in them. The awe and love [with which they are performed] lift the Torah study and *mitzvot* and allow the will of God to be revealed in them.

TEXT 9

THE REBBE, RABBI MENACHEM MENDEL SCHNEERSON, *LIKUTEI SICHOT* 3:955

מִצְוֹות זַיינֶען גֶעגֶעבְּן גֶעוָוארְן בִּכְדֵי "לְצָרֵף בָּהֶן אֶת הַבְּרִיּוֹת", בִּכְדֵי אַז דֶער אִיד וָואס טוּט דִי מִצְוָה זָאל וֶוערְן אוֹיסְגֶעאֵיידְלְט אוּן פַארְבּוּנְדְן מִיטְן אוֹיבֶּערְשְׁטְן. וָואס דֶער פַארְבּוּנְד פוּן דֶעם אִידְן מִיט דֶעם אוֹיבֶּערְשְׁטְן דַארְף אַרוּמְנֶעמֶען אַלֶע זַיינֶע כֹּחוֹת, בִּיז צוּ פְּנִימִיּוּת הַנֶּפֶשׁ.

וּבְמֵילָא, אוֹיב עֶר וֶועט טָאן דִי מִצְוֹות נָאר לָצֵאת יְדֵי חוֹבָתוֹ, אָן אַ חַיּוּת, וֶוערְט דָאךְ דֶעמָאלְט דִי מִצְוָה גֶעטָאן בְּלוֹיז מִיטְן כֹּחַ הַמַּעֲשֶׂה אַלֵיין, אִיז עֶר דָאךְ דַאן פַארְבּוּנְדְן מִיטְן אוֹיבֶּערְשְׁטְן נָאר מִיט זַיין כֹּחַ הַמַּעֲשֶׂה אַלֵיין - דֶער רָצוֹן הָעֶלְיוֹן אִיז אָבֶּער, אַז דֶער **גַאנְצֶער** אִיד מִיט **אַלֶע** זַיינֶע כֹּחוֹת זָאל וֶוערְן פַארְבּוּנְדְן מִיטְן אוֹיבֶּערְשְׁטְן, דוּרְךְ דֶעם וָואס **אַלֶע** זַיינֶע כֹּחוֹת וֶועלְן מְקַיֵּים זַיין דִי מִצְוָה . . .

אִיז אָבֶּער פָארְט דִי עֲבוֹדָה מִיט דִי כֹּחוֹת פְּנִימִיִּים, אַהֲבָה וְיִרְאָה, נִיט אַן עִנְיָן פַאר זִיךְ, וָוארוּם דֶער תַּכְלִית פוּן דֶער אַהֲבָה וְיִרְאָה אִיז, זֵיי זָאלְן בְּרֶענְגֶען חַיּוּת אִין קִיּוּם הַמִּצְוֹות בְּפוֹעַל; וַוייל תַּכְלִית הַכַּוָּונָה אִיז: דִירָה **בְּתַחְתּוֹנִים** דַוְקָא, וָואס דָאס קוּמְט דוּרְךְ כֹּחַ הַתַּחְתּוֹן שֶׁבָּאָדָם - דוּרְךְ מַעֲשֶׂה הַמִּצְוֹות בְּפוֹעַל. דִי **שְׁלֵימוּת** הַכַּוָּונָה פוּן דִירָה בְּתַחְתּוֹנִים אָבֶּער וֶוערְט אוֹיסְגֶעפִירְט - בִּשְׁעַת אַז דֶער קִיּוּם הַמִּצְוֹות אִיז בְּכָל כֹּחוֹתָיו.

Mitzvot were given to enable the "refinement of humanity." The performance of *mitzvot* refines us and connects us with God. This connection should permeate all our faculties and extend to the depths of the soul.

Now, if one performs a mitzvah simply to discharge their obligation, without passion, only their faculties of action are engaged. Consequently, their connection to God will be limited to their action faculties. It is God's will, however, that the *entirety* of the person and *all* of

RABBI MENACHEM MENDEL SCHNEERSON 1902–1994

The towering Jewish leader of the 20th century, known as "the Lubavitcher Rebbe," or simply as "the Rebbe." Born in southern Ukraine, the Rebbe escaped Nazi-occupied Europe, arriving in the U.S. in June 1941. The Rebbe inspired and guided the revival of traditional Judaism after the European devastation, impacting virtually every Jewish community the world over. The Rebbe often emphasized that the performance of just one additional good deed could usher in the era of Mashiach. The Rebbe's scholarly talks and writings have been printed in more than 200 volumes.

their faculties should be connected. This is accomplished by involving *all* of one's faculties in the performance of *mitzvot*. . . .

Nevertheless, serving God with one's higher faculties, love and awe, is not an end unto itself. The purpose of love and awe is to infuse mitzvah performance with life and enthusiasm. The objective of Creation is to make a divine abode specifically of the *lower* worlds, which can only be achieved through utilizing one's *lowest* faculty, action, in doing *mitzvot*. The goal is only *fully* achieved, however, when the *mitzvot* are performed with all of one's capacities and faculties.

Sabbath Prayer, Joseph Wolins, oil painting, c. 1940.

TEXT 10

I CHRONICLES 28:9

וְאַתָּה שְׁלֹמֹה בְנִי, דַע אֶת אֱלֹקֵי אָבִיךָ וְעָבְדֵהוּ בְּלֵב שָׁלֵם וּבְנֶפֶשׁ חֲפֵצָה.

And you, my son Solomon, know the God of your father and worship Him with a whole heart and with an eager soul.

TEXT 11

ZOHAR 1:103B

"נוֹדַע בַּשְּׁעָרִים בַּעֲלָהּ" (מִשְׁלֵי לא, כג) . . . וַדַאי, "נוֹדָע בַּשְּׁעָרִים בַּעֲלָהּ"
דָא קוּדְשָׁא בְּרִיךְ הוּא, דְאִיהוּ אִתְיַדַע וְאִתְדַבֵּק לְפוּם מַה דִמְשַׁעֵר בְּלִבֵּיהּ,
כָּל חַד כַּמָה דְיָכִיל לְאַדְבָּקָא בְּרוּחָא דְחָכְמְתָא.

"Her husband is known at the gates (*she'arim*)" (PROVERBS 31:23). The "husband" in this verse refers to God, Who makes Himself known and connects with every individual in accordance with what that person's heart can contain (*mesha'er*), each person to the extent they can cleave to the spirit of wisdom.

ZOHAR

The seminal work of kabbalah, Jewish mysticism. The *Zohar* is a mystical commentary on the Torah, written in Aramaic and Hebrew. According to the Arizal, the *Zohar* contains the teachings of Rabbi Shimon bar Yochai, who lived in the Land of Israel during the second century. The *Zohar* has become one of the indispensable texts of traditional Judaism, alongside and nearly equal in stature to the Mishnah and Talmud.

TEXT 12

RABBI SHNE'UR ZALMAN OF LIADI, *TANYA*, CHAPTER 46

וְהוּא, כַּאֲשֶׁר יָשִׂים אֶל לִבּוֹ מַה שֶּׁאָמַר הַכָּתוּב: "כַּמַּיִם הַפָּנִים לַפָּנִים כֵּן לֵב הָאָדָם אֶל הָאָדָם" (מִשְׁלֵי כז, יט). פֵּירוּשׁ, כְּמוֹ שֶׁכִּדְמוּת וְצוּרַת הַפָּנִים שֶׁהָאָדָם מַרְאֶה בַּמַּיִם כֵּן נִרְאֶה לוֹ שָׁם בַּמַּיִם אוֹתָהּ צוּרָה עַצְמָהּ, כָּכָה מַמָּשׁ לֵב הָאָדָם הַנֶּאֱמָן בְּאַהֲבָתוֹ לְאִישׁ אַחֵר, הֲרֵי הָאַהֲבָה זוּ מְעוֹרֶרֶת אַהֲבָה בְּלֵב חֲבֵרוֹ אֵלָיו גַּם כֵּן לִהְיוֹת אוֹהֲבִים נֶאֱמָנִים זֶה לָזֶה, בִּפְרָט כְּשֶׁרוֹאֶה אַהֲבַת חֲבֵרוֹ אֵלָיו. וְהִנֵּה זֶהוּ טֶבַע הַנָּהוּג בְּמִדַּת כָּל אָדָם, אַף אִם שְׁנֵיהֶם שָׁוִים בְּמַעֲלָה.

וְעַל אַחַת כַּמָּה וְכַמָּה אִם מֶלֶךְ גָּדוֹל וָרַב מַרְאֶה אַהֲבָתוֹ הַגְּדוֹלָה וְהָעֲצוּמָה לְאִישׁ הֶדְיוֹט וְנִבְזֶה וּשְׁפַל אֲנָשִׁים וּמְנֻוָּל הַמּוּטָל בָּאַשְׁפָּה, וְיוֹרֵד אֵלָיו מִמְּקוֹם כְּבוֹדוֹ עִם כָּל שָׂרָיו יַחְדָּיו, וּמְקִימוֹ וּמְרִימוֹ מֵאַשְׁפָּתוֹ, וּמַכְנִיסוֹ לְהֵיכָלוֹ הֵיכַל הַמֶּלֶךְ חֶדֶר לִפְנִים מֵחֶדֶר, מָקוֹם שֶׁאֵין כָּל עֶבֶד וָשַׂר נִכְנָס לְשָׁם, וּמִתְיַחֵד עִמּוֹ שָׁם בְּיִחוּד וְקֵירוּב אֲמִתִּי וְחִיבּוּק וְנִישּׁוּק, וְאִתְדַּבְּקוּת רוּחָא בְּרוּחָא בְּכָל לֵב וָנֶפֶשׁ -

עַל אַחַת כַּמָּה וְכַמָּה שֶׁתִּתְעוֹרֵר מִמֵּילָא הָאַהֲבָה כְּפוּלָה וּמְכוּפֶּלֶת בְּלֵב הַהֶדְיוֹט וּשְׁפַל אֲנָשִׁים הַזֶּה אֶל נֶפֶשׁ הַמֶּלֶךְ, בְּהִתְקַשְּׁרוּת הַנֶּפֶשׁ מַמָּשׁ מִלֵּב וָנֶפֶשׁ מֵעִמְקָא דְלִבָּא לְאֵין קֵץ. וְאַף אִם לִבּוֹ כְּלֵב הָאֶבֶן הִמֵּס יִמַּס וְהָיָה לְמַיִם, וְתִשְׁתַּפֵּךְ נַפְשׁוֹ כַּמַּיִם בִּכְלוֹת הַנֶּפֶשׁ מַמָּשׁ לְאַהֲבַת הַמֶּלֶךְ.

וְהִנֵּה כְּכָל הַדְּבָרִים הָאֵלֶּה וּכְכָל הַחִזָּיוֹן הַזֶּה, וְגָדוֹל יֶתֶר מְאֹד בְּכִפְלֵי כִּפְלַיִים לְאֵין קֵץ עָשָׂה לָנוּ אֱלֹקֵינוּ. כִּי לִגְדוּלָּתוֹ אֵין חֵקֶר, וְאִיהוּ מְמַלֵּא כָּל עָלְמִין וְסוֹבֵב כָּל עָלְמִין . . .

כִּי הִנִּיחַ הַקָּדוֹשׁ בָּרוּךְ הוּא אֶת הָעֶלְיוֹנִים וְאֶת הַתַּחְתּוֹנִים, וְלֹא בָּחַר בְּכוּלָּם כִּי אִם בְּיִשְׂרָאֵל עַמּוֹ, וְהוֹצִיאָם מִמִּצְרַיִם עֶרְוַת הָאָרֶץ, מְקוֹם הַזּוּהֲמָא וְהַטּוּמְאָה, לֹא עַל יְדֵי מַלְאָךְ וְלֹא עַל יְדֵי כוּ', אֶלָּא הַקָּדוֹשׁ בָּרוּךְ הוּא בִּכְבוֹדוֹ וּבְעַצְמוֹ יָרַד לְשָׁם, כְּמוֹ שֶׁכָּתוּב: "וָאֵרֵד לְהַצִּילוֹ וגו'" (שְׁמוֹת ג, ח), כְּדֵי לְקָרְבָם אֵלָיו בְּקֵירוּב וְיִחוּד אֲמִיתִּי, בְּהִתְקַשְּׁרוּת הַנֶּפֶשׁ מַמָּשׁ.

בִּבְחִינַת נְשִׁיקִין פֶּה לְפֶה, לְדַבֵּר דְּבַר ה' זוּ הֲלָכָה, וְאִתְדַּבְּקוּת רוּחָא בְּרוּחָא, הִיא הַשָּׂגַת הַתּוֹרָה וִידִיעַת רְצוֹנוֹ וְחָכְמָתוֹ, דְּכוּלָּא חַד מַמָּשׁ. וְגַם בִּבְחִינַת חִיבּוּק, הוּא קִיּוּם הַמִּצְוֹת מַעֲשִׂיּוֹת בִּרְמַ"ח אֵבָרִים, דִּרְמַ"ח פִּקּוּדִין הֵן רְמַ"ח אֵבָרִין דְּמַלְכָּא, כְּנִזְכַּר לְעֵיל.

[One way to arrive at a love for God is to] take to heart the verse: "As water reflects a face, so does the heart of man reflect another heart" (PROVERBS 27:19). This means that just as water reflects the very image and features that a person presents before it, so too, a heart that is loyal in its love for another awakens a corresponding loving response, cementing the mutual love and loyalty. This is especially true when the love is observable. This is a universal law of human nature that applies even if the two people involved are equal.

How much more so this law applies if a great and mighty king shows immense love for a commoner, who is scorned, lowly, covered in filth, and lying in a dunghill. [Imagine the king] leaving his [royal palace] and, accompanied by his entire retinue of ministers, approaching the commoner. The king extracts him from the dunghill and brings him into the innermost chamber

Bride's Prayer, Yossi Rosenstein, oil painting, 2004.

of his royal palace, a room where no servant or minister is permitted entry. There the king embraces and kisses him, and shares with him the closest of friendships, a spiritual attachment of the heart and soul.

How great will be the love of this common, lowly individual for the king? He will most certainly be attached to the king with heart and soul, with infinite heartfelt sincerity. Even if his heart is made of stone, it will surely melt and become water, and it will pour with soulful longing for the love of the king.

Now, God has done with us all of this precisely, exactly as described. But it is infinitely greater, because His greatness defies comprehension, and He pervades all worlds and transcends all worlds. . . .

God disregarded the higher and lower worlds and their inhabitants, and chose none else but Israel, His nation. He brought them out of Egypt—the most decadent place on earth, a place of spiritual filth and impurity. He did not send an angel to take them out; rather, He alone in His majesty and glory descended there, as God said, "I have come down to rescue them, etc." (EXODUS 3:8). He took them out to bring them near to Him with true closeness and unity, to share with them a soul connection.

This connection includes:

kisses, mouth to mouth, which occurs when we speak the word of God, namely, the halachah;

the *fusion of spirits*, which occurs when we comprehend the Torah and know His will and wisdom, all of which is truly one with God;

and also *embracing*, which occurs when we use our 248 limbs to fulfill the 248 positive *mitzvot* of the Torah, which symbolize God's "organs" [and thus when fulfilling them, we embrace God's "body"].

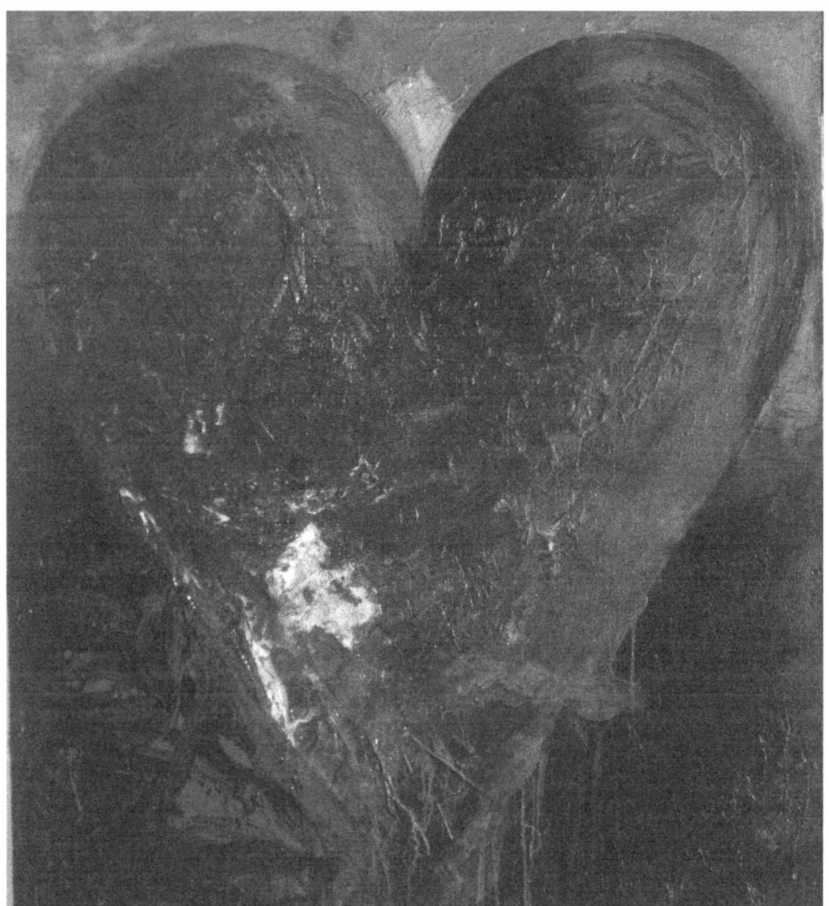

Cruising (La Chasse) (4 parts) (detail), Jim Dine, acrylic on canvas with objects, 1981.

KEY POINTS

1 Our relationship with God invokes an array of emotions. One of these, love, plays a central role in the relationship. Love and awe—collectively known as *kavanah*—motivate and vitalize mitzvah observance; without *kavanah*, our sages tell us, a mitzvah is a soulless body.

2 *Kavanah* alone does not connect a person with God; such a connection is forged specifically through the *act* of a mitzvah. But when a mitzvah is done with feeling, the connection is enhanced and expands to embrace the person's innermost feelings as well.

3 It can be difficult to generate emotions toward an abstract and intangible entity such as God. Yet, an emotional bond can be achieved through focusing the mind. Meditation allows one to experience a heartfelt and individualized relationship with God.

4 One meditation hinges on the human instinct to spontaneously respond to another's love in reciprocal fashion. Contemplating God's greatness and His remarkable—even illogical—love for us causes us to mirror that love toward Him.

Additional Readings

LAWS OF REPENTANCE, CHAPTER 10

EXCERPTED FROM MAIMONIDES'S MAGNUM OPUS, *MISHNEH TORAH*

2. One who serves G-d out of love observes the Torah and *mitzvot* and follows the paths of wisdom for no reason in the world—not for fear of negative consequences and not to obtain any benefit—but does what is right because it is the truth. The good results then certainly follow [though this is not the person's objective]. Such service is a significant goal that not every wise person can obtain. It is how Abraham conducted himself: his entire service of G-d was a result of love. Because of his high level of service, G-d referred to him as "My lover." G-d instructed us through Moses to strive for this love, as the verse states: "You shall love your G-d" (Deuteronomy 6:5). One who has an appropriate degree of love for G-d will perform all the *mitzvot* with love.

3. What is the proper degree of love that we ought to have for G-d? Our love for Him should be powerful and intense to the point that the entirety of our being is consumed with this love, such that it is constantly on our mind. Imagine a man who falls deeply in love with a woman, to the point that he cannot remove her from his thoughts—he thinks of her when he sits, when he stands up, when he eats and drinks, [etc.]. One's love for G-d ought to exceed this love! Thus we are commanded: "[You shall love your G-d] with all your heart and with all your soul." King Solomon referred to this degree of love for G-d when he exclaimed, "I am lovesick" (Song of Songs 2:5). Indeed, the entire Song of Songs is a parable that describes this intense love.

4. Our early sages have stated: A person might say, "I will study Torah in order to become wealthy, or to gain the title 'rabbi,' or to receive a share in the World to Come." That is why the Torah reminds us, "To love G-d" (Deuteronomy 11:13)—whatever you do, do only out of love. The sages added: "'[Fortunate is the one who fears G-d and] who greatly desires His commandments' (Psalms 112:10). [This infers that one ought to desire the commandments, themselves] not the reward for the commandments." Our greatest sages would privately instruct the wisest and the most intellectual of their students: "Do not be as servants who serve their masters in order to receive a reward; rather because He is your master, He is worthy of being served" (*Ethics of the Fathers* 1:3). In other words, serve Him with love.

5. If one observes Torah in order to receive a reward, or in order to prevent tragedy from befalling him, he has not served G-d for its own sake. However, if one observes [Torah] neither due to fear nor in order to receive a reward, but only out of love of the Master of the Universe Who commanded so—this is considered service for its own sake. Still, our sages have stated: "A person should always observe Torah, even for ulterior purposes, because ultimately that will lead to observing Torah for its own sake." Therefore, when Torah is taught to young children and women and the ignorant population, they are taught to observe out of fear and in order to receive reward. Then, once they grow in wisdom and knowledge, we reveal to them this secret, little by little, and get them used to the concept until they grasp it and are able to serve G-d out of love.

RABBI MOSHE BEN MAIMON (MAIMONIDES, RAMBAM), 1135–1204

Halachist, philosopher, author, and physician. Maimonides was born in Córdoba, Spain. After the conquest of Córdoba by the Almohads, he fled Spain and eventually settled in Cairo, Egypt. There, he became the leader of the Jewish community and served as court physician to the vizier of Egypt. He is most noted for authoring the *Mishneh Torah,* an encyclopedic arrangement of Jewish law, and for his philosophical work, *Guide for the Perplexed.* His rulings on Jewish law are integral to the formation of halachic consensus.

6. It is patently clear that love for G-d will not become entrenched in a person's heart until he is constantly preoccupied with it, leaving everything else in the world behind. As we were commanded: "[Love your G-d] with all your heart and all your soul." One's love of G-d depends on the level of knowledge of G-d; if there is a little [knowledge] then [the love is] small, and with more [knowledge] there is more [love]. For this reason one must make a conscious effort to understand and grasp intellectual concepts that will lead us to understand G-d to the extent that is humanly possible, as was explained in [*Mishneh Torah, Sefer Mada—The Book of Knowledge*] the Laws of the Foundations of the Torah.

TORAH STUDIES: MISHPATIM

ADAPTED BY RABBI LORD JONATHAN SACKS; FROM THE TEACHINGS OF THE LUBAVITCHER REBBE

Our Sidra begins with the words, "And these are the judgments which you shall set before them," and the last phrase of this sentence has troubled many commentators. What is the precise meaning of the expression "set before them?" Several different answers have traditionally been given, and the Rebbe explores the relationship between them. The word "judgments" (mishpatim) *also requires comment, for this is a technical term in Torah, referring in general to social legislation of the kind which, had it not been given by G-d, man could have devised for himself on rational grounds. It is to be contrasted with "testimonies"* (edut) *such as the Shabbat and the festivals, which though they are rationally comprehensible, could not have been invented by man; and with "statutes"* (chukim) *which are laws whose purpose lies altogether beyond our understanding. Why are only "judgments" singled out to be "set before" the people? In answering this, the Rebbe explores the difficult and much misunderstood relationship between our obedience to and our understanding of G-d's law.*

RABBI LORD JONATHAN SACKS, PHD, 1948–

Former chief rabbi of the United Kingdom. Rabbi Sacks attended Cambridge University and received his doctorate from King's College, London. A prolific and influential author, his books include *Will We Have Jewish Grandchildren?* and *The Dignity of Difference.* He received the Jerusalem Prize in 1995 for his contributions to enhancing Jewish life in the Diaspora, was knighted and made a life peer in 2005, and became Baron Sacks of Aldridge in 2009.

1. The Meaning of "Before Them"

"And these are the judgments which you shall set before them."[1] The Rabbis have given several explanations of the phrase "before them."

The first[2] is that every legal dispute amongst Jews should be tried "before them," before a *Jewish* court of law, which tries cases according to the Torah. They should not take the case before non-Jewish judges, even if their law in this instance coincides with that of the Torah.

The second[3] is that when one is teaching the Torah to a pupil, he should "show the face"; in other words, he should explain the reasons for the law,[4] so that the pupil understands it rather than receiving it as a dogma.

The third, given by the Alter Rebbe,[5] is that "before them" means "to their innermost selves."[6] The verse therefore means that the knowledge of G-d should enter the most inward reaches of the Jewish soul. There is an allusion to this in the Jerusalem Talmud,[7] which relates the phrase "You shall set" (*tasim*) to the word "treasure-house" (*simah*). The treasure-house of the Torah should thus awaken the treasure-house of the soul, that is, its innermost core.[8]

2. Three Kinds of Law

It is a general principle that different interpretations of the same words of Torah bear an inner relationship to one another.[9] What, then, is the connection between these three explanations?

Also, why should the words "before them," however they are interpreted, be attached specifically to "judgments?" There are three kinds of commandments contained in the Torah: Judgments, testimonies and statutes.[10] *Statutes* are laws which transcend our understanding and which we obey simply because they are the word of G-d. *Testimonies* can be rationally explained, but they are not necessitated by rational considerations: Had G-d not decreed them, man would not have invented them. *Judgments*, however, are laws which reason would have compelled man to devise even if they had not been Divinely revealed. As the Rabbis say, "If the Torah had not been given, we would have learned modesty from the cat and honesty from the ant. . . ."[11] Why, then, is it judgments that the Torah singles out to be set "before them?"

If we take the first interpretation of "before them," this is easy to understand. It is only in the sphere of judgments that Jewish and non-Jewish law are likely to coincide. Hence the necessity to urge, specifically of judgments, that disputes concerning them be taken to a Jewish court. In the case of testimonies and statutes, which can be derived only from Divine revelation, there would be no possibility of taking disputes to a non-Jewish court which based its laws on human reason.

In the second interpretation, however, we run up against a difficulty. If "set before them" means to teach them with explanations, then this is surely more applicable to testimonies and statutes, which are difficult to understand, than to judgments. It is *obvious* that judgments should be explained. Whereas it would be a significant point to demand that testimonies (which can be comprehended, even if they are not necessitated, by reason) and statutes (which reason cannot grasp) should also be taught as far as possible through explanation and rational acceptance.

The same difficulty arises with the third explanation. It surely is not necessary to awaken the innermost reaches of the soul to be able to obey judgments, when reason is sufficient to compel adherence to them. But obedience to testimonies and statutes is not demanded by reason, and so it requires the arousal and assent of the inward self if it is to be done with a feeling of involvement rather than simply in blank response to coercion. Again, the connection between judgments and the phrase "before them" seems misplaced.

3. Action and Intention

An important truth about the Divine command is that "the principal thing is the act" [*Ethics of the Fathers* 1:17]. If, for example, a person has made all the appropriate mental preparations for putting on Tefillin but stops short of actually putting them on, he has not fulfilled the commandment. And if on the other hand he has put them on, but without the proper intentions, he has nonetheless performed the Mitzvah, and must make a blessing over it.

Despite this, it is also G-d's will that every facet of man be involved in the Mitzvah; not only his power of action and speech, but also his emotion, intellect, will and delight. This applies not only to the commandments which obviously involve feeling and understanding—like the Mitzvot of loving and fearing, believing in and knowing G-d—but to every command, including those which require a specific action. Each Mitzvah must be affirmed by the deepest reaches of man's being, especially by his delight, so that he performs it with joy[12] and a willing heart. This is true, furthermore, even of statutes, which by nature lie beyond his understanding. It is not enough to obey them in action only, as if he had no choice but to submit to G-d's will without sense or comprehension. Nor is it enough to say: I do not understand them, but G-d must certainly have a reason for decreeing them, and that is sufficient for me. For this attitude is not one of unconditional obedience. It is as if to say: I will obey only what is reasonable, but I will allow a mind greater than mine to decide what is reasonable and what is not. Instead, the true acceptance of statutes is one which goes beyond reason, and which makes no conditions. It is one in which the desire to serve G-d for His own sake is so strong that even the intellect positively assents to the call of He who is beyond it.

In the light of this we can understand the Rabbinical saying about the word "statute": "It is a decree before Me: You have no right to speculate about it."[13]

This is strange because, since "the principal thing is the act" it would have been more natural to say, "You have no right to *disobey* it." However, the saying implies that the physical act is not enough: It must be accompanied by the assent of the mind. And this means more than the silencing of doubt, more than the prudential acquiescence in G-d's wisdom. It means that simple faith floods his mind, leaving no room for second thoughts.

This is why statutes need the awakening of a Jew's innermost soul. Without it, there would still be room for "speculation" or doubt even if outwardly he continued to obey. With it, his thoughts and feelings are fired by an inner enthusiasm. And this is the connection between the second and third interpretations of "before them": "Inwardness" leads to "understanding," to an acceptance of the law by mind and heart.

But a question remains. Why are these insights attached by the Torah to judgments instead of statutes, where they would seem more appropriate? There is no difficulty in understanding judgments, and reason—without inwardness—is sufficient to lead a man to obey willingly.

4. Faith and Reason

The answer is to be found in another Rabbinic commentary to our verse. Noticing that the Sidra begins with the word "and" ("And these are the judgments. . . .") they said, "'And these' indicates a continuation of the previous subject."[14] In other words, the judgments, of which our Sidra speaks, are a continuation of the Ten Commandments, and were, like them, given at Sinai.

The Ten Commandments fall into two categories. The first commands concern the highest principles of the unity of G-d. But the others state simple, social laws like "Thou shalt not murder" and "Thou shalt not steal," judgments whose purpose is immediately intelligible. By fusing these extremes, the principles of faith and the judgments of reason, the Torah teaches that even commands such as "Thou shalt not steal" should be obeyed not simply because they are *reasonable* but because they are the will of He who said, "I am the L-rd thy G-d."

Thus, when the Rabbis said that the words "And these are the judgments. . . ." were a continuation of the Ten Commandments, they meant that these judgments should be obeyed not because they are understood, but because they were commanded by G-d at Sinai.

This explains the first interpretation, that one should not bring a Jewish dispute before a non-Jewish court. Even if the laws coincide in practice, a law which has its source in reason is not the same as one which is based on the words, "I am the L-rd thy G-d," and its verdicts do not emanate from Torah.

The third interpretation also becomes clear. Even judgments, which can be obeyed for the sake of reason, must be obeyed from the inwardness of the soul. Judgments must be obeyed like testimonies and statutes: Not from reason alone but from an inward response which animates every facet of one's being.

And this explains the force and subtlety of the second interpretation: That the judgments should be taught so that the pupil understands them. The point is that on the one hand they should not be regarded as the mere dictates of reason; on the other, they should not be thought of as irrational. They are to be obeyed *with* but not *because of* the mind's assent. The mind is to be shaped by what lies beyond it.

Why is human reason not sufficient in itself? Firstly because it has no absolute commitment: "Today it (one's evil inclination) says to him, Do this; tomorrow it tells him, Do that; until it bids him, Go and serve idols."[15] This description of the gradual erosion of spiritual standards is interpreted by the previous Lubavitcher Rebbe, Rabbi Yosef Yitzchak, thus: The Jew's evil impulse cannot begin with enticement to a forbidden act. Rather, it bids him "Do this," "Do that," i.e., a *Mitzvah*, but do it because your intellect and ego concur. Thus, gradually the framework is developed in one, whereby even a forbidden act is not excluded.

Secondly, because even though it might lead a man to obey judgments, it would not bring him to closeness with G-d. This is the difference between an act which is reasonable and an act which is a Mitzvah. "Mitzvah" means "connection": It is the link between man and G-d. Speaking of G-d's statutes and judgments, the Torah tells the Jew: "He shall live by them." If he brings the *whole* of his life—action, emotion, reason and inwardness—into the performance of a

Mitzvah because it was given at Sinai, he recreates Sinai: The meeting of man and G-d.

(*Source: Likkutei Sichot, Vol. III, pp. 895–901*)

Excerpt from Torah Studies: Discourses by the Lubavitcher Rebbe, Rabbi Menachem Mendel Schneerson, adapted by Rabbi Lord Jonathan Sacks (Brooklyn, N.Y.: Kehot Publication Society, 1996), pp. 112–118.

Reprinted with permission of Kehot Publication Society

Endnotes

1 Shemot 21:1.
2 Gittin, 88b. Cited by Rashi, Shemot 21:1.
3 Eruvin, 54b.
4 Based on the word *lifneihem* (before them), which literally means "before their faces."
5 *Torah Or, Mishpatim* .
6 Based on the verbal similarity between *lifneihem* (before them) and *lipnimiusam* (to their innermost selves).
7 Avodah Zarah, 2:7.
8 Zohar, Part III, 73a. *Likkutei Torah, Vayikra* , 5c.
9 Cf. supra, p. 30.
10 Cf. commentaries, Devarim 6:20.
11 Eruvin, 100b.
12 Cf. *Rambam*, end of *Hilchot Lulav*.
13 Rashi, Bamidbar 19:2.
14 *Shemot Rabbah*; *Tanchuma and Mechilta*, ad loc.
15 Shabbat, 105b.

INTENTION

BY RABBI ADIN EVEN-ISRAEL STEINSALTZ

According to Halacha, meditating on a word or idea is not the same as saying it. Even concentrating with *kavanah,* or spiritual alignment, does not release one from reciting the words of a prayer or blessing. On the other hand, if one does say the words but does not manage to align oneself spiritually, one has fulfilled one's obligations. To be sure, the religious demand is for both outer and inner participation; but—aside from the recitation of the first verse of the Shema prayer and the first benediction of the Amidah prayer—one does not have to repeat the prayer even if it was recited without proper *kavanah,* intention or directed concentration.

All of this may seem rather unspiritual, that is, for prayer to suffice with an external expression rather than with an inner intensity of purpose. The explanation is that the soul does not really need to do exercises, expressing love of God, and so forth; but the physical body does. Every mitzvah has its material component, an outer action in the world. The other components—mostly spiritual in essence—are not considered as having the same importance in terms of doing. Not that the spiritual components are without value; they simply have a different task or function. For, as we are well aware, nothing in the world of action can be accomplished only by good intentions. Man has been given a garden to cultivate, and no matter how sublime his thoughts about the plants (and even the possible beneficial effect these thoughts may have on the plants), yet it still seems to be necessary to do some hoeing, planting, and weeding. In other words, the task of man is connected with the essence of the world of substance, with those things that his

RABBI ADIN EVEN-ISRAEL STEINSALTZ, 1937–

Talmudist, author, and philosopher. Rabbi Even-Israel Steinsaltz is considered one of the foremost Jewish thinkers of the 20th century. Praised by *Time* magazine as a "once-in-a-millennium scholar," he has been awarded the Israel Prize for his contributions to Jewish study. He lives in Jerusalem and is the founder of the Israel Institute for Talmudic Publications, a society dedicated to the translation and elucidation of the Talmud.

soul cannot deal with in the abstract. Acknowledging this connection, we are stopped short by the paradox that there doesn't seem to be any need for the soul. Good thoughts and good intentions are ultimately no more than the scaffolding of the structure and not the structure itself.

On the other hand, as a Kabbalistic image puts it, the spiritual qualities of love and fear of God are like the two wings which enable every act to fly; without them, one remains bound to the earth. True, it is the purpose of man to descend and correct or repair the inadequacies of matter; but the lower the material problem, the higher he can rise in solving it, in effecting its Tikun. Ultimately, this may be reduced to the simple performance of mitzvot—the recitation of each of the letters of the Shema, the actual performance of certain basic actions, like offering a penny to charity, and so forth.

Now, it is known that God sustains the souls of all living things, giving to each its specific form and vitality. For all things possess a "soul" of some sort, having been given their existence by God. Nevertheless, the light of the Divine Soul in man is something else entirely.

The difference between the two kinds of soul lies in the degree of hiddenness of the light in the physical and in the whole process of being clothed in matter. Just as there are various stages of mental being—the first, of total concealment of light (the ignorant man), the second, where God is still hidden but is clothed or outwardly manifested in some definite shape (the humanist-atheist), and the third, which is the rational world of the philosophers, sufficing with systems and explanations of reality and leaving no room for God—so too, and how much more so, in terms of the soul, do the stages of the knowledge of God range from extreme darkness to light.

In any case, God is inevitably present, whether in nature or man, whether in body or in soul. One of the qualitative differences in the various forms of existence is in the capacity to sin. A more common classification, not necessarily qualitative, of the forms of existence includes: (1) non-consciousness (inorganic), (2) life (plant and animal), and (3) speech (man), where the difference is in the degree of life force in them. True, there is no relation between these two kinds of difference; something of no value in terms of good and evil may have considerable significance in terms of its potential for holiness and vice versa.

In mathematics, one can speak of an absolute number; besides this, one can determine the power or size of a specific number by adding zeroes or by giving the specific number a root or power sign. So too, in the moral life, one can relate to each action by itself—either it is a transgression or a mitzvah—and its power or significance is something that is measured by oneself, by what one gives to it in terms of intention, inner effort, joy, or participation. In performing an act of charity, for example, it is a matter of what it has cost one to obtain the money, the quality of the spiritual accompaniment to the act, and so forth. The differences between the levels of charity are far more than in the value of the money; the coin remains the same; it is a matter of the smile or the groan with which it is given. Thus, there is a meaningful distinction between body and soul, between intention and act.

Nevertheless, there is no contradiction between this and the fact that the physical performance of the mitzvah is paramount. Therefore, to return to a previous distinction, the body and the soul can be on the same level in terms of holiness (good and evil), but in terms of life force, the soul has infinitely more power than the body. There is more life in the spiritual soul than in any physical body, more "power" and potency. As for intellectual activity, its importance lies in that it accompanies the body. But a body that has a living soul in it lives far more intensely than one that has no soul. On the whole then, a mitzvah performed by someone with knowledge and understanding is a holy action and very different from one performed in ignorance.

This brings us back to the intention of the mitzvah, which gives the mitzvah wings and enables it to rise. The more love and fear of God involved in the act, the higher the level of the performance—ranging from a mitzvah that remains in the World of Action and changes something in the realm of good and evil to the mitzvah that rises above the world of matter and causes a shifting of things in the higher worlds.

Since the aim of human life on earth is precisely that—to redeem this world by bringing it up to some level of contact with the Divine aspiring to higher levels by proper intention is a vital aspect of this process of Tikun or correction. Thus, if a person has the opportunity to perform a mitzvah, either he chooses to do it only with his body, with its circumscribed field of force and of life, or he chooses to harness it to the power of his thought and feeling, giving it a certain orientation and additional potency. Like any act which one may perform—such as digging with one's hands or digging with a tractor—the action is the same, but its power is different. So too, the mitzvah, whether it is giving charity or reciting a blessing, is always itself; its strength and capacity depend on the life force one puts into it, and this is mainly a matter of the heart's intention and the thoughts of the knowledgeable mind. True, the intention without the body can have no effect whatsoever; but together with the physical act, it can effect a crucial change in the essence of the world.

Excerpt from Adin Even-Israel Steinsaltz, *The Long Shorter Way: Discourses on Chasidic Thought* (Jerusalem: Koren Publishers Jerusalem, Ltd., 1988).

Acknowledgments

"G-d said to Moses: 'Do not question the Jewish people's faith. They all are believers, the children of believers.'"

—TALMUD, SHABBAT 97A

"A Jew naturally recognizes the divine and senses the supernatural. Consequently, a Jew neither desires nor is able to be torn away from G-d."

—RABBI YOSEF YITSCHAK SCHNEERSOHN, CITED IN *HAYOM YOM*

Belief may be natural to the Jew and rooted in his or her deepest self, but it is often buried a little too deep. This results in uneasy tension: a Jew who longs to embrace belief but does not know how, who deconstructs faith into a hopeless tangle by embracing some tenets and rejecting others, or who equates Jewishness with acute discomfort.

The challenges to faith in contemporary life are unprecedented and multifold, rooted in confusions fueled by the pain of terrorism, the shadow of the Holocaust, the emotional dysfunction of a smartphone generation, the smugness of a highly scientific and informed society, and more.

The *Rohr Jewish Learning Institute* is meeting this critical challenge with *Wrestling with Faith*, a revolutionary course that speaks to today's Jew. Asking the burning questions that many are hesitant to articulate, *Wrestling with Faith* probes to the core of each issue honestly, without fear or obfuscation. More than any other course previously offered, participants are invited to wrestle with their faith and are dared to emerge inspired for a lifetime.

We are grateful to the following individuals for helping shape this innovative course:

We extend our thanks to **Rabbis Mordechai Dinerman** and **Naftali Silberberg,** co-directors of the JLI Curriculum Department and the Flagship editorial team; **Rabbi Dr. Shmuel Klatzkin**, JLI's senior editor; and **Rabbi Zalman Abraham**, who skillfully provides the vision for strategic branding and marketing of JLI course offerings.

We are also grateful to **Rabbis Lazer Gurkow, Naftali Silberberg, Boruch Werdiger**, and **Yosi Wolf**, who wrote and edited the lessons, as well as **Rabbis Yakov Gershon** and **Benyomin Walters**, for extensively researching the topics for this course and making substantial contributions to course content.

Rabbi Chaim Block, Rabbi Mendel Cohen, Rabbi Yosef Levine, Rabbi Mendel Lifshitz, Mrs. Esther Schanowitz, and **Mrs. Mindy Wallach**, members of the JLI Editorial Board, provided many useful suggestions that enhanced the course and ensured its suitability for a wide range of students.

Rivki Mockin streamlined the curriculum process and ensured the smoothness and timeliness of the product, and **Chana Dechter,** JLI Flagship's administrator and project manager, contributed immeasurably to the production and professionalism of the entire project. **Zelda Abelsky** and **Rabbi Michoel Shapiro** provided editorial assistance, and **Shterna Karp, Mimi Palace, Shmuel Telsner, Ya'akovah Weber,** and **Rachel Witty** enhanced the quality and accuracy of the writing with their proofreading. **Shternie Morozow** designed the textbooks with taste and expertise, and the textbook images were researched and selected by **Rabbi Zalman Abraham** and **Chany Tauber**. **Mendel Sirota** directed the book's publication and distribution.

Mushka Minsky oversaw multimedia production for the course. **Mushka Druk, Baila Pruss,** and **Chany Tauber** designed the aesthetically pleasing PowerPoints, and **Moshe Raskin** and **Getzy Raskin** produced the videos; the video scripts were masterfully written by **Rabbi Yaakov Paley** and **Tonia Lazaroff.**

We are immensely grateful for the encouragement of JLI's visionary chairman, and vice-chairman of *Merkos L'Inyonei Chinuch*—Lubavitch World Headquarters, **Rabbi Moshe Kotlarsky**. Rabbi Kotlarsky has been highly instrumental in building the infrastructure for the expansion of Chabad's international network and is also the architect of scores of initiatives and services to help Chabad representatives across the globe succeed in their mission. We are blessed to have the unwavering support of JLI's principal benefactor, **Mr. George Rohr**, who is fully invested in our work, continues to be instrumental in JLI's monumental growth and expansion, and is largely responsible for the Jewish renaissance that is being spearheaded by JLI and its affiliates across the globe.

The commitment and sage direction of JLI's dedicated Executive Board—**Rabbis Chaim Block, Hesh Epstein, Ronnie Fine, Yosef Gansburg, Shmuel Kaplan, Yisrael Rice**, and **Avrohom Sternberg**—and the countless hours they devote to the development of JLI are what drive the vision, growth, and tremendous success of the organization.

Finally, JLI represents an incredible partnership of more than 1,400 *shluchim* and *shluchot* in more than one thousand locations across the globe, who contribute their time and talent to further Jewish adult education. We thank them for generously sharing feedback and making suggestions that steer JLI's development and growth. They are our most valuable critics and our most cherished contributors.

Inspired by the call of the **Lubavitcher Rebbe**, of righteous memory, it is the mandate of the Rohr JLI to **provide a community of learning** for all Jews throughout the world where they can participate in their precious heritage of Torah learning and experience its rewards. May this course succeed in fulfilling this sacred charge!

On behalf of the Rohr Jewish Learning Institute,

RABBI EFRAIM MINTZ
Executive Director

RABBI YISRAEL RICE
Chairman, Editorial Board

12 Tamuz, 5778

The Rohr Jewish Learning Institute

AN AFFILIATE OF MERKOS L'INYONEI CHINUCH,
THE EDUCATIONAL ARM OF THE CHABAD-LUBAVITCH MOVEMENT
822 EASTERN PARKWAY, BROOKLYN, NY 11213

JLI INTERNATIONAL

Rabbi Avrohom Sternberg
CHAIRMAN

Rabbi Dubi Rabinowitz
DIRECTOR

Rabbi Berry Piekarski
ADMINISTRATOR

Rabbi Levi Kaplan
PROJECT MANAGER

Rabbi Yosef Yitzchok Noyman
ADMINISTRATOR, JLI ISRAEL
IN PARTNERSHIP WITH
MIVTZA TORAH—ISRAEL

Rabbi Eli Wolf
ADMINISTRATOR, JLI IN THE CIS
IN PARTNERSHIP WITH
THE FEDERATION OF JEWISH
COMMUNITIES OF THE CIS

Rabbi Shevach Zlatopolsky
EDITOR, JLI IN THE CIS

Rabbi Nochum Schapiro
REGIONAL REPRESENTATIVE,
AUSTRALIA

Rabbi Avraham Golovacheov
REGIONAL REPRESENTATIVE,
GERMANY

Rabbi Shmuel Katzman
REGIONAL REPRESENTATIVE,
NETHERLANDS

Rabbi Avrohom Steinmetz
REGIONAL REPRESENTATIVE,
BRAZIL

Rabbi Bentzi Sudak
REGIONAL REPRESENTATIVE,
UNITED KINGDOM

Rabbi Mendel Edelman
LIAISON TO FRENCH-SPEAKING
COUNTRIES

NATIONAL JEWISH RETREAT

Rabbi Hesh Epstein
CHAIRMAN

Mrs. Shaina B. Mintz
DIRECTOR

Mrs. Mushka Minsky
PROJECT MANAGER

Bruce Backman
HOTEL LIAISON

Rabbi Menachem Klein
PROGRAM COORDINATOR

Rabbi Shmuly Karp
SHLUCHIM LIAISON

Rabbi Mendel Rosenfeld
LOGISTIC COORDINATOR

Rochel Karp
Aliza Landes
Mrs. Mussie Sputz
SERVICE AND SUPPORT

JLI LAND & SPIRIT
ISRAEL EXPERIENCE

Rabbi Shmuly Karp
DIRECTOR

Mrs. Shaina B. Mintz
ADMINISTRATOR

Rabbi Yechiel Baitelman
Rabbi Dovid Flinkenstein
Rabbi Chanoch Kaplan
Rabbi Levi Klein
Rabbi Mendel Lifshitz
Rabbi Mendy Mangel
Rabbi Sholom Raichik
Rabbi Ephraim Silverman
STEERING COMMITTEE

SHABBAT IN THE HEIGHTS

Rabbi Shmuly Karp
DIRECTOR

Mrs. Shulamis Nadler
SERVICE AND SUPPORT

Rabbi Chaim Hanoka
CHAIRMAN

Rabbi Mordechai Dinerman
Rabbi Zalman Marcus
STEERING COMMITTEE

MYSHIUR
ADVANCED LEARNING INITIATIVE

Rabbi Shmuel Kaplan
CHAIRMAN

Rabbi Levi Kaplan
DIRECTOR

TORAHCAFE.COM
ONLINE LEARNING

Rabbi Levi Kaplan
DIRECTOR

Rabbi Mendy Elishevitz
WEBSITE DEVELOPMENT

Moshe Levin
CONTENT MANAGER

Avrohom Shimon Ezagui
FILMING

MACHON SHMUEL
THE SAMI ROHR RESEARCH INSTITUTE

Rabbi Avrohom Bergstein
DEAN

Rabbi Zalman Korf
ADMINISTRATOR

Rabbi Gedalya Oberlander
Rabbi Chaim Rapoport
Rabbi Levi Yitzchak Raskin
Rabbi Chaim Schapiro
Rabbi Moshe Miller
RABBINIC ADVISORY BOARD

Rabbi Yakov Gershon
RESEARCH FELLOW

FOUNDING DEPARTMENT HEADS

Rabbi Mendel Bell
Rabbi Zalman Charytan
Rabbi Mendel Druk
Rabbi Menachem Gansburg
Rabbi Meir Hecht
Rabbi Yoni Katz
Rabbi Chaim Zalman Levy
Rabbi Benny Rapoport
Dr. Chana Silberstein
Rabbi Elchonon Tenenbaum
Rabbi Mendy Weg

Faculty Directory

ALABAMA

BIRMINGHAM
Rabbi Yossi Friedman 205.970.0100

MOBILE
Rabbi Yosef Goldwasser 251.265.1213

ALASKA

ANCHORAGE
Rabbi Yosef Greenberg
Rabbi Mendy Greenberg 907.357.8770

ARIZONA

CHANDLER
Rabbi Mendy Deitsch 480.855.4333

FLAGSTAFF
Rabbi Dovie Shapiro 928.255.5756

FOUNTAIN HILLS
Rabbi Mendy Lipskier 480.776.4763

ORO VALLEY
Rabbi Ephraim Zimmerman 520.477.8672

PHOENIX
Rabbi Zalman Levertov
Rabbi Yossi Friedman 602.944.2753

SCOTTSDALE
Rabbi Yossi Levertov 480.998.1410

TUCSON
Rabbi Yehuda Ceitlin 520.881.7956

ARKANSAS

LITTLE ROCK
Rabbi Pinchus Ciment 501.217.0053

CALIFORNIA

AGOURA HILLS
Rabbi Moshe Bryski
Rabbi Yisroel Levine 818.991.0991

BAKERSFIELD
Rabbi Shmuli Schlanger
Mrs. Esther Schlanger 661.331.1695

BEL AIR
Rabbi Chaim Mentz 310.475.5311

BERKELEY
Rabbi Yosef Romano 510.396.4448

BURBANK
Rabbi Shmuly Kornfeld 818.954.0070

CARLSBAD
Rabbi Yeruchem Eilfort
Mrs. Nechama Eilfort 760.943.8891

CHATSWORTH
Rabbi Yossi Spritzer 818.718.0777

CONTRA COSTA
Rabbi Dovber Berkowitz 925.937.4101

CORONADO
Rabbi Eli Fradkin 619.365.4728

ENCINO
Rabbi Aryeh Herzog 818.784.9986
Chapter founded by Rabbi Joshua Gordon, OBM

FOLSOM
Rabbi Yossi Grossbaum 916.608.9811

FREMONT
Rabbi Moshe Fuss 510.300.4090

GLENDALE
Rabbi Simcha Backman 818.240.2750

HUNTINGTON BEACH
Rabbi Aron David Berkowitz 714.846.2285

LA JOLLA
Rabbi Baruch Shalom Ezagui 858.455.5433

LOMITA
Rabbi Eli Hecht
Rabbi Sholom Pinson 310.326.8234

LONG BEACH
Rabbi Abba Perelmuter 562.621.9828

LOS ANGELES
Rabbi Leibel Korf 323.660.5177

MALIBU
Rabbi Levi Cunin 310.456.6588

MARINA DEL REY
Rabbi Danny Yiftach-Hashem
Rabbi Dovid Yiftach 310.859.0770

NORTH HOLLYWOOD
Rabbi Nachman Abend 818.989.9539

NORTHRIDGE
Rabbi Eli Rivkin 818.368.3937

OJAI
Rabbi Mordechai Nemtzov 805.613.7181

PACIFIC PALISADES
Rabbi Zushe Cunin 310.454.7783

PALO ALTO
Rabbi Yosef Levin
Rabbi Ber Rosenblatt 650.424.9800

PASADENA
Rabbi Chaim Hanoka
Rabbi Sholom Stiefel 626.539.4578

PLEASANTON
Rabbi Raleigh Resnick 925.846.0700

POWAY
Rabbi Mendel Goldstein 858.208.6613

RANCHO MIRAGE
Rabbi Shimon H. Posner 760.770.7785

RANCHO PALOS VERDES
Rabbi Yitzchok Magalnic 310.544.5544

RANCHO S. FE
Rabbi Levi Raskin 858.756.7571

REDONDO BEACH
Rabbi Yossi Mintz
Rabbi Zalman Gordon 310.214.4999

S. CLEMENTE
Rabbi Menachem M. Slavin 949.489.0723

S. CRUZ
Rabbi Yochanan Friedman 831.454.0101

S. DIEGO
Rabbi Rafi Andrusier 619.387.8770
Rabbi Motte Fradkin 858.547.0076

S. FRANCISCO
Rabbi Shlomo Zarchi 415.752.2866

S. LUIS OBISPO
Rabbi Chaim Leib Hilel 805.229.1836

S. MONICA
Rabbi Boruch Rabinowitz 310.394.5699

S. RAFAEL
Rabbi Yisrael Rice 415.492.1666

SOUTH LAKE TAHOE
Rabbi Mordechai Richler 530.314.7677

SUNNYVALE
Rabbi Yisroel Hecht 408.720.0553

TUSTIN
Rabbi Yehoshua Eliezrie 714.508.2150

VENTURA
Rabbi Yakov Latowicz 805.658.7441

WEST HOLLYWOOD
Rabbi Mordechai Kirschenbaum 310.275.1215

WEST LOS ANGELES
Rabbi Mordechai Zaetz 424.652.8742

YORBA LINDA
Rabbi Dovid Eliezrie 714.693.0770

COLORADO

ASPEN
Rabbi Mendel Mintz 970.544.3770

DENVER
Rabbi Yossi Serebryanski 303.744.9699

FORT COLLINS
Rabbi Yerachmiel Gorelik 970.407.1613

HIGHLANDS RANCH
Rabbi Avraham Mintz 303.694.9119

LONGMONT
Rabbi Yakov Borenstein 303.678.7595

VAIL
Rabbi Dovid Mintz 970.476.7887

WESTMINSTER
Rabbi Benjy Brackman 303.429.5177

CONNECTICUT

FAIRFIELD
Rabbi Shlame Landa 203.373.7551

GLASTONBURY
Rabbi Yosef Wolvovsky 860.659.2422

GREENWICH
Rabbi Yossi Deren
Rabbi Menachem Feldman 203.629.9059

NEW LONDON
Rabbi Avrohom Sternberg 860.437.8000

STAMFORD
Rabbi Yisrael Deren
Rabbi Levi Mendelow 203.3.CHABAD

WEST HARTFORD
Rabbi Shaya Gopin 860.232.1116

WESTPORT
Rabbi Yehuda L. Kantor 203.226.8584

DELAWARE

WILMINGTON
Rabbi Chuni Vogel 302.529.9900

DISTRICT OF COLUMBIA

WASHINGTON
Rabbi Levi Shemtov
Rabbi Shua Hecht 202.332.5600

FLORIDA

ALTAMONTE SPRINGS
Rabbi Mendy Bronstein 407.280.0535

BAL HARBOUR
Rabbi Dov Schochet 305.868.1411

BOCA RATON
Rabbi Zalman Bukiet
Rabbi Arele Gopin 561.994.6257
Rabbi Moishe Denburg 561.526.5760
Rabbi Ruvi New 561.394.9770

BOYNTON BEACH
Rabbi Yosef Yitzchok Raichik 561.732.4633

BRADENTON
Rabbi Menachem Bukiet 941.388.9656

SOUTHWEST BROWARD COUNTY
Rabbi Aryeh Schwartz 954.252.1770

CAPE CORAL
Rabbi Yossi Labkowski 239.963.4770

CORAL GABLES
Rabbi Avrohom Stolik 305.490.7572

CORAL SPRINGS
Rabbi Yankie Denburg 954.471.8646

DELRAY BEACH
Rabbi Sholom Ber Korf 561.496.6228

FLEMING ISLAND
Rabbi Shmuly Feldman 904.290.1017

FORT LAUDERDALE
Rabbi Yitzchok Naparstek 954.568.1190

FORT MYERS
Rabbi Yitzchok Minkowicz
Mrs. Nechama Minkowicz 239.433.7708

HALLANDALE BEACH
Rabbi Mordy Feiner 954.458.1877

HOLLYWOOD
Rabbi Leizer Barash 954.965.9933
Rabbi Leibel Kudan 954.801.3367

KENDALL
Rabbi Yossi Harlig 305.234.5654

LAKELAND
Rabbi Moshe Lazaros 863.510.5968

LONGWOOD
Rabbi Yanky Majesky 407.636.5994

MAITLAND
Rabbi Sholom Dubov
Rabbi Levik Dubov 470.644.2500

MIAMI
Rabbi Yakov Fellig 305.445.5444

MIAMI BEACH
Rabbi Yisroel Frankforter 305.534.3895

N. MIAMI BEACH
Rabbi Eli Laufer 305.770.4412

OCALA
Rabbi Yossi Hecht 352.330.4466

ORLANDO
Rabbi Yosef Konikov 407.354.3660

ORMOND BEACH
Rabbi Asher Farkash 386.672.9300

PALM BEACH GARDENS
Rabbi Dovid Vigler 561.624.2223

PALM CITY
Rabbi Shlomo Uminer 772.288.0606

PALM HARBOR
Rabbi Pinchas Adler 727.789.0408

PALMETTO BAY
Rabbi Zalman Gansburg 786.282.0413

PARKLAND
Rabbi Mendy Gutnick 954.796.7330

PEMBROKE PINES
Rabbi Mordechai Andrusier 954.874.2280

PLANTATION
Rabbi Pinchas Taylor 954.644.9177

PONTE VEDRA BEACH
Rabbi Nochum Kurinsky 904.543.9301

S. AUGUSTINE
Rabbi Levi Vogel 904.521.8664

S. PETERSBURG
Rabbi Alter Korf 727.344.4900

SARASOTA
Rabbi Chaim Shaul Steinmetz 941.925.0770

SATELLITE BEACH
Rabbi Zvi Konikov 321.777.2770

SOUTH PALM BEACH
Rabbi Leibel Stolik 561.889.3499

SOUTH TAMPA
Rabbi Mendy Dubrowski 813.922.1723

SUNNY ISLES BEACH
Rabbi Alexander Kaller 305.803.5315

TALLAHASSEE
Rabbi Schneur Oirechman 850.523.9294

VENICE
Rabbi Sholom Ber Schmerling 941.493.2770

WELLINGTON
Rabbi Mendy Muskal 561.333.4663

WESTON
Rabbi Yisroel Spalter 954.349.6565

WEST PALM BEACH
Rabbi Yoel Gancz 561.659.7770

GEORGIA

ALPHARETTA
Rabbi Hirshy Minkowicz 770.410.9000

ATLANTA
Rabbi Yossi New
Rabbi Isser New 404.843.2464

ATLANTA: INTOWN
Rabbi Eliyahu Schusterman
Rabbi Ari Sollish 404.898.0434

CUMMING
Rabbi Levi Mentz 310.666.2218

GWINNETT
Rabbi Yossi Lerman 678.595.0196

MARIETTA
Rabbi Ephraim Silverman 770.565.4412

IDAHO

BOISE
Rabbi Mendel Lifshitz 208.853.9200

ILLINOIS

CHICAGO
Rabbi Mendy Benhiyoun 312.498.7704
Rabbi Meir Hecht 312.714.4655
Rabbi Dovid Kotlarsky 773.495.7127
Rabbi Yosef Moscowitz 773.772.3770
Rabbi Levi Notik 773.274.5123

DES PLAINES
Rabbi Lazer Hershkovich 224.392.4442

ELGIN
Rabbi Mendel Shemtov 847.440.4486

GLENVIEW
Rabbi Yishaya Benjaminson 847.910.1738

HIGHLAND PARK
Mrs. Michla Schanowitz 847.266.0770

NORTHBROOK
Rabbi Meir Moscowitz 847.564.8770

OAK PARK
Rabbi Yitzchok Bergstein 708.524.1530

PEORIA
Rabbi Eli Langsam 309.692.2250

ROCKFORD
Rabbi Yecheskel Rothman 815.596.0032

SKOKIE
Rabbi Yochanan Posner 847.677.1770

VERNON HILLS
Rabbi Shimmy Susskind 847.984.2919

WILMETTE
Rabbi Dovid Flinkenstein 847.251.7707

INDIANA

INDIANAPOLIS
Rabbi Avraham Grossbaum
Rabbi Dr. Shmuel Klatzkin 317.251.5573

IOWA

BETTENDORF
Rabbi Shneur Cadaner 563.355.1065

KANSAS

OVERLAND PARK
Rabbi Mendy Wineberg 913.649.4852

KENTUCKY

LOUISVILLE
Rabbi Avrohom Litvin 502.459.1770

LOUISIANA

BATON ROUGE
Rabbi Peretz Kazen 225.267.7047

METAIRIE
Rabbi Yossie Nemes
Rabbi Mendel Ceitlin 504.454.2910

MARYLAND

BALTIMORE
Rabbi Velvel Belinsky 410.764.5000
Classes in Russian

BEL AIR
Rabbi Kushi Schusterman 443.353.9718

BETHESDA
Rabbi Sender Geisinsky 301.913.9777

CLARKSBURG
Rabbi Yehuda Glick 301.337.0514

COLUMBIA
Rabbi Hillel Baron
Rabbi Yosef Chaim Sufrin 410.740.2424

FREDERICK
Rabbi Boruch Labkowski 301.996.3659

GAITHERSBURG
Rabbi Sholom Raichik 301.926.3632

OLNEY
Rabbi Bentzy Stolik 301.660.6770

OWINGS MILLS
Rabbi Nochum H. Katsenelenbogen 410.356.5156

POTOMAC
Rabbi Mendel Bluming 301.983.4200
Rabbi Mendel Kaplan 301.983.1485

ROCKVILLE
Rabbi Moishe Kavka 301.836.1242

MASSACHUSETTS

BOSTON
Rabbi Yosef Zaklos 617.297.7282

CAPE COD
Rabbi Yekusiel Alperowitz 508.775.2324

HINGHAM
Rabbi Levi Lezell 617.862.2770

LONGMEADOW
Rabbi Yakov Wolff 413.567.8665

NEWTON
Rabbi Shalom Ber Prus 617.244.1200

SUDBURY
Rabbi Yisroel Freeman 978.443.0110

SWAMPSCOTT
Rabbi Yossi Lipsker
Rabbi Yisroel Baron 781.581.3833

MICHIGAN

ANN ARBOR
Rabbi Aharon Goldstein 734.995.3276

BLOOMFIELD HILLS
Rabbi Levi Dubov 248.949.6210

GRAND RAPIDS
Rabbi Mordechai Haller 616.957.0770

WEST BLOOMFIELD
Rabbi Elimelech Silberberg 248.855.6170

MINNESOTA

MINNETONKA
Rabbi Mordechai Grossbaum
Rabbi Shmuel Silberstein 952.929.9922

S. PAUL
Rabbi Shneur Zalman Bendet 651.998.9298

MISSOURI

S. LOUIS
Rabbi Yosef Landa 314.725.0400

NEVADA

LAS VEGAS
Rabbi Yosef Rivkin 702.217.2170

SUMMERLIN
Rabbi Yisroel Schanowitz
Rabbi Tzvi Bronchtain 702.855.0770

NEW JERSEY

BASKING RIDGE
Rabbi Mendy Herson
Rabbi Mendel Shemtov 908.604.8844

CHERRY HILL
Rabbi Mendel Mangel 856.874.1500

CLINTON
Rabbi Eli Kornfeld 908.623.7000

FAIR LAWN
Rabbi Avrohom Bergstein 201.362.2712

FORT LEE
Rabbi Meir Konikov 201.886.1238

FRANKLIN LAKES
Rabbi Chanoch Kaplan 201.848.0449

GREATER MERCER COUNTY
Rabbi Dovid Dubov
Rabbi Yaakov Chaiton 609.213.4136

HASKELL
Rabbi Mendy Gurkov 201.696.7609

HOLMDEL
Rabbi Shmaya Galperin 732.772.1998

MADISON
Rabbi Shalom Lubin 973.377.0707

MANALAPAN
Rabbi Boruch Chazanow
Rabbi Levi Wolosow 732.972.3687

MEDFORD
Rabbi Yitzchok Kahan 609.451.3522

MOUNTAIN LAKES
Rabbi Levi Dubinsky 973.551.1898

MULLICA HILL
Rabbi Avrohom Richler 856.733.0770

OLD TAPPAN
Rabbi Mendy Lewis 201.767.4008

ROCKAWAY
Rabbi Asher Herson
Rabbi Mordechai Baumgarten 973.625.1525

RUTHERFORD
Rabbi Yitzchok Lerman 347.834.7500

SCOTCH PLAINS
Rabbi Avrohom Blesofsky 908.790.0008

SOUTH BRUNSWICK
Rabbi Levi Azimov 732.398.9492

TEANECK
Rabbi Ephraim Simon 201.907.0686

TENAFLY
Rabbi Mordechai Shain 201.871.1152

TOMS RIVER
Rabbi Moshe Gourarie 732.349.4199

WEST ORANGE
Rabbi Mendy Kasowitz 973.325.6311

WOODCLIFF LAKE
Rabbi Dov Drizin 201.476.0157

NEW MEXICO

LAS CRUCES
Rabbi Bery Schmukler 575.524.1330

NEW YORK

BAY SHORE
Rabbi Shimon Sztillerman 631.913.8770

BEDFORD
Rabbi Arik Wolf 914.666.6065

BINGHAMTON
Mrs. Rivkah Slonim 607.797.0015

BRIGHTON BEACH
Rabbi Moshe Winner 718.946.9833

CEDARHURST
Rabbi Zalman Wolowik 516.295.2478

COMMACK
Rabbi Mendel Teldon 631.543.3343

DOBBS FERRY
Rabbi Benjy Silverman 914.693.6100

EAST HAMPTON
Rabbi Leibel Baumgarten
Rabbi Mendy Goldberg 631.329.5800

ELLENVILLE
Rabbi Shlomie Deren 845.647.4450

FOREST HILLS
Rabbi Yossi Mendelson 917.861.9726

GREAT NECK
Rabbi Yoseph Geisinsky 516.487.4554

KINGSTON
Rabbi Yitzchok Hecht 845.334.9044

LARCHMONT
Rabbi Mendel Silberstein 914.834.4321

LITTLE NECK
Rabbi Eli Shifrin 718.423.1235

LONG BEACH
Rabbi Eli Goodman 516.897.2473

NYC KEHILATH JESHURUN
Rabbi Elie Weinstock 212.774.5636

NYACK
Rabbi Chaim Zvi Ehrenreich 845.356.6686

OCEANSIDE
Rabbi Levi Gurkow 516.764.7385

OSSINING
Rabbi Dovid Labkowski 914.923.2522

OYSTER BAY
Rabbi Shmuel Lipszyc
Rabbi Shalom Lipszyc 347.853.9992

PARK SLOPE
Rabbi Menashe Wolf 347.957.1291

PORT WASHINGTON
Rabbi Shalom Paltiel 516.767.8672

PROSPECT HEIGHTS
Rabbi Mendy Hecht 347.622.3599

ROCHESTER
Rabbi Nechemia Vogel 585.271.0330

ROSLYN
Rabbi Yaakov Reiter 516.484.8185

SEA GATE
Rabbi Chaim Brikman 917.975.2792

SOUTHAMPTON
Rabbi Chaim Pape 917.627.4865

STATEN ISLAND
Rabbi Mendy Katzman 718.370.8953

STONY BROOK
Rabbi Shalom Ber Cohen 631.585.0521

SUFFERN
Rabbi Shmuel Gancz 845.368.1889

YORKTOWN HEIGHTS
Rabbi Yehuda Heber 914.962.1111

NORTH CAROLINA

ASHEVILLE
Rabbi Shaya Susskind 828.505.0746

CARY
Rabbi Yisroel Cotlar 919.651.9710

CHAPEL HILL
Rabbi Zalman Bluming 919.630.5129

CHARLOTTE
Rabbi Yossi Groner
Rabbi Shlomo Cohen 704.366.3984

GREENSBORO
Rabbi Yosef Plotkin 336.617.8120

RALEIGH
Rabbi Pinchas Herman
Rabbi Lev Cotlar 919.637.6950

OHIO

BEACHWOOD
Rabbi Shmuli Friedman 216.282.0112

BLUE ASH
Rabbi Yisroel Mangel 513.793.5200

COLUMBUS
Rabbi Yitzi Kaltmann 614.294.3296

DAYTON
Rabbi Nochum Mangel
Rabbi Shmuel Klatzkin 937.643.0770

OKLAHOMA

OKLAHOMA CITY
Rabbi Ovadia Goldman 405.524.4800

TULSA
Rabbi Yehuda Weg 918.492.4499

OREGON

PORTLAND
Rabbi Mordechai Wilhelm 503.977.9947

SALEM
Rabbi Avrohom Yitzchok Perlstein 503.383.9569

PENNSYLVANIA

AMBLER
Rabbi Shaya Deitsch 215.591.9310

BALA CYNWYD
Rabbi Shraga Sherman 610.660.9192

LAFAYETTE HILL
Rabbi Yisroel Kotlarsky 484.533.7009

LANCASTER
Rabbi Elazar Green 717.368.6565

MONROEVILLE
Rabbi Mendy Schapiro 412.372.1000

NEWTOWN
Rabbi Aryeh Weinstein 215.497.9925

PHILADELPHIA: CENTER CITY
Rabbi Yochonon Goldman 215.238.2100

PITTSBURGH
Rabbi Yisroel Altein .... 412.422.7300 EXT. 269

PITTSBURGH: SOUTH HILLS
Rabbi Mendy Rosenblum 412.278.3693

RYDAL
Rabbi Zushe Gurevitz 267.536.5757

WYNNEWOOD
Rabbi Moishe Brennan 610.529.9011

PUERTO RICO

CAROLINA
Rabbi Mendel Zarchi 787.253.0894

RHODE ISLAND

WARWICK
Rabbi Yossi Laufer 401.884.7888

SOUTH CAROLINA

COLUMBIA
Rabbi Hesh Epstein
Rabbi Levi Marrus 803.782.1831

MYRTLE BEACH
Rabbi Doron Aizenman 843.448.0035

TENNESSEE

CHATTANOOGA
Rabbi Shaul Perlstein 423.490.1106

MEMPHIS
Rabbi Levi Klein 901.754.0404

TEXAS

ARLINGTON
Rabbi Levi Gurevitch 817.451.1171

BELLAIRE
Rabbi Yossi Zaklikofsky 713.839.8887

DALLAS
Rabbi Mendel Dubrawsky
Rabbi Moshe Naparstek 972.818.0770

FORT WORTH
Rabbi Dov Mandel 817.263.7701

FRISCO
Rabbi Mendy Kesselman 214.460.7773

HOUSTON
Rabbi Dovid Goldstein
Rabbi Zally Lazarus 281.589.7188
Rabbi Moishe Traxler 713.774.0300

HOUSTON: RICE UNIVERSITY AREA
Rabbi Eliezer Lazaroff 713.522.2004

LEAGUE CITY
Rabbi Yitzchok Schmukler 281.724.1554

MISSOURI CITY
Rabbi Mendel Feigenson 832.758.0685

PLANO
Rabbi Mendel Block
Rabbi Yehudah Horowitz 972.596.8270

S. ANTONIO
Rabbi Chaim Block
Rabbi Levi Teldon 210.492.1085

THE WOODLANDS
Rabbi Mendel Blecher 281.719.5213

UTAH

SALT LAKE CITY
Rabbi Benny Zippel 801.467.7777

VERMONT

BURLINGTON
Rabbi Yitzchok Raskin 802.658.5770

VIRGINIA

ALEXANDRIA/ARLINGTON
Rabbi Mordechai Newman 703.370.2774

FAIRFAX
Rabbi Leibel Fajnland 703.426.1980

GAINESVILLE
Rabbi Shmuel Perlstein 571.445.0342

NORFOLK
Rabbi Aaron Margolin
Rabbi Levi Brashevitzky 757.616.0770

TYSONS CORNER
Rabbi Chezzy Deitsch 703.829.5770
Chapter founded by Rabbi Levi Deitsch, OBM

WASHINGTON

BELLINGHAM
Rabbi Yosef Truxton 617.640.8841

MERCER ISLAND
Rabbi Elazar Bogomilsky 206.527.1411

SPOKANE COUNTY
Rabbi Yisroel Hahn 509.443.0770

WISCONSIN

KENOSHA
Rabbi Tzali Wilschanski 262.359.0770

MADISON
Rabbi Avremel Matusof 608.231.3450

MILWAUKEE
Rabbi Mendel Shmotkin 414.961.6100

WAUKESHA
Rabbi Levi Brook 925.708.4203

ARGENTINA

BUENOS AIRES
Mrs. Chani Gorowitz 54.11.4865.0445
Rabbi Mendi Mizrahi 54.11.4963.1221
Rabbi Mendy Gurevitch 55.11.4545.7771
Rabbi Pinhas Sudry 54.1.4822.2285
Rabbi Shloimi Setton 54.11.4982.8637
Rabbi Shiele Plotka 54.11.4634.3111
Rabbi Yosef Levy 54.11.4504.1908

SALTA
Rabbi Rafael Tawil 54.387.421.4947

AUSTRALIA

NEW SOUTH WALES

DOUBLE BAY
Rabbi Yanky Berger
Rabbi Yisroel Dolnikov 612.9327.1644

QUEENSLAND

BRISBANE
Rabbi Levi Jaffe 617.3843.6770

DOVER HEIGHTS
Rabbi Motti Feldman 614.0400.8572

NORTH SHORE
Rabbi Nochum Schapiro
Mrs. Fruma Schapiro 612.9488.9548

VICTORIA

MOORABBIN
Rabbi Elisha Greenbaum 614.0349.0434

WESTERN AUSTRALIA

PERTH
Rabbi Shalom White 618.9275.2106

AZERBAIJAN

BAKU
Mrs. Chavi Segal 994.12.597.91.90

BELARUS

BOBRUISK
Mrs. Mina Hababo 375.29.104.3230

MINSK
Rabbi Shneur Deitsch
Mrs. Bassie Deitsch 375.29.330.6675

BRAZIL

CURITIBA
Rabbi Mendy Labkowski 55.41.3079.1338

S. PAULO
Rabbi Avraham Steinmetz 55.11.3081.3081

CANADA

ALBERTA

CALGARY
Rabbi Mordechai Groner 403.281.3770

EDMONTON
Rabbi Ari Drelich
Rabbi Mendy Blachman 780.200.5770

BRITISH COLUMBIA

KELOWNA
Rabbi Shmuly Hecht 250.575.5384

RICHMOND
Rabbi Yechiel Baitelman 604.277.6427

VANCOUVER
Rabbi Dovid Rosenfeld 604.266.1313

VICTORIA
Rabbi Meir Kaplan 250.595.7656

MANITOBA

WINNIPEG
Rabbi Shmuel Altein 204.339.8737

ONTARIO

LAWRENCE/EGLINTON
Rabbi Menachem Gansburg 416.546.8770

MAPLE
Rabbi Yechezkel Deren 647.883.6372

MISSISSAUGA
Rabbi Yitzchok Slavin 905.820.4432

NIAGARA FALLS
Rabbi Zalman Zaltzman 905.356.7200

OTTAWA
Rabbi Menachem M. Blum 613.843.7770

RICHMOND HILL
Rabbi Mendel Bernstein 905.770.7700

GREATER TORONTO REGIONAL OFFICE & THORNHILL
Rabbi Yossi Gansburg 905.731.7000

THORNHILL WOODS
Rabbi Chaim Hildeshaim 905.881.1919

WATERLOO
Rabbi Moshe Goldman 226.338.7770

WHITBY
Rabbi Tzali Borenstein 905.493.9007

YORK MILLS
Rabbi Levi Gansburg 416.551.9391

QUEBEC

HAMPSTEAD
Rabbi Moshe New
Rabbi Berel Bell 514.739.0770

MONTREAL
Rabbi Ronnie Fine
Pesach Nussbaum 514.738.3434

S. LAZARE
Rabbi Nochum Labkowski 514.436.7426

TOWN OF MOUNT ROYAL
Rabbi Moshe Krasnanski
Rabbi Shneur Zalman Rader 514.342.1770

WESTMOUNT
Rabbi Yossi Shanowitz
Mrs. Devorah Leah Shanowitz 514.937.4772

SASKATCHEWAN

REGINA
Rabbi Avrohom Simmonds 306.585.1359

SASKATOON
Rabbi Raphael Kats 306.384.4370

CAYMAN ISLANDS

GRAND CAYMAN
Rabbi Berel Pewzner 717.798.1040

COLOMBIA

BOGOTA
Rabbi Chanoch Piekarski 57.1.635.8251

COSTA RICA

S. JOSÉ
Rabbi Hershel Spalter
Rabbi Moshe Bitton 506.4010.1515

CROATIA

ZAGREB
Rabbi Pinchas Zaklas 385.1.4812227

DENMARK

COPENHAGEN
Rabbi Yitzchok Loewenthal 45.3316.1850

ESTONIA

TALLINN
Rabbi Shmuel Kot 372.662.30.50

FRANCE

BOULOGNE
Rabbi Michael Sojcher 33.1.46.99.87.85

DIJON
Rabbi Chaim Slonim 33.6.52.05.26.65

MARSEILLE
Rabbi Eliahou Altabe 33.6.11.60.03.05
Rabbi Menahem Mendel Assouline 33.6.64.88.25.04
Rabbi Emmanuel Taubenblatt 33.4.88.00.94.85

PARIS
Rabbi Avraham Barou'h Pevzner 33.6.99.64.07.70
Rabbi Asher Marciano 33.1.45.26.87.60

GEORGIA

TBILISI
Rabbi Meir Kozlovsky 995.32.2429770

GERMANY

BERLIN
Rabbi Yehuda Tiechtel 49.30.2128.0830

DUSSELDORF
Rabbi Chaim Barkahn 49.173.2871.770

HAMBURG
Rabbi Shlomo Bistritzky 49.40.4142.4190

HANNOVER
Rabbi Binyamin Wolff 49.511.811.2822

GREECE

ATHENS
Rabbi Mendel Hendel 30.210.323.3825

GUATEMALA

GUATEMALA CITY
Rabbi Shalom Pelman 502.2485.0770

ISRAEL

ASHKELON
Rabbi Shneor Lieberman 054.977.0512

BALFURYA
Rabbi Noam Bar-Tov 054.580.4770

CAESAREA
Rabbi Chaim Meir Lieberman 054.621.2586

EVEN YEHUDA
Rabbi Menachem Noyman 054.777.0707

GANEI TIKVA
Rabbi Gershon Shnur 054.524.2358

GIV'ATAYIM
Rabbi Pinchus Bitton 052.643.8770

KARMIEL
Rabbi Mendy Elishevitz 054.521.3073

KFAR SABA
Rabbi Yossi Baitch 054.445.5020

KIRYAT BIALIK
Rabbi Pinny Marton 050.661.1768

KIRYAT MOTZKIN
Rabbi Shimon Eizenbach 050.902.0770

KOCHAV YAIR
Rabbi Dovi Greenberg 054.332.6244

MACCABIM-RE'UT
Rabbi Yosef Yitzchak Noiman 054.977.0549

NES ZIYONA
Rabbi Menachem Feldman 054.497.7092

NETANYA
Rabbi Schneur Brod 054.579.7572

RAMAT GAN-KRINITZI
Rabbi Yisroel Gurevitz 052.743.2814

RAMAT GAN-MAROM NAVE
Rabbi Binyamin Meir Kali 050.476.0770

RAMAT YISHAI
Rabbi Shneor Zalman Wolosow 052.324.5475

RISHON LEZION
Rabbi Uri Keshet 050.722.4593

ROSH PINA
Rabbi Sholom Ber Hertzel 052.458.7600

TEL AVIV
Rabbi Shneur Piekarski 054.971.5568

JAPAN

TOKYO
Rabbi Mendi Sudakevich 81.3.5789.2846

KAZAKHSTAN

ALMATY
Rabbi Shevach Zlatopolsky 7.7272.77.59.49

KYRGYZSTAN

BISHKEK
Rabbi Arye Raichman 996.312.68.19.66

LATVIA

RIGA
Rabbi Shneur Zalman Kot
Mrs. Rivka Glazman 371.6720.40.22

LITHUANIA

VILNIUS
Rabb Sholom Ber Krinsky 370.6817.1367

LUXEMBOURG

LUXEMBOURG
Rabbi Mendel Edelman 352.2877.7079

NETHERLANDS

ALMERE
Rabbi Moshe Stiefel 31.36.744.0509

AMSTERDAM
Rabbi Yanki Jacobs 31.644.988.627
Rabbi Jaacov Zwi Spiero 31.652.328.065

EINDHOVEN
Rabbi Simcha Steinberg 31.63.635.7593

HAGUE
Rabbi Shmuel Katzman 31.70.347.0222

HEEMSTEDE-HAARLEM
Rabbi Shmuel Spiero 31.23.532.0707

MAASTRICHT
Rabbi Avrohom Cohen 31.43.390.0575

NIJMEGEN
Rabbi Menachem Mendel Levine 31.621.586.575

ROTTERDAM
Rabbi Yehuda Vorst 31.10.265.5530

PANAMA

PANAMA CITY
Rabbi Ari Laine
Rabbi Gabriel Benayon 507.223.3383

RUSSIA

ASTRAKHAN
Rabbi Yisroel Melamed 7.851.239.28.24

BRYANSK
Rabbi Menachem Mendel Zaklas 7.483.264.55.15

CHELYABINSK
Rabbi Meir Kirsh 7.351.263.24.68

MOSCOW: MARINA ROSHA
Rabbi Mordechai Weisberg 7.495.645.50.00

NIZHNY NOVGOROD
Rabbi Shimon Bergman 7.920.253.47.70

OMSK
Rabbi Osher Krichevsky 7.381.231.33.07

PERM
Rabbi Zalman Deutch 7.342.212.47.32

ROSTOV
Rabbi Chaim Danzinger 7.8632.99.02.68

S. PETERSBURG
Rabbi Zvi Pinsky 7.812.713.62.09

SAMARA
Rabbi Shlomo Deutch 7.846.333.40.64

SARATOV
Rabbi Yaakov Kubitshek 7.8452.21.58.00

TOGLIATTI
Rabbi Meier Fischer 7.848.273.02.84

UFA
Rabbi Dan Krichevsky 7.347.244.55.33

VORONEZH
Rabbi Levi Stiefel 7.473.252.96.99

SINGAPORE

SINGAPORE
Rabbi Mordechai Abergel 656.337.2189
Rabbi Netanel Rivni 656.336.2127
Classes in Hebrew

SOUTH AFRICA

CAPE TOWN
Rabbi Levi Popack 27.21.434.3740

JOHANNESBURG
Rabbi Dovid Masinter
Rabbi Ari Kievman 27.11.440.6600

SWEDEN

MALMO
Rabbi Shneur Kesselman 46.707.366.770

STOCKHOLM
Rabbi Chaim Greisman 468.679.7067

SWITZERLAND

BASEL
Rabbi Zalmen Wishedsky 41.41.361.1770

LUZERN
Rabbi Chaim Drukman 41.41.361.1770

THAILAND

BANGKOK
Rabbi Yosef C. Kantor 6681.837.7618

UKRAINE

DNEPROPETROVSK
Rabbi Dan Makagon 380.504.51.13.18

NIKOLAYEV
Rabbi Sholom Gotlieb 380.512.37.37.71

ODESSA
Rabbi Avraham Wolf
Rabbi Yaakov Neiman .... 38.048.728.0770 EXT. 280

ZHITOMIR
Rabbi Shlomo Wilhelm 380.504.63.01.32

UNITED KINGDOM

BOURNEMOUTH
Rabbi Bentzion Alperowitz 44.749.456.7177

CHEADLE
Rabbi Peretz Chein 44.161.428.1818

LEEDS
Rabbi Eli Pink 44.113.266.3311

LONDON
Rabbi Mendel Cohen 44.777.261.2661
Rabbi Nissan D. Dubov 44.208.944.1581
Rabbi Dovid Katz 44.207.624.2770
Rabbi Yisroel Lew 44.207.060.9770
Rabbi Gershon Overlander
Rabbi Hillel Gruber 44.208.202.1600
Rabbi Shlomo Odze 44.791.757.3558
Rabbi Yossi Simon 44.208.458.0416

MANCHESTER
Rabbi Levi Cohen 44.161.792.6335
Rabbi Shmuli Jaffe 44.161.766.1812

URUGUAY

MONTEVIDEO
Rabbi Mendy Shemtov 598.2628.6770

The Jewish Learning Multiplex

Brought to you by the Rohr Jewish Learning Institute

In fulfillment of the mandate of the Lubavitcher Rebbe, of blessed memory, whose leadership guides every step of our work, the mission of the Rohr Jewish Learning Institute is to transform Jewish life and the greater community through the study of Torah, connecting each Jew to our shared heritage of Jewish learning.

While our flagship program remains the cornerstone of our organization, JLI is proud to feature additional divisions catering to specific populations, in order to meet a wide array of educational needs.

THE ROHR JEWISH LEARNING INSTITUTE,
a subsidiary of *Merkos L'Inyonei Chinuch*,
is the adult education arm of the Chabad-Lubavitch Movement.

Torah Studies provides a rich and nuanced encounter with the weekly Torah reading.

MyShiur courses are designed to assist students in developing the skills needed to study Talmud independently.

This rigorous fellowship program invites select college students to explore the fundamentals of Judaism.

Jewish teens forge their identity as they engage in Torah study, social interaction, and serious fun.

The Rosh Chodesh Society gathers Jewish women together once a month for intensive textual study.

TorahCafe.com provides an exclusive selection of top-rated Jewish educational videos.

This yearly event rejuvenates mind, body, and spirit with a powerful synthesis of Jewish learning and community.

Participants delve into our nation's rich past while exploring the Holy Land's relevance and meaning today.

Select affiliates are invited to partner with peers and noted professionals, as leaders of innovation and excellence.

Machon Shmuel is an institute providing Torah research in the service of educators worldwide.